Oedipus in Britain

Oedipus in Britain: Edward Glover and the Struggle over Klein

Paul Roazen

Other Press
New York

Production Editor: Robert D. Hack

This book was set in 11 pt. Berkeley by Alpha Graphics of Pittsfield, NH.

Copyright © 2000 by Paul Roazen

10 9 8 7 6 5 4 3 2 1

All rights reserved, including the right to reproduce this book, or parts thereof, in any form, without written permission from Other Press, Llc except in the case of brief quotations in reviews for inclusion in a magazine, newspaper, or broadcast. Printed in the United States of America on acid-free paper. For information write to Other Press, Llc, 377 W. 11th Street, New York, NY 10014. Or visit our website: www.otherpress.com.

Library of Congress Cataloging-in-Publication Data

Roazen, Paul, 1936–
    Oedipus in Britain : Edward Glover and the struggle over Klein / by Paul Roazen.
    p. cm.
    Includes bibliographical references and index.
    ISBN 1-892746-66-2 (hardcover)
    1. Glover, Edward, b. 1888. 2. Psychoanalysts—Great Britain—Biography. 3. Psychoanalysis—Great Britain—History. I. Title.
BF109.G56 R63 2000
150.19'5'092—dc21
[B]   00-035661

For Hans Mohr

They say best men are moulded out of faults,

And, for the most, become much more the better

For being a little bad. . . .
Measure for Measure (V, i)

Contents

Illustrations		xi
Introduction		xxvii
1.	An Outsider on Wimpole Street	1
2.	Ernest Jones As a Leader	23
3.	The Controversial Discussions–I "A New *Weltanschauung*"?	45
4.	The Controversial Discussions–II "Double-barrelled Training"	79
5.	Freud in Exile and Technique	109
6.	Star Pupil: Dr. Lawrence S. Kubie	131
Epilogue		167
Notes		179
Acknowledgments		191
Index		193

Edward Glover as a schoolboy, second row, extreme left. He was brought up for his first six years in a Presbyterian Manse, and thereafter studied in the schoolhouse of his father. (Dr. Paul Byers)

Edward Glover in a photograph for his final year dinner at Glasgow University, Jan. 14, 1909. (Dr. Paul Byers)

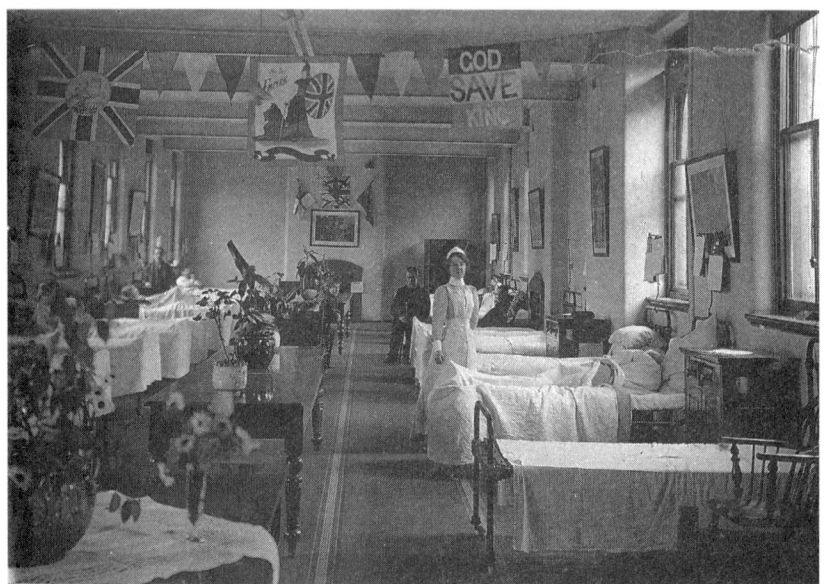

In 1912 Glover was an assistant physician at the King Edward VII sanatorium for Chest Diseases. (Dr. Paul Byers)

Dr. Edward Glower (London)

Glover in a caricature for the 8th Congress of the International Psychoanalytic Association, April 21–23, 1924, Salzburg, Austria. (Olga Dormandi)

Melitta Schmideberg—Melanie Klein's daughter—with her husband Walter, July 7, 1923. (The Wellcome Trust)

Melanie Klein, June 29, 1925, the year she first lectured in England. (The Wellcome Trust)

Glover with Melitta and Walter Schmideberg at the 13th Congress of the International Psychoanalytic Association, Lucerne, Switzerland, August 26–31, 1934. (N. T. Gidal)

Melanie Klein with Sylvia Payne at the Lucerne Congress. After World War II, Payne would mediate the terms setting up Anna Freud's separate training group within the British Psychoanalytic Society. (N. T. Gidal)

Philipp Sarasin and Ernest Jones at the Lucerne Congress. Sarasin supported Glover in the clash with Jones over the propriety of Glover becoming a full member of the Swiss Psychoanalytic Society following Glover's 1944 resignation from the British Psychoanalytic Society. (N. T. Gidal)

James Strachey at the Lucerne Congress. The photographer had a sense of humor about Strachey's reclusive bookishness. (N. T. Gidal)

Anna Freud with Marie Bonaparte at the 15th Congress of the International Psychoanalytic Association, Paris, France, August 1–5, 1938. They would be allied in backing Glover's being able to remain within the IPA, just as they were to be later united in helping to drive Jacques Lacan out. (The Freud Museum)

Glover's amiability was combined with considerable theoretical capacities and a willingness to struggle doctrinally. (Dr. Paul Byers)

Ernest Jones, near his death in 1958. By the end of his life, Jones could write appreciatively about Glover's public contributions to psychoanalysis. (The Freud Museum)

Anna Freud in 1971, drawn by the same artist who did all the caricatures for the 1924 Salzburg Congress. It would have been "not done" to have included Freud's youngest child in such a 1924 book. (Olga Dormandi)

D. W. Winnicott in 1971. Although he became one of the most original and talented analysts in the world, Winnicott had initially been highly critical of Glover's 1944 decision to leave the British Psychoanalytic Society. By 1965 Winnicott regretted Glover's withdrawal. (Olga Dormandi)

Glover was a pipe smoker who also enjoyed a glass of good wine. (Dr. Paul Byers)

Glover, with a large and distinguished clinical practice, had courtly Old World Manners. (Dr. Paul Byers)

Glover at a desk in 1967. (Stephen Moreton-Prichard)

Glover in 1967. The photographer wrote in 1999: "He was a lovely man . . . one shot in particular, I remember, exemplified this, regardless of the ash on his waistcoat!" (Stephen Moreton-Prichard)

Glover in 1967, inscribed by him to Dr. & Mrs. Paul Byers: "Exemplar I — to my dearest friends, Valery and Paul, with regretful recognition of the wholesale degeneration of his features. Eddie. Edward Glover circa his 80th birthday." (Stephen Moreton-Prichard)

Glover in 1967, also inscribed by him to Dr. & Mrs. Paul Byers: "Examplar II — a rather lardaceous picture which at the same time indicates clearly what a moral scoundrel is. Eddie (Edward Glover). To Paul and Valery. Jan. 1968." (Stephen Moreton-Prichard)

Glover in 1967, also inscribed by him to Dr. & Mrs. Paul Byers: "Examplar III — Now here is what I dare to call a bonnie picture of a decaying Lowland Scot, pretending that he can read the Queen's English in blatant opposition to the facts of the case. To Paul & Valery, Eddie." (Stephen Moreton-Prichard)

Lawerence S. Kubie, who stands out as Glover's most eminent pupil, near the end of his own life. (*Psychoanalytic Quarterly*)

The bust of Glover done by Peter Lambda for the ISTD not long before Glover's death in 1972.

Introduction

Psychoanalysis has a secure place in the history of twentieth-century intellectual life, and it is a sure bet that we have by no means heard the last of it. The influence of Sigmund Freud's work cannot be contested, even if a good part of his impact has been expressed by criticisms of what he accomplished. For slightly over a hundred years now psychoanalytic thinking has been spreading around the world. When, in the early 1960s, I first got interested in the significance of Freud's ideas, almost all the leading American psychiatric positions were then held by analysts. Since this was by no means the case in Britain, where I had briefly studied for graduate work, it was easy to be intrigued by the contrast between the reception of psychoanalysis in the United States and in Great Britain. Comparative national history, including the different ways in which those two countries responded to Freud's concepts, seemed to me a fascinating cultural puzzle.

By now, however, the story that can be followed has grown far more extensive. There has been recently a notable falling-off in psychoanalysis's standing in America, largely due to the approval of advances in psychopharmacology in therapy; and the harshest sorts of polemics against Freud have appeared to appeal to a general audience.[1] In Britain, on the other hand, oddly enough largely because of the Conservative governments of Margaret Thatcher, psychoanalytic studies centers have been set up at over a dozen of the newer, "redbrick" universities. While she reduced previous public funds to the ancient and rich institutions at Oxford and Cambridge, she facilitated grants to the newer places of higher learning. Once a subject gets established as part of a formal academic curriculum, bureaucratic lethargy alone is such that these units should be likely to continue indefinitely to do research and train therapists. (In the United States there are still only three academic psychoanalytic studies centers, at the New School for Social Research in New York City, Emory in Atlanta, and the University of Chicago.)

Private institutes for psychoanalytic training staffed by experienced practitioners have existed since the early 1920s, but Freud was not eager to see them give up their autonomy for the sake of gaining normal university recognition. America has, despite Freud's suspiciousness about what the New World would do to his ideas, remained so faithful to his intentions that it is rarely found that any psychoanalytic institutes there are affiliated with medical schools. I think that the recent success of psychoanalysis within the British academic world has become a notable cultural event in the communication of his teachings. Freud's commitment to the significance of nonmedical (lay) analysts may have complicated the short-range problem of arranging for the institutionalizing of the new profession, but in the long run it has proven feasible in Britain, which has all along endorsed lay analysis. The acceptance of lay analysis in the States has until recently been grudging, and nonmedical practitioners have never had the status in America that they attained in Britain.

To broaden the tale of the comparative impact of Freud, it is noteworthy that while psychoanalysis was once flourishing in Russia, Stalin put a temporary end to the movement in the late 1920s; now again, with the collapse of the old Soviet Union, Freud's ideas have undergone a notable revival in Russia. And in France, a country originally slow to respond to the significance of Freud, no modern system of thought is more important in Paris today than the psychoanalytic world view. Parisian bookstores brim with new texts and journals connected with Freud. Disappointments with Marxist ideology and Communist practice have helped fuel the fashionability of psychoanalytic reasoning. Freud has become required reading as part of examinations for entrance to the most famous French universities, and psychoanalysis is widely popular as part of philosophic studies. This enthusiasm for psychoanalysis in France has had an effect among Francophilic readers elsewhere, so that literary studies in America, for example, are more influenced by Freud than ever. Italy has been especially influenced by French developments as well as those in the States.

Elsewhere the tale of the impact of Freudianism is equally interesting. Valuable books have appeared on psychoanalysis in the Netherlands, Germany, and other countries as well. Latin America presents intellectual historians with a special case of its own, since Argentina is now one of the liveliest centers of psychoanalytic psychology. (In contrast to almost everywhere else, psychoanalysis is taught there as part of academic psychology programs.) The presidency of the International Psychoanalytic Association (known as the IPA), an organization first established by Freud in 1910, now regularly rotates between three locations: Latin America, Europe, and the United States. (The followers of the analyst Jacques Lacan, once a French member of the IPA, alone almost number those of the IPA itself, not to mention the numerous adherents of such former disciples of Freud as Alfred Adler, Carl G. Jung, Otto Rank, and Erich Fromm.)

One of the enduring problems with writing about the history of psychoanalysis has been not only the way different communities have chosen to highlight special aspects of Freud's conceptualization, but it has been all too easy for pioneering figures to get ignored. One should perhaps not be surprised to find that the past gets retold from present-day perspectives, so that it is possible for people who were once obviously most significant to be later neglected, if not forgotten. The writings of the French may seem particularly arbitrary about who is or who is not considered part of the psychoanalytic canon, as genuine continuities are disrupted, but that is probably because psychoanalysis in France is so much more highly intellectual than anywhere else.

For some years now I have thought of publishing a book about Dr. Edward Glover (1888–1972), since I spent so many productive hours interviewing him in the mid-1960s in London. At the time he was best known to me as the author of, among other writings, a famous text on psychoanalytic technique as well as of a popular book, *Freud or Jung?* (which has recently been reprinted).[2] If he was then notable for being a maverick, having resigned from the British Psychoanalytic Society in 1944 after a frustrating public struggle with Melanie Klein and her supporters, his reputation has slumped even more since then. The one biography of Klein is unremittingly hostile and unfair to Glover.[3] And the 1991 publication of the proceedings of *The Freud–Klein Controversies 1941–45* only accentuated the degree of Glover's historical isolation; he is characterized there as having been "fanatical," and his forecasts for the British Psychoanalytic Society supposedly "apocalyptic and ferociously one-sided."[4] A reviewer of *The Freud–Klein Controversies* was able to dismiss Glover, without challenge, by the tendentious characterization of him as "an abrasive and unpopular man."[5] Another reviewer used words like "pugnacious," as well as "spiteful and rebarbative" to describe Glover.[6] While the papers presented in behalf of Klein got reprinted in a book, Glover's own critiques of Kleinianism, published separately, do not even get cited in the bibliography to *The Freud–Klein Controversies*.[7]

A central point that has so far escaped the literature is that Glover was an exceptionally kindly spirit, someone with charmingly courtly Old World manners. (One obituary of him I have seen accurately described him as "a warm-hearted, courteous man of natural elegance and generosity." Another characterized him as an "essentially gentle and sympathetic personality." The death notices in *The Times* were almost insultingly brief.[8]) When I once proposed to one of Glover's most fair-minded contemporaries, Dr. Sylvia Payne, that he was the last person one might ever imagine to have taken part in such a fight over Klein, I got full agreement, and the assertion that it had to be "seen to be believed."[9] So an unusually amiable man is in danger of going down in the history books as only a partisan and dogmatist.

In reality I think it makes almost as much sense to see Glover as a historical victim of what happened. Initially attracted by Klein's originality, he later had felt that Klein's work became a betrayal of Freud's own conceptions; Freud himself took a similar viewpoint, although he did not want to make a fuss like that associated with the earlier so-called renegades, such as Adler and Jung. Once Freud had come to England, having fled in 1938 from the threat of Nazism, Glover's situation did seem to have improved. Freud personally confirmed to Glover how intensely distasteful the founder of psychoanalysis deemed Klein's approach.

In the end the legacy of Klein, who died in 1960, succeeded so fruitfully in enlivening and enriching psychoanalysis that today few contemporary analysts in Britain are likely to want to acknowledge just how much Freud in reality distanced himself from her ideas, since that would entail accepting a lack of legitimizing lineage in their heritage.[10] Klein had, to put it in a nutshell, rejected Freud's own view of the centrality of the classical Oedipus complex, although in other ways she could be more royal than the king. It was hardly a secret, when Freud emigrated with his family, including his child analyst daughter Anna, along with other Viennese disciples, how his ardent loyalist pupils felt about Kleinianism. In the 1930s there had been formal exchanges of lecturers between the Vienna and British Psychoanalytic Societies, as the rival points of view were presented; it was apparent that the Viennese representative, who had spoken in London against Klein, was unwelcome there at the time of the migration of analysts in 1938.

After Freud's death in 1939 the World War, for a time, took precedence over psychoanalytic politics. Ernest Jones, the creator of British psychoanalysis and its president until 1944, was trying to be protective of Klein, at the same time that he sought to maintain good relations with Anna Freud, whom he had helped rescue from Vienna. (She later proved a key resource when Jones became Freud's official biographer.) Although Anna, like her father, felt like a guest in the British Society, she had been at odds with Klein (whose specialty was also in child analysis) since the mid-1920s. Freud had in private, for example in correspondence with Jones, indicated his intense displeasure with the direction of Klein's thinking. Freud thought that Klein's battle with Anna was a disguised displacement from real differences with himself. He had promised Jones, though, at the time of the move to England, that Anna would not prove disruptive to the British Society.

Glover took up Freud's banner, with the support of others, notably Klein's analyst daughter; but in the end it was Glover who was squeezed out. He resigned from the British Society, and—over Jones's objections as President of the IPA—Glover succeeded in becoming a full member of the Swiss Psychoanalytic Society, and therefore entitled to participate in IPA meetings. Glover continued to practice as an analyst in London, and Anna Freud created her own training program within the British Society.

But the upshot has been that while both Klein and Anna Freud have had their respective adherents, and biographies of them both have appeared, Glover was left historically to twist in the wind. He finally chose not to found a new group of his own, although at the time Klein had thought he was likely to do so. As Glover's most distinguished student, the American psychiatrist Lawrence S. Kubie, wrote, "it never tempted Glover, as so many others, to launch his own messianic school."[11] Throughout the history of psychoanalysis it has been those embattled enough to have partisan followers who have been best remembered, while the least sectarian and organizationally tenacious tend to have fallen by the wayside.

So Glover, after having participated in probably the single most important defining moment in British psychoanalysis, is in danger of becoming one of the lost sheep of the story of the development of Freud's school. In Nicholas Wright's 1988 play *Mrs. Klein*, which telescopes events to the year 1934, she describes Glover as "not a dunce exactly but he's too dogmatic. Like some mid-Victorian, mutton-chop-whiskered tyrant of the breakfast table, ghastly." And Mrs. Klein throws wine in her daughter's face when she discovers that she has changed to having Glover as her analyst.[12] I think that it needs to be remembered now that, in addition to his extensive specialized bibliography of books, articles, editorials, and reviews, he once also prolifically wrote for the *Listener*, *Lancet*, *Horizon*, the *Spectator*, the London *Times*, the *New York Times*, and elsewhere.[13] He was one of the great publicists for psychoanalysis in the English language, he spoke on radio programs, and books of his were also translated—into French, German, Italian, Spanish, Chinese. The example of Glover indicates that an interesting history of British psychoanalysis could be written on the basis of a list of those who left or were driven out of the British Society.

Glover's private life was such that circumstances also contrived to obliterate his memory. His second wife had been an invalid for many years before she predeceased him, and their one child was "backward." So at Glover's death in 1972 there was no one on hand to make sure that his papers got secured. When analysts die, if only for purposes of protecting the privacy of former patients, it often happens that documents get destroyed in an indiscriminate way. Despite all the years that Glover had practiced and helped promote psychoanalysis, there was no effort made to preserve any of his extensive literary remains.

Curiously enough the largest body of Glover's documentary legacy can today be found in the United States. Around the time I was meeting him for the sake of my research into the history of the psychoanalytic movement, Glover gave some interviews to the Columbia Oral History Project. He was, unfortunately, so discreet then, in front of a tape recorder, that it is hard to find his authentic-sounding voice in those transcriptions. But in the Library of Congress in Washington, D.C., amidst the uncombed papers of Anna Freud and Lawrence Kubie, I found the largest collection of Glover's letters that I have ever encountered, and my coming upon them, and some related material at the Library of Congress, have moved me now to carry out the project I have long entertained of putting down my account of what Glover told me. (An interview with Glover at the Library of Congress, conducted by the late Kurt R. Eissler, has been sealed until 2013.)

Once, in 1977, I presented a preliminary bit of this material before the Topeka Psychosocial Group, which was led by people associated with the Menninger Clinic; I remember being surprised by how fascinated the small audience was. On the North American side of the Atlantic Glover was always considered a reliable pillar of orthodoxy, and his name was formally listed on the editorial mastheads of the annual *The Psychoanalytic Study of the Child* and the journal *Psychoanalytic Quarterly*. At the time I saw Glover scarcely anyone in the States knew about the struggles Glover had had within British analysis. Yet as a reviewer of *The Freud–Klein Controversies*, unsympathetic to Glover, noted, those debates charted "the course . . . of the ensuring fifty years of psychoanalytic history."[14] With this book I hope to restore historical balance about Glover without trying to paint him as any kind of saint.

1

An Outsider on Wimpole Street

Out of all the people I ever met in the course of my interviewing work on the history of psychoanalysis, it is a special pleasure for me now to concentrate on the material I gathered from Edward Glover. As I have indicated, in the mid-1960s he was a well-known and influential psychoanalytic writer, especially because of his important contributions to the issue of therapeutic technique. Even if nobody were ever to conduct formal analyses again, Glover's considered experience as a clinician would have something to add to the folklore of wisdom about the art of psychotherapy. General practitioners, nurses, counselors, and social workers, not just psychiatrists with pills, can benefit from the example of Glover's humaneness.

Even now in North America Glover is considered a sound and important theoretician of the so-called mainstream within psychoanalysis. Yet in London I found in the 1960s he was relegated to being an outsider, someone who seemed to have gotten a raw deal from everyone. Since my interviews with him his historical reputation has been even more tarnished, and ever since his death I have felt an obligation to try to help set the record straight. I found him to be unusually gentle, someone who it was exceptionally nice to meet, and the time I spent with him stands out in my mind as particularly instructive.

Glover played a leading role not only in the early history of psychoanalysis in Great Britain, but he also was a long-standing officer of the International Psychoanalytic Association; he was Secretary from 1934 until 1944. In addition, it is known how he took a major part in the controversies surrounding the work of Melanie Klein, a dispute that came to a head toward the end of World War II. The fight over Mrs. Klein's innovations is still best comprehended in England, but the influence of her ideas had an impact elsewhere as well, particularly in Latin America. Since Klein's psychology (known as "the English school" of psychoanalysis) is often considered one of the most important contributions made since Freud's own, an examination of Glover's part in the criticism of Kleinianism becomes correspondingly significant.

As sweet a man as I found Glover to be, I already knew about his combative book against Jung, which alerted me to the existence of another, polemical side to the mild and courteous man I met. (A Jungian psychiatrist in London, Dr. Michael Fordham, told me that whenever he wanted to see what was wrong in Jung Fordham looked it up in Glover's book.) Jung himself read Glover's 1950 pamphlet, which had originally been proposed by the literary critic Cyril Connolly. Jung reponded to Glover's indictment in a letter to an American:

> Glover's book—apart from its more venomous qualities—is quite amusing: it is exactly like those pamphlets people used to write against Freud in the early days. It was quite obvious then that they were merely expressing their resentments on account of the fact that Freud had trodden on their toes. The same is true of Glover. A critique like his is always suspect as a compensation for an unconscious inclination in the other direction. He is certainly not stupid enough not to see the point I make, but I touched on a weak spot in him, namely where he represses his better insight and his latent criticism of his Freudian superstition. He is just a bit too fanatical. Fanaticism always means overcompensated doubt. He merely shouts down his inner criticism and that's why his book is amusing.[1]

It is impressive to me how Jung was able to take Glover's indictment in stride. One observer notes of Glover's writing against Jung that it "is antagonistic, witty, sarcastic, and animated. And there is intellectual substance beneath the acidic surface; he has a deep acquaintance with Jung's ideas, and he provides the most thorough case against Jung that has ever been written."[2] Jungians on the whole have been less bellicose among themselves than the Freudians in their own intramural contests, precisely on Jung's grounds here that any too decided convictions betray a latent unconscious inclination in an opposite direction. But that has not stopped biographers and historians of science from trying to take apart Jung, almost even before he has been safely established among intellectual historians; a critical biography of Jung has recently credited Glover for having mounted "the most sustained attack on Jung's theories of psychological types. . . ."[3] (Still, the general public has absorbed Jung's famous distinction between introverts and extraverts.) Jung-bashing has recently become almost as fashionable as assaults on Freud.[4]

Glover, I think, would have defended himself over his critique of Jung because, like Freud, Glover thought it was critically important to be aware of the "dangers" of analysis being "watered down" into an old-fashioned conscious psychology; the idea was that psychoanalysis is a unique system under constant threat of being "lost" amidst alternative approaches. (Klein's passionate disciples felt exactly the same about her own ideas.) In his Freudian period Jung too could be combative, but his response to Glover was a sign of how well Jung had matured. For example, while Jones was writing his biography of Freud, and pursuing Jung as a "deviationist," Jung himself had appealed to Jones (without success) for the sake of letting bygones be bygones. Glover explained to me that he was willing to go along with "the traditional principles of psychoanalysis" rather than "rush into new concoctions." Glover was one of the most literate of traditionalists, and clear enough as a writer for Connolly to have commissioned him to write about Jung in his *Horizon*.

My transcriptions of the detailed notes I took from Glover, informed by the available scholarly literature, means that only at remarkably few points have I had to add a phrase, word, or clause in order to make what he said comprehensible; Glover was that articulate and sequential in what he had to say. Nevertheless I have put in quotation marks certain more striking of Glover's expressions, even though it would not be amiss to place even more by him that follows within quotes. I hesitate to take such license because I cannot be certain that every word would be just as he said it, although I am confident that my note-taking was an accurate rendition of what went on. Whenever, however, for the sake of my own memory, I had put something specially into quotation marks, I have repeated that here; also when what he told me is likely to seem too unexpected or controversial, I have used quotations as well. I hope that the detail, and coherency, of what I am presenting will add plausibility to my record. It is possible partially to corroborate what I report here with some of Glover's other reminiscences and historical reflections, as well as to find confirmations in the course of his theoretical writings.[5] The letters to Anna Freud and Lawrence S. Kubie should amplify what I have tried to reconstruct earlier.

When in my interviewing I asked Glover a direct question, I have adopted the device of italicizing it so that the reader will understand some of the connecting links introduced into the narrative I present. In order to give as full an account as possible of what I learned, I have at places enclosed within parentheses some commentary of my own; these asides represent either ideas that now occur to me, over thirty years later, or historical suggestions that were brought to my attention by other people I interviewed, as well as by publications as they eventually came out. And documents I recently found at the Library of Congress, consisting of correspondence between Glover and Anna Freud, as well as letters by Sylvia Payne and Ernest Jones to Anna Freud, tracing the origins of the separate training system for Anna Freud's students, will require an extended digression from my interview material. The chapter made up of the Glover–Kubie letters can, in the light of everything that will have preceded it, be taken to speak for itself, although of course I have made my selections in the light of what I have considered most noteworthy.

During the summer of 1965, after my initial interviews with Anna Freud, I stayed in London for the sake of gathering background on the history of psychoanalysis.[6] A small grant from Harvard University, where I had just been promoted to full-time faculty rank, was covering my basic expenses, so that money enabled me to relax about exactly where my research might ultimately lead. Regularly sitting in on case conferences at Anna Freud's clinic in Hampstead took up only a small part of my work; my contact with her, restricted as it was, seemed to legitimize my ongoing research in the eyes of many. The good fortune in my stumbling across Jones's papers that went to make up his three-volume biography of Freud meant that I spent many exciting hours sorting them out in the basement of the British Psychoanalytic Society. Everything was so exactly as Jones had left it, after his death in 1958, that there was even an original pack of Freud's letters to a boyhood friend of his (Emil Fluss), which I turned over to the Librarian, who was then Masud Khan, at that time unaware what precious items he had under his control.

It was only in the course of dinner table conversations with Geoffrey Gorer, whom I saw several times that summer, that I decided that I must be sure, among the other people I met, to contact Glover. Gorer was an exceptionally intelligent commentator on British psychoanalysis, and altogether a fascinating figure himself; he was also a fine writer who had been a friend of people like George Orwell, W. H. Auden, and the Sitwells. Among Gorer's other books he had co-authored one on Russia with the analyst John Rickman; Gorer knew Margaret Mead well, he had once been taken through Freud's house on Maresfield Gardens by Gorer's friend Ernst Kris, and Gorer was acquainted with lots of other interesting people from his days at the British Embassy in Washington, D. C. during World War II. (Gorer was modest enough to be deferential about the way Vladimir Nabokov and Sir Isaiah Berlin had competed at outsparkling each other as conversationalists.) Currently Gorer, who lived in a beautiful country house where he had accumulated a fine collection of modern paintings and raised prize flowers, was on good terms with Freud's grandson Lucian, who was already then a leading painter. Among Gorer's other talents was a serious interest in cultural anthropology, and he insisted to me that it was "a sociological law" of all fieldwork inquiry that "mavericks" make the best sources of information. By 1965 Glover seemed to Gorer someone who had drawn a particularly bad hand in life, and I therefore, at Gorer's urging, resolved to see Glover. (By now Gorer, who died in 1985, is himself in danger of being neglected; he pursued his work independently of a research university, or any established school of thought, and such an old-fashioned gentleman-scholar can easily be forgotten.)

When I first met Glover I had no intention of ever publishing what he told me, but I thought of the time he gave me as useful for my speaking with other early analysts, and in ensuring that I successfully made my way through the existing documentation that could be uncovered. In those days I had in mind revising for publication my Ph.D. dissertation, which had been on "Freud and Political Theory,"[7] though I also vaguely hoped that my interviews might lead to other possibilities for manuscripts that I might write.

Glover succeeded in living to be 84, dying of stomach cancer in 1972, seven years after I first met him. I have selected the set of interviews I conducted with him partly because as time passed I have come to think he was right in feeling that his own version of events was important and unrepresented. In order to structure the information that I gathered I have had to group the material under separate headings. Yet it did not take much artifical reconstruction on my part to assemble his interviews in a coherent way. Glover gave me nine separate interviews in the summer of 1965, and then I saw him for two more when I returned to London in the fall of 1966. After we met Glover and I exchanged some friendly correspondence, and he suggested another early analyst on the continent—Dr. Philipp Sarasin—whom I should see. (It was typical of Glover's style that he wrote me, "If you write, mention my name. I knew him well: he had a voice like a brass band but very nice and helpful.")

There has to be an inevitably subjective component in this report of my encounter with Glover. Yet in the course of my extensive other interviewing, as well as my reading, I think there was a disciplined check on what I learned. It would be misleading, however, not to concentrate as much as possible exactly on what I saw and heard, if this account is going to be most useful to others.

Although Glover's office was located in a medically posh part of London, 18 Wimpole Street, which is right near the perhaps more internationally famous Harley Street, there was no separate entrance and exit for patients, as Freud had arranged for at his Vienna apartment to protect each person's anonymity. One was expected to sit in a general waiting room with other physicians' medical patients until a receptionist for all the doctors came to announce that it was now time to go in; she accompanied one to his consulting room. (A psychoanalytic patient's privacy was protected in that most of the other patients were seeing regular medical doctors.)

I find in my notes that I describe his office as "Miss Haversham's place," thinking of Dickens's *Great Expectations*. For I had the first impression of being present in a room that was a kind of living tomb. (Glover had practiced there since 1926.) Books and papers were piled all over, almost tumbling in on themselves. The furniture was largely eighteenth and nineteenth century, including a Chippendale desk, but everything seemed well used rather than on display. The furnishings communicated by themselves something about Glover as a real person.

Personally, in contrast to someone like my patron Helene Deutsch's lively set of witty *bon mots*,[8] I found in Glover an air of somberness, which seemed like a comparative absence of humor. Although unlike in *Great Expectations* Glover's quarters had no literal cobwebs, I did have the feeling that I had stepped back into the past. His analytic couch, as customary then in London analytic consulting rooms of the earliest pioneers, was by North American standards enormous and obtrusively placed. Glover was himself a large (slightly overweight) reserved old gentleman who always wore a bow tie. He spoke with a quietly striking Scottish accent; he was born (1888) in Lesmahagow, part of the rural county of Lanarkshire, twenty-five miles from Glasgow. (It has to be odd to find him, in an otherwise excellent set of editorial notes to a fragmentary diary of Freud's, referred to in 1992 as an "English"[9] analyst.) To a Jungian-sounding pen-pal he acquired in the mid-1960s, Glover wrote of himself as a lowland Scot: "I am a *peasant* by birth—my father a schoolmaster and my mother simultaneously the daughter of an old farming family and the adopted niece of a Scottish Calvinistic parson who died, naturally, of alcoholic cirrhosis of the liver. Hence my contumacy."[10] Later I learned from a medical colleague of Glover's at 18 Wimpole Street that it had been Glover's habitual practice as a writer to read his letters aloud to a secretary to ensure that his style had been easy and correct.

These letters he wrote in old age contain other autobiographical fragments not available elsewhere. His father, Matthew Glover (who knew among other subjects Greek, Latin, Hebrew, and French), taught him a good deal about writing English; his mother, Elizabeth Smith Shanks, was the niece of a Scottish Presbyterian minister who had adopted her as a child. Edward was the last of three sons. The middle one (John) died at the age of 6 when Edward himself was 4. The first-born of the brothers was James, 5½ years older than Edward, with whom by the age of 15 Edward had what he called "the beginnings of a permanent alliance—all earlier jealousies forgotten or buried."[11] Edward's father, who "always thought I was a moron compared to Brother James, said to me when I was about 10 'Well, never mind, you are such an inquisitive and critical little boy that I am sure some day you will do scientific research.'"[12] James "in after years continued to maintain" that their mother's Scottish Presbyterian minister uncle was her lover, but "I didn't believe it . . . if he had really been her lover she would have eaten him down to the watch chain and fob . . . I concluded that he wasn't her lover and that I was legitimate . . . we made it up, my brother and I. . . . And I loved him dearly and he me from when I was 10 till he died of diabetes in Spain . . . in 1926."[13]

At the age of 16 Glover started medical school at the University of Glasgow, as ancient a center of learning as Oxford or Cambridge. He claimed to his pen-pal that it had right away "dawned on me that professional life was a battle between myself and THE EXAMINERS and so I put my goods in the shop window and spent the rest of the time on the University Magazine & similar extravagances to the permanent benefit of my soul."[14] Somehow an issue of *The Socialist Torch*, published by the University Socialist Society and dated March 19, 1908, managed to survive the destruction of his psychoanalytic papers. Edward was a success as a student, and graduated "with distinction" in 1909 when he was 21. (An impressive booklet from the final-year medical dinner also survived, and the drawings in it look like Edward's; the high level of erudition in that pamphlet in itself is a demonstration to me of the decline of literacy since then.) By 1915 he was licensed to practice medicine.

At the outset of our relationship none of this biography was known to me; I could never have imagined that in his childhood no musical instruments were allowed in church, or that "even to whistle on Sunday was a 'mortal sin,' to use a Roman Catholic" concept.[15] I had a favorable first impression about him, and Glover asked me to draw up a prospectus of future questions. Such an ideally rational approach proved unnecessary since every time I saw him I had more than enough inquiries to keep the interview moving. I did write him a couple of letters to indicate lines of inquiry that interested me, but as I remember it the specific issues I mentioned invariably led to a dead end, since he so often made it plain that he was not intrigued by the subjects I had mentioned. Flying by the seat of my pants proved a more successful way of ensuring his spontaneity. Early on he pointed out that he was 77 years old, and that he could not know how much time was left to him. He explained that if someone were to pay him $20,000 a year he would gladly do nothing else but write about the early history of psychoanalysis.

That money seems like a small sum, but my own new teaching salary was itself a fraction of that figure. London analysts, no matter how distinguished or renowned, have rarely collected the fees customary in America and Canada. Unlike their New York City colleagues, for example, who earned enough money for many to live spaciously on Park and Fifth Avenues, only those few analysts with private inherited means could enjoy luxury in England. American celebrities like Marilyn Monroe, Jacqueline Kennedy, or Woody Allen might then be going to analysts, and Hollywood had long glamorized the profession. But in my experience British analysts had far more of a financial struggle than was then customarily the case in the New World. But though they were not nearly so successful in worldly terms, I found that the intellectual quality of British psychoanalysis was unusually high. In places or periods when analysis is less popular it attracts practitioners for motives aside from merely getting ahead professionally.

After our first meeting I noted that Glover had done almost all the talking. (One is bound to wonder whether the normal restraints on their talkativeness in the course of their practice of analytic therapy does not leave analysts with a special bent for holding forth on other occasions.) There had been a continual flow of material from Glover, but to my mild distress I found out that he did not want to discuss the subject of my Ph.D. thesis at all. Instead he told me that there were about twenty other members of the British Psychoanalytic Society in its early days, but according to Glover few of them really mattered. (We both knew that he was implicitly excluding Ernest Jones from this characterization.) He soon said he "trusted" me, and loaned copies of an autobiographical manuscript as well as an unpublished paper of his about his own analyst in Berlin, Karl Abraham; he also gave me a draft of an article by an old New York analyst about the Hungarian favorite of Freud's, Sandor Ferenczi. Glover explained in passing that it was proving difficult to find a place to publish a piece about himself by Dr. Melitta Schmideberg, Melanie Klein's daughter, whom I had known as once having been a psychoanalytic supporter of Glover's. (Politics can play more of a role in the acceptance of psychoanalytic papers than one might expect, and extends even to the nature of the bibliographies that are considered advantageous for getting articles accepted in professional journals. But by 1965 Schmideberg was wholly out of sympathy with psychoanalysis, and indeed psychiatry, as a whole.)

When I indicated that I had made appointments to see analysts like Dr. Michael Balint, Ferenczi's leading follower, as well as James and Alix Strachey, Freud's translators,[16] Glover did not seem to want to hear what I had said. I found in my interviews, and I am saying this although it is bound to sound immodest, that although people were often eager to hear what I had learned from others, there was also apt to be an unspoken fear that I might drift away elsewhere; an inevitable human vanity is involved in talking about one's past, and this factor both facilitated my interviews as well as rendered some of the material suspect.

With Glover I spent a good deal of time going over old membership lists of the British Society; I tried to ask questions even though I never knew what might turn up. In retrospect I think the names that I raised proved to be mainly a waste of time; it took up valuable interviewing space, and most of those people were not active enough participants in psychoanalysis to have been worth the effort. Yet the reminders of these various people did keep Glover interested, as it revived old memories of past associates.

I never discussed with Glover the details of the personal tragedies in his life. His autobiographical paper told me that his first wife, Christine, had died in childbirth, and the baby was stillborn. (After eighteen months of marriage to his "first and only love,"[17] she had a burst appendix that was operated on; she aborted, and then died of septicemia.) Those traumas had preceded his decision to go into analysis in late 1920; it facilitated things, Glover thought, since his first wife had had "academic ambitions" for him, and with her dead he could more readily go to the continent to undertake the training necessary to join a new field. Later in 1926 his admired older brother James, who was an analyst before Edward (both were tubercular), died. (A reliable analyst maintained that James drank, which would be deadly for a diabetic; on the other hand, one incident in which James was picked up on drunk driving charges was attributed to an insulin deficiency.) It would be a sign of what an extraordinary professional recluse Edward was that, although his brother (who published little) had a nine-page obituary in the *International Journal of Psycho-Analysis*, that journal allowed Edward's own death to go unrecorded. (It published "instead of the usual obituary notice" Kubie's biographical sketch, which had been intended for his 85th birthday.)

To flesh out the theme of sadness in Edward's life, his second wife (Gladys), "after four years of sterility" had "a horrifying pregnancy,"[18] which ended in her giving birth to a mentally retarded daughter. The Glovers heroically kept the girl (Ann) at home, caring for her themselves, in order to let her develop as far as she could; she was musical and knew some French, and they would take her with them on visits to analytic colleagues they felt at ease with. Gladys eventually became bedridden, which put even more of a burden on him. According to Kubie she had suffered "for nearly three years from a brain tumour in which her attacks of pain and particularly her terror could be controlled only by his presence."[19] When I later happened to hear that she had died (1966), I wrote him a sincere letter of condolence. He replied with a kindliness I had come to expect: "Many thanks for your letter. I was much touched by it. It is the end of a long story for me. How are you getting on? Well I hope."

Although we never talked about his troubles, nor do I remember ever speaking with him about any aspects of my own private life, we both took for granted the reality of his current professional isolation. It took courage on Glover's part, in keeping with his convictions, for him to leave the British Psychoanalytic Society in 1944. At the time I knew him he was not only a member of the Swiss psychoanalytic group but an honorary member of the American Psychoanalytic Society. (His prior contacts within the international movement had enabled him to find safe havens abroad. Glover had been, however, voted down as president of the IPA in 1957; an Englishman, William Gillespie, proposed by the nominating committee, won the election in which Glover's name, along with that of a French analyst, had been proposed from the floor. After Glover's defeat on the first ballot he declined also to stand for a vice-presidential race.) I never saw in Glover any bitterness about the surface pathos of his situation. If all true believers share a horror at excommunication (and each of the pioneering analysts had to some extent to be fanatics to overcome the barriers to their undertaking new careers), Glover semed content enough with his self-imposed exile. He had resisted invitations to get him to lecture once again at the British Society. Glover and I both assumed my familiarity with his writings and his specific contributions to psychoanalytic thought. He seemed to have a busy clinical practice, although since there was no telephone in his office we could never be interrupted. (Traditionally it has been far more of an intrusion to telephone someone in England than America; the mails were so reliable there that one could then invite someone to tea by letter for the same day.)

When he asked me at our first interview for a list of questions, I had responded by writing him a letter in which I inquired into his ideas about the contrasting ways psychoanalysis had been received and changed in different national cultures, such as England and the United States. He responded at the outset of our second interview by telling me that my question sounded like a "racial" theory. (There was no unpleasant edge to his comment, and in retrospect I would concede that in the late nineteenth century racist connotations were often associated with an emphasis on dominant national traits; Jung could be indicted for believing, even more than Freud, in the power and significance of a racial inheritance. But I would still contend that the dangers of racism should not be considered the end of the proposal to look at psychoanalysis within the perspective of the cultural differences among various countries.)

On behalf of psychoanalysis's cosmopolitanism Glover cited Jones, who had remarked that after World War I, when military "shell-shock" became a clinical problem, "independently of each other investigators in different countries had interpreted war neurosis in similar ways." Glover did concede immediately, without any prompting from me, that that was not all there was to it; the analysts were "pupils of the same men," and "their ideas all came from the same place." Glover preferred, instead of taking a national character line of reasoning, to trace whatever differences there were to "the influence of individuals." (Freud had his own reasons, as a Jew struggling to escape from the narrow confines of his background, for insisting on universalizing whatever he thought he knew about human psychology. When I saw Anna Freud that summer, I had brought up the existence of a psychoanalytic group in Japan. She said that although she had met some of them she could not understand what they were doing, and that she did not think they comprehended her either, but she thought it was impossible to be sure what was going on there under the rubric of psychoanalysis. I thought to myself then that greater clarity between the Japanese and the rest of the psychoanalytic movement might only have risked the expulsion of the Japanese from the IPA; Lacan in France had suffered the fate of being effectively excluded, but then Paris was so close to London as to appear threatening, whereas having a Japanese society looked good for the international and cross-cultural standing of psychoanalysis. Glover was so unassuming as not ever to have mentioned to me his having analyzed Yaekichi Yabe, founder of Japanese psychoanalysis. I later found out that some of the most distinctive contributions of the Japanese analysts were in line with some of Kleinian thinking.)

As much as Glover had not been keen in following up on my inquiry about the comparative national receptions of psychoanalytic doctrine, he himself did however once comment about how good the situation of analysis in Holland was. The Dutch society was largely non-Jewish, as were the Swiss and the early British groups, which was noteworthy compared to the rest of the movement. (The Dutch had welcomed Freud's ideas to an unusual degree even before World War I, and by the 1960s psychoanalysis was flourishing there; Anna Freud had mentioned to me that some psychiatric professorships had recently gone to analysts not "in spite" of their Freudian allegiances but "because of them.")

Later that summer I found myself beginning my notes about an interview with Glover: "I've grown to quite like the chap—curious, though, how he announces the end of the interview; he just rises and expects me to know that I am to leave." (I have often wondered how important a clinical reality such nonverbal acts can constitute; one other example would be Freud's continental European custom of shaking hands with patients before and after every analytic hour. In his book on technique Glover discussed, with great subtlety, the issue of handshakes,[20] and how it is apt to affect different kinds of patients, yet he ignored the role of the practice in helping to ensure reality testing. It is still the custom to shake hands today in someplace like Heidelberg in Germany. I now suspect that Glover, who failed to talk about the implications of a receptionist accompanying patients, was missing the woods for the trees. When I saw Erich Fromm, he thought of Glover as a leading exponent of classical analytic technique, and made fun of some of his observations about how psychologically helpless analysts can be without the help of the free associations of patients.) Although I felt a power element implicit in Glover's way of terminating an interview, I was happy to undertake such a tilted contract between us as unequals for the sake of what I was learning. But the built-in authoritarianism in his somewhat peculiar way of ending an interview was accompanied, I later reflected, by another oddity: I never knew beforehand how long each interview would last, and it would vary from time to time, although on each occasion I had the distinct impression that I had been sandwiched in between Glover's regular appointments.

Toward the end of our time together I find in my notes: "Glover enjoyed this session—like the one before last." That summer I went off on a short holiday to Greece, coinciding with the beginning of the temporary holiday closing of the British Psychoanalytic Society's library facilities (located then almost around the corner from Glover's office); Glover told me he envied me the trip, since he had only himself been as far east as Albania. When I confessed at one point that I was beginning to run out of questions, Glover had confidence in my abilities, he simply suggested that I get my "grey-matter moving," and in fact I found myself able to pose new queries.

At the outset Glover had been especially interested in talking about his training at the Berlin Psychoanalytic Institute, which was newly established, during 1921. He felt that in retrospect he and his colleagues had all taken for granted an objectively remarkable experience. Glover had had to wait a year in order to get Karl Abraham as his analyst, and it took time to get visas after World War I was over. (Glover, a pacifist, had also been attached as a physician to an English Quaker Relief Commission. Although Abraham, unlike Ferenczi in Budapest, had made no special point about writing on technique, Abraham was widely esteemed as a sound clinician.) I asked why he had not gone to Freud, but it turned out that Glover had heard from his brother James that Freud's list of patients was already "full-up," and Abraham was considered "second-best." In those days, according to Glover, it was so pleasant when one went abroad that it was tempting "to stay as long as one could."

Evidently Abraham took a personal interest in his patients; after awhile he had invited Glover to his house. Yet even there Abraham "never let up" interpreting psychoanalytically, but Abraham was, according to Glover, "gentle about it." (Glover wrote that it was "a genuine Freudian analysis, although my relation to him was more in the form of undergraduate to Oxford tutor."[21]) Glover remembered that in one of Abraham's letters to Freud, Abraham was worried about "slow progress" in a case, even though Glover said that Abraham had only seen the patient twice. Freud replied by saying that Abraham should not get discouraged too soon. (In my opinion—which is a minority one—Abraham is now an overestimated figure in the history of psychoanalysis, a point that is hard for Kleinians to accept since she herself thought that Abraham's work was a key to authenticating the link between her own ideas and those of Freud. Although it is true that Abraham seems to have had a stable character structure, in his letters to Freud he often comes across as a boring straight-man, and his attitude toward Freud appears to me to have been, strictly speaking, infantile. Nonetheless, Klein as well as Glover and many other early analysts had chosen to go to him for an analysis.)

Did Abraham, like Freud, talk about the early history of psychoanalysis? No, except that Abraham was "always crazy" about Wilhelm Fliess. (Freud's own falling out with the Berlin physician Fliess had taken place in 1902, but Fliess had played a notable role in Freud's creation of psychoanalysis; Freud's middle son Oliver told me that his father had always kept a photo of Fliess hanging in his apartment, but Oliver—usually correct about details—may have been mixed up by a picture of another bearded gentleman. Although Fliess's last known contact with Freud came in 1904, Fliess stayed abreast of psychoanalysis, and one of Fliess's sons for a time later joined the field.) Abraham had talked to Glover quite a lot about Fliess's theory of periodicity, a notion that once especially intrigued Freud, and also Abraham had discussed Fliess's ideas on psychosexual development, which had also been an influence on Freud's views.

But mainly as a clinical analyst Abraham would use illustrative material, "thumb-nail sketches of other cases, to help you open up"; according to Glover, Abraham used this technique frequently in order "to loosen up resistances." (As a Freudian Glover accepted Freud's idea that to the degree people lack self-knowledge it means that they are "resisting" insight.) In Glover's view any technique that helps "overcome resistances" is in itself a valuable approach, and he thought that Abraham's technique as an analyst was "an easy, quiet, standard" one.

In 1965 Glover had just written the Introduction to the Freud–Abraham correspondence,[22] a book that I was reading in page proofs that summer; since I already knew from James Strachey that important letters had been censored from the about-to-be-published volume, I poked around in questioning Glover to see if I could find out more of what had been left out. Although Glover told me he had read the complete version of the Freud–Abraham letters, I got nowhere with him in trying to elicit more about the tendentiously edited correspondence; Glover may have been in reality an outsider, but he was still behaving as a loyal establishmentarian.

I even mentioned the late angry letter by Freud to Abraham (not long before Abraham's premature death) that Strachey had informed me about. (For the sake of his *Standard Edition of the Complete Psychological Works of Sigmund Freud* Strachey had had access to the complete Freud–Abraham correspondence; Strachey was such a secure insider that he could safely afford an occasional indiscretion.) But with me Glover remained the soul of correctness without making any display at all of his determination to be silent. About all I could evoke from Glover was some discussion of the psychoanalytic film that Abraham, and also his Berlin colleague Hanns Sachs, were interested in; Glover said that Freud had had "a rooted objection" to the project. Otherwise, Glover agreed with Abraham in saying that the only disagreements between Abraham and Freud had been in some differences of "estimations of character." (Glover was still on close terms with Abraham's widow and children in London. Abraham's wife and son had changed their last names on moving to England; thanks to Glover's help I had a chance to interview Mrs. Abraham, and her analyst daughter Hilda was present as well. Hilda Abraham, a woman I found not at all bright, insisted on such strange translations of the Freud–Abraham letters that her professional co-translator, Eric Mosbacher, told me he had refused to have his real name appear on the credit page of the book. A revised edition of this whole correspondence, edited by Ernst Falzeder, is due out one of these days.)

Glover mentioned, in reminiscing about his Berlin days, that Karen Horney had been prominent then. He somehow thought that her ideas had eventually "died out" in America, although in future decades the feminist movement would carry her reputation to altogether new heights of prominence.[23] Glover had written critically of her work in which she suggested that Freud's biological approach needed a cultural corrective. Glover considered that what he took to be the American tendency "to let everyone have their say" was better than the British way of splitting into separate training groups because of theoretical differences. (As we shall see, such a split was the main consequence of the debate over Klein that Glover had helped precipitate in the British Psychoanalytic Society at the end of World War II. And Horney, once demoted at the New York Psychoanalytic Society, had proceeded to found her own group.) Glover said that he was "rather shocked" at the idea of "throwing people out" of a psychoanalytic society. (Yet he did not seem to realize that essentially that is what Freud had done with Adler and Jung, as well as their respective supporters; in 1965 it was not yet clear to me what had happened in those pre-World War I squabbles.[24] I did not realize that Klein's supporters might have feared an intention on Glover's part formally to exclude them from the British Psychoanalytic Society. Jones at least worried about the possibility that some might feel forced to resign.)

I do not think that Glover knew at all much about America. He did appreciate the different reaction official psychiatry had had toward psychoanalysis in the States as opposed to Great Britain. Even before World War I psychiatrists in America were using Freud's concepts in their clinical practice; American receptivity to new ideas partly helps account for Freud's early impact. The American tradition of psychotherapy was optimistic and reform-minded; although by the 1970s the clinical tide would be going in an opposite direction, away from Freud, up until then American psychiatry and the whole general culture had been thoroughly imbued with at least a surface level of psychoanalytic teachings. In England, on the contrary, both neurologists and psychiatrists had by and large stood aloof from Freud's influence, relying instead on their own traditions of dealing with clinical issues. (Neurology has been one of the glories of British medicine.) Glover did know about one book on psychoanalysis in America, the early survey by Clarence Oberndorf,[25] which Glover thought "very good." (I later found out that Oberndorf had been one of Freud's least-favored patients. According to some it was he that Freud had once dismissed from treatment on the grounds that he "had no unconscious"; such ironic condemnation was almost the worst Freud could say about anyone. Freud got off to a bad start with Oberndorf, born in the South, by making an early tactless dream interpretation that linked race with Obderndorf having remained a bachelor.[26] Evidently Freud did not appreciate the racial sensitivities of white Southerners; part of Freud's devaluation of America was to view it as Indian territory that would one day become a Negro republic.[27])

The more Glover and I chatted, the more pro-American he seemed to become. The anti-American issue came up time and again that summer, in a number of different interviewing contexts. Anna Freud's own prejudices were mild compared to the diatribe against all things American I heard from someone like Masud Khan.[28] (Glover was impressed by Khan, although a bit mystified how Khan could successfully navigate between Klein and Anna Freud.) Glover told me that in America analysts were more "generous" and "democratic" about competing views than would be the case elsewhere.

Why was American psychoanalysis so different from on the continent? He thought it was hard to say. I suggested that perhaps because, for a variety of partly fortuitous reasons, no one had come to the States straight from Freud, with his unqualified blessings, American psychoanalysis had taken its own independent course. (But I now think that that explanation does not stand up well. Freud had after World War I chosen Horace W. Frink to lead his American followers, but Frink's mental collapse put a quick end to his leadership.[29] Freud's general distaste for America helps explain why he did not settle, even after the debacle with Frink, on a new chosen disciple for the New World. But perhaps Freud had accurately felt the way the American response to him could skirt the European view of tragedy which was so intrinsically a part of Freud's world outlook.[30])

Max Eitingon was a memorable figure among the Berlin analysts during Glover's own training. Yet Eitingon "never spoke at meetings." (From others I learned that Eitingon had a stammer.) Although Eitingon was not the equal of the most famous Berlin analysts, he did have a great deal of money, and that ensured his standing within Freud's movement. Although in Glover's view Eitingon was "a silent man," Glover pointed out that Eitingon had been the first to join up with Abraham; Eitingon, like Abraham, had had some psychiatric training in Switzerland, which was unusual for analysts of that generation. (North Americans are still likely to underestimate the immense professional gap throughout continental Europe between neurology, the field in which Freud got his own training, and psychiatry; psychoanalysis was itself a wholly separate discipline. In Britain psychiatry has always been intimately related to neurology.) Evidently Abraham viewed Eitingon as "rather a dilettante"; Eitingon did not produce much, which Abraham "did not like." The only thing that Eitingon ever did of "any consequence" in the psychoanalytic movement was in the area of establishing an international training system for analysts; Glover thought that Eitingon had been keen on "a fairly rigid system," which later got rejected.

(In 1988 a controversy arose about whether Eitingon could have ever once been a secret agent for the Soviets under Stalin. It would surely be remarkable if the K.G.B. had indirectly funded the whole psychoanalytic training system. Within psychoanalysis Eitingon functioned as the perfect *apparatchik*—a man of the apparatus—and a generous benefactor of Freud's cause, as well as a close personal friend. A sophisticated historian of Russian psychoanalysis has recently observed, "There is no proof that Max Eitingon was a Soviet agent; however, there are sufficient grounds for such a hypothesis."[31])

Eitingon did have a strong tie to Freud, as did Hanns Sachs, who was another luminary from Glover's Berlin period. He considered Sachs, who was originally a lawyer and not medically trained, a "cultural *flâneur*." Glover held it against Sachs that he had trained Franz Alexander for only "three months"; Sachs then supposedly concluded that Alexander was "a brilliant mind who needs no more analysis." Glover insisted that it was simple-minded to decide on the basis of such a short time that Alexander was "fully normal." (Alexander later had come to epitomize recommended changes in psychoanalytic technique that Glover detested,[32] and Anna Freud did too,[33] which may help account for Glover's singling out this so-called clinical misjudgment of Sachs's. Alexander was later to be the life and soul of an interesting period in the history of analysis in Chicago, but Alexander is unduly neglected today.) Glover felt that by 1965 any such three months of analysis as Sachs supposedly gave Alexander would be deemed only the beginning of things.

Yet at the same time Glover could fall into a curious contradiction, for he asked in the context of Alexander's brief analysis with Sachs how it can be that, if we know so much more now, people got well in the early days of psychoanalysis? He liked to quote A. A. Brill as having been "not far off the mark when he expressed the opinion that psycho-analysis was already a finished product in 1907."[34] (In 1931 Glover had published a well-known paper on "The Therapeutic Effect of Inexact Interpretation: A Contribution to the Theory of Suggestion,"[35] which was more than an opening shot at Melanie Klein, which is the way it is usually seen.) Glover meant to be saying in seeing me that basically we do not understand much more about therapy than in the early 1920s. But the example he offered of Alexander's short analysis did not at all prove what he wanted to demonstrate, for if in the 1920s Sachs had in fact been naively optimistic about treatment, then perhaps the state of psychoanalytic therapy in the old days left something to be desired. Glover was, however, insistent that the early analyses had been too short; he illustrated this proposition with the additional instance of Jones, who Glover recalled being with Ferenczi in analysis for only "four months." (Newly available evidence indicates that Jones was even at that exaggerating how long he spent with Ferenczi.[36]) I have no doubt that it was true that in the beginning a nine-month analysis was, as Glover contended, considered a long one.

Sachs was Viennese, and had gone to Berlin not out of any discontent with Freud's immediate circle but rather to "lift" some of the training "burdens" from Abraham's shoulders, once the Berlin Institute was underway as a training center. Whenever Sachs went on vacation in those days he would be accompanied by a "caravan" of trainees, who in turn had patients with them as well. Glover claimed that Sachs had a "chip on the shoulder" because of the allied blockade of Central Europe during World War I; Glover said that Sachs attributed a tubercular relapse of his own (Glover's first medical papers were on tuberculosis) to that blockade, and Glover remembered Sachs as "a man with a grievance." (Sachs was one of the first people in analysis to concern himself with problems of technique, a special area of Glover's interest. I had to wonder about Glover's account of Sachs's so-called grievance, since it did not jibe with accounts others gave me of Sachs's relatively easy-going personality.) According to Glover Theodor Reik was also someone with a "grievance," because of a famous lawsuit against him in Vienna. (Reik, not a doctor, was sued in Vienna under a law against quackery; it was on this occasion that Freud wrote his essay in defense of the practice of lay analysis.) Glover said that Reik could not see why there were fewer English and American patients in Vienna than in the early days, and Glover told me that he thought that Reik felt it was somehow Glover's "fault." (Although Glover's status as an outsider in London seemed to give him the advantage of distance as an observer, the relative frustrations of his professional life meant he might have been projecting some of his own feelings onto others.)

Glover of course had his idiosyncracies, and blind spots, but I found him one of the most refreshingly direct of all the early analysts I interviewed. Despite his reputation as a polemicist he was unusually even-handed about most of those he talked about. I suppose, in thinking back on it now, that his relative isolation in London made him more receptive to responding to my historical inquiries. In hindsight it has to be remarkable how British scholars had not been more inquisitive about what Glover might have had to add to the saga of the early days of psychoanalysis. People with different interests than my own would doubtless have elicited from him a rather separate set of responses, yet I always remained grateful for the time he was willing to give me and what he enabled me to learn. (My own 1969 work on Victor Tausk, which proved to be highly controversial, seems to have left Glover—according to a letter to Kubie—relatively unperturbed.[37])

2

Ernest Jones As a Leader

For years Glover had been Scientific Secretary of the British Society, and in effect Jones's second-in-command. (Glover had also served as Honorary Secretary of the Bulletin of the International Psychoanalytic Association, Director of the Clinic of the British Society, Director of its Research, Chairman of its Training Committee, as well as Scientific Secretary—a roster of offices like something out of Gilbert and Sullivan.) Glover said that his office-holding had imposed on him the burden of being politically "tactful," not only to the other members but to Jones in particular as President. In Glover's view (and here others plentifully confirmed him) Jones could be "peppery." When I asked what kind of analyst Jones was, Glover replied that he was "a standard Freudian—until perhaps the last ten years of his life," when Glover thought Jones had "wavered" in being a "staunch" follower of Freud's. (Jones had died in 1958; by Jones's "wavering" Glover was referring to his differences with Jones about whether Melanie Klein constituted a "deviation" from Freud.)

When, after I knew Glover better, I inquired about Jones's clinical technique, Glover replied that Jones was "a rather tough" analyst, "in a way" one could say that he was "ritualistic." Jones did "not mind patients suffering a bit"; even in the context of Freud's written principle that suffering is an incentive to insight, I thought Glover was saying something stronger about Jones's willingness to stand back from trying to alleviate human misery. But Glover also maintained that Jones had a fairly "standard" approach. (I knew that one reason that Jones had had relatively few students in London was that he charged consulting fees in analysis, and therefore was a very costly analyst to have.)

Jones had, in Glover's opinion, one "pet" disciple, Dr. Elizabeth Rosenberg-Zetzel, and Glover told me that he thought this was probably "just plain counter-transference" on Jones's part. (She was objectively very talented, and came from an immensely rich and prominent American family. I heard from her sister, Anne Geismar, who was in analysis in New York with Brill at the same time in the 1930s that Elizabeth was with Jones, that Jones was capable of using confidential family information with Zetzel. When the two sisters started analysis they both were single, until Brill's patient married a literary critic—Maxwell Geismar—who held a fellowship restricted to unmarried candidates; Anne Geismar insisted that Brill would have had to communicate the news of the marriage with the proviso that secrecy was essential. Jones went right ahead and told Elizabeth about her only sibling's marriage, so the information had not come either from her sister or her parents; Anne interpreted Jones's action as designed to drive Elizabeth further away from her family, at the same time that Jones was able to assert his own power over his patient.[1])

Glover did, despite what he might think of Jones personally or Jones's judgment about Zetzel, make a point of praising Jones's qualities as an expositor. In Glover's view Jones's article on symbolism[2] had never been bettered. (This was a point echoed by other Freudians in London as well.) *What about Jones's biography of Freud?* (In those days Jones's three-volume biography was absolutely essential to understanding the history of Freud's school; it still remains an outstanding source, but Jones's biases are now more evident, and there has been an immense expansion of the literature in general.) Glover thought that the Jones biography contained too much "detail" but that it would be a great help to future biographers.

Glover thought it was significant, given how difficult Jones could be, that it took Freud a long time to like or trust Jones. Glover's point got underlined when the Freud–Jung correspondence appeared in print during 1974. We then learned that Freud had written Jung:

> Jones is undoubtedly a very interesting and a worthy man, but he gives me a feeling of, I was almost going to say, racial strangeness. He is a fanatic and doesn't eat enough. 'Let me have men about me that are fat,' says Caesar, etc. He almost reminds me of the lean and hungry Cassius. He denies all heredity; to his mind even I am a reactionary. How, with your moderation, were you able to get on with him?

(Freud had no compunction about identifying with Shakespeare's Caesar.) Jung wrote to Freud about Jones that he was "an intellectual liar (no moral judgment intended!) hammered by the vicissitudes of fate and circumstance into too many facets. But the result? Too much adulation on one side, too much opportunism on the other." As late as 1927, and in contrast to his public praise of Jones, Freud was capable of writing to a disciple, Max Eitingon, "I don't believe that Jones is consciously ill-intentioned; but he is a disagreeable person, who wants to display himself in ruling, angering and agitating, and for this his Welsh dishonesty ('the Liar from Wales') serves him well."[3]

It turns out that Jones had confessed early on to Freud, "the originality complex is not strong with me; my ambition is rather to know, to be 'behind the scenes,' and 'in the know,' rather than to find out. I realize that I have very little talent for originality . . . my work will be to try to work out in detail, and to find new demonstrations for the truth of ideas . . . that others have suggested."[4] One of his lady friends, analyzed by Freud, could write about Jones to Freud, "I wonder why he is such an incorrigible fibber (to put it politely!)." Freud once put the matter firmly to Jones, "accuracy and plainness is [sic] not in the character of your dealings with people. Slight distortions and evasions, lapses of memory, twisted denials, a certain predilection for sidetracks prevail. . . ."[5] Whatever lack of personal affection Freud may have had for Jones, Freud knew he could rely on Jones to forward the cause of psychoanalysis in Britain.

What does one make of the secret Committee founded by Jones before World War I? Glover did not think there was anything peculiar in such a secret group of people. (In subsequent years even more would be made of this Committee, even though it should always have been clear that Freud had never intended to yield an ounce of his real power. The members of the original Committee, besides Freud and Jones, were Otto Rank, Sandor Ferenczi, Hanns Sachs, Karl Abraham, and Max Eitingon.) Glover thought that Jones's proposal of that Committee had been designed to relieve Freud of some of the leadership "burdens" involved in running an international movement. Since I thought the secrecy was peculiar in a science, I questioned Glover about the two Greek letters that, I had only recently realized, had once been used in private to stand for the name of psychoanalysis. Glover, however, did not think any of this was important. To him psychoanalysis had "not been secret enough." Yet more than once he gestured at a big cabinet in his office, which he implied was full of confidential training material, and which I might seek permission from the British Society to quote. (After his death all this got destroyed.)

Glover did readily concede that sometimes Jones's books could be historically unreliable, and he immediately began talking about Jones's account of "the Ferenczi episode." At one point I pressed Glover on this point, since it was appalling to me how Jones could have unfairly attributed the ideas of Ferenczi's last phase, which had been the source of controversy, to some underlying "psychosis" having supposedly finally asserted itself.[6] Glover thought that Ferenczi had had "quite good results" prior to his advocating a more "active" therapy. ("Activity" meant that Ferenczi was experimenting with giving up some of the distance and neutrality that Freud had recommended for analytic beginners; Freud's own clinical practices with patients, such as Ferenczi himself, were at substantial odds with his published "rules."[7])

As far as Ferenczi's health went, to Glover as a physician it was "obvious," having met Ferenczi at an international meeting shortly before his death, that he was suffering from pernicious anemia; the change was "startling," and that affliction, rather than any emotional disorder, could account for whatever behavioral problems Ferenczi had experienced. (In his biography of Freud Jones had underplayed the existence of physical illness in Ferenczi's final period; Jones made no mention of the pernicious anemia, cited by Freud in his formal obituary.[8] But Jones may have been following Freud's own private lead, since Freud seems to have seen the physical affliction as somehow an expression of psychotic conflicts.[9] Ferenczi's own diary from his last year[10] does not sustain any of the diagnostic name-calling that Jones undertook about Ferenczi in Jones's Freud biography.)

Glover said that he "trusted" Dr. Michael Balint, who was Ferenczi's student and literary executor, in his judgment on behalf of Ferenczi's mental stability. Ferenczi was always "charming" and "imaginative," and he had a special capacity for thinking out and elaborating his ideas. (Anna Freud wrote Jones that she had not observed the better side of Ferenczi, even though people uniformly endorsed with me the characterization of him by one of Freud's relatives as "the milk of human kindness.") As far as the falling out between Freud and Ferenczi, when Freud came to "loggerheads" over something important with an intimate friend, Freud could not be at all friendly anymore.

Jones was, Glover told me in the context of discussing Ferenczi, a "spiteful, jealous little man." (Glover was speaking about Jones absolutely matter-of-factly, without any trace of emotion or hatred. Another interviewee of mine, Dr. Smiley Blanton, called Jones "querulous, nasty, a mean son of a bitch."[11]) During Jones's analysis with Ferenczi, it turns out, Ferenczi had written Freud, "his dreams are full of mockery and scorn toward me, which he has to admit, without being able really to believe in these hidden characteristics of his . . . he forbids himself any independence, which then avenges itself by means of an inclination toward intrigue and secret triumphs, treachery."[12] Ferenczi was astute about how ruthless, single-minded, and unscrupulous Jones could be as a power-seeker. It was characteristic for Jones to have written to Anna Freud in 1956 about the famous literary critic Lionel Trilling, who had almost obsequiously hosted Jones for a program on Freud's hundredth anniversary: "Trilling (television) was charming, easy and docile, but he is not very bright—neurotic and self-conscious. I had to tell him what to say!"[13]

Jones, Glover reported, could not see how Glover could go to meetings of the academic psychologist J. A. Hadfield. (In general I found that each of Freud's disciples were apt to pride themselves, as

Glover was doing in contrast to Jones, in being less doctrinaire than others within their movement.) Glover thought he should at least "go to the pub" with people like Hadfield who were critical of psychoanalysis. (It was reported to me by another source that Glover had analyzed Hadfield.[14]) Even when Jones wrote an obituary, for example the one on Abraham, Jones could not stop himself from "throwing a few daggers." Jones had expressed his amazement at Abraham's supposed concern for academic advancement when it was Jones himself who had been bent on getting a university appointment. (Jones's embitterment by his lack of academic recognition was confirmed by others. His failure at a London hospital was the prelude to his going to Canada before World War I, and then at the University of Toronto he had once again gotten into hot water.) Another London analyst had already pointed out to me how Jones had been sure to insert some swipes at Sachs in his official obituary of him too. (Sachs had introduced Jones to his second wife, and translated a couple of Jones's books. Jones commented that "a considerable narcissism formed an unmistakeable feature of Sachs's personality, though it was expressed in amusing rather than disturbing ways. For instance, every place where he lived became the most desirable in the world. . . ."[15] Jones had paid for Sachs to recuperate once in Switzerland.[16]) Glover, in spite of everything, thought that since Jones had "a fine mind" he had been a good man to have "behind the ramparts." (Freud had himself used military-sounding metaphors when it came to promoting psychoanalysis.) In the campaign for psychoanalysis Glover had backed Jones up, and still felt that he had been "entitled" to that support.

Jones, physically relatively undersized compared to Glover, struck him as "a fiery little man." (Another London psychiatrist, rather sour, told me he was repelled by how "slick and certain" Jones was of everything, and considered Jones a "snake in the grass."[17] The bit of Brill's correspondence I have seen shows how Jones could double-cross the gullible Brill at international meetings.) Glover said that he had not opposed Jones in public, except for once. (Glover was excepting the eighteen months of debate over Klein within the British Society.) Jones and Glover used to walk home together after psychoanalytic meetings, and that one time Jones had observed, "Edward, tonight was the first time you have opposed me." Glover added for my benefit, "Little did he know." (But I thought to myself that Glover was, compared to Jones, hopelessly naïve at political infighting. In this connection I am reminded of Leo Durocher's principle that "nice guys finish last.")

Working under Jones was not easy for Glover to take. For example, he mentioned how much he had liked David Eder, a Jewish analyst who, although analyzed in Vienna by Freud as well as Tausk, had become a Jungian for a time.[18] (Eder's wife had been analyzed by Jung.) Eder always felt torn in his allegiance between Zionism and psychoanalysis. By 1920 Eder had, according to Jones, despite earlier doctrinal wavering, "become an analyst again."

Glover said that Jones had been "a little bit jealous" of Eder, even though Jones had introduced him to psychoanalysis. Eder could be notably obstinate. (In his autobiography Jones documents this obstinancy; before World War I Eder could not, to Jones's frustration, appreciate the full significance of the differences between Freud and Jung. It is noteworthy, I think, how Glover's own name does not come up once in Jones's autobiography.) At a meeting Eder, who was then serving as Secretary of the British Society, clashed once with Jones; they had by then given Jones a presidential chair, and Glover was leaning on it, undoubtedly, Glover now thought, unconsciously trying to "elbow" Jones out. On that occasion of Eder's difference with Jones Glover felt "a strange vibration"; for "by God" Jones was literally shaking with anger at Eder. After Eder's death in 1936 Freud had written to Eder's sister-in-law, the analyst Barbara Low, "he belonged to the people one loves without having to trouble about them. One's heart warmed at the thought of him. . . ."[19] Jones also once wrote that Eder had "a heart of gold."[20] Yet it becomes comprehensible how Jones could have thought Freud had betrayed him in publicly crediting Eder with having been "the first, and for a time the only doctor to practice the new therapy in England."[21] (Jones was naturally protective of his own historical role, and when he saw the passage in print he was quick to write in protest to Anna Freud.)

"If Jones got a dislike then he never got over it." Glover claimed that Jones feared things when there was no need; but "Jones did not show fear but rather fight." (This was a characteristically generous interpretation of Glover's.) Ever since Jones's earliest career, before going to Canada, Jones had felt threatened. His worry and professional unhappiness took the form, Glover said, of "slaughtering anyone who came across his path." (This description would have been shared by other of Jones's contemporaries in London; despite Glover's own capacities as a polemicist, no one I met thought of him in the same partisan category as Jones.) Eder had been an old friend, but Jones came to "despise" him. Eder's stubborness meant to Glover that Eder had "a mind like a bear"; and when Eder used his abstract capacities to oppose Jones, it was then that Jones had quaked in his chair with anger and hatred.

Glover said that he had known Jones for many years, but felt he never succeeded in knowing him well, and Glover thought that for a long time he had been probably Jones's nearest friend. (Another analyst, Dr. Sylvia Payne, remarked to me that Jones had filled her with cases once she started practicing in London, and she never had a vacancy; Jones spoke "awfully well," and "everybody respected his mind," but she also said that she had "never gotten anything from him as a friend." Although he believed in her work "people did not get very attached to Jones.") Glover might give me details about the difficulties within the British Society, but then also draw back and say that such controversies can afflict any group, and that he preferred that those quarrels get buried. I felt this was a genuine feeling on Glover's part, and that he was mild and lacking in spite.

The original pre-World War I London Psychoanalytic Society had "come to grief," and Glover said that Jones was "only too glad" to abolish it and then start over again in 1919. Early that year Jones wrote to Freud about Jones's intention to "expel the Jung 'rump.'" Freud was agreeable to Jones's proceeding to "throw out the majority of former members." When Jones wrote about "the question of constituting a new society (purged of Eder, etc.) . . .", Freud heartily went along: "Your intention to purge the London society of the jungish members is excellent."[22] (Fromm once singled out this sentence, highlighting the word "purge."[23]) Freud was hesitant to accept Eder's wife for analysis: "I am not sure that her case may be worth my time or her money, being aware of Eder's impotence, etc."[24] By 1923 however Eder was readmitted to the new British Society, and after his death Freud contributed money to the Eder Memorial Fund that was set up. Glover thought that Jones "rather overdid" the necessities of psychoanalysis being self-protective out of his being "a disappointed man." (Glover struck me as immensely kind, but his repeated references to the disappointments of others must have said something of how he felt about himself, which may have been appropriate to his advanced age. But in Jones's case I think Glover was dead right.)

In Berlin Glover remembered that there had been literary figures who had been interested in psychoanalysis. But neither there, nor in London, did Glover think that "associate" members of the Society had been of any "use." (When I once read him an old list of those names for one year's membership, he expressed with some astonishment that he "had never seen these people!") At the same time Glover objected to the "social discrimination" against nonanalysts, and thought it persisted as a historical hangover; he pointed out how in America there were even "famous" names like Smith Ely Jelliffe,[25] "a first-class mind," who lent some support to psychoanalysis. (Subsequently I found out that because of Jelliffe's interest in Jung, Freud developed personal contempt for Jelliffe. The correspondence between Jelliffe and Glover indicates that Jelliffe could refer patients to Glover.) I never did point out to Glover enough of the contradictions in his thinking; I was too busy trying to keep straight what he had told me. But perhaps if I had seen more of Glover's inconsistencies at the time they came up it would have undermined our rapport. For example, without any challenge from me, Glover wound up this particular line of reasoning of his, in connection with what kind of adherents psychoanalysis needed, by opposing outsiders who were not fully committed, on the grounds that "botanists have no place in a society of analytic chemists." (It certainly seems strange to me that Glover could so readily compare psychoanalysis by analogy to any of the pure sciences.)

Jones had, in Glover's view, been exceptionally good at holding together the international movement, at a time when there was "a real danger" of a split between America and Europe over training matters.

The controversy over the legitimacy of lay analysis went on for Congress after Congress, which Freud no longer attended after first getting cancer of the jaw in 1923. The Americans, determined to keep a medical monopoly for psychoanalysis, never yielded to Freud's own personal point of view. Jones, despite his "slightly unkind and satirical wit," was a "good chairman," and Glover readily volunteered that Jones had been faced with a hard job. But according to Glover Jones had been "very cute," once the *Psychoanalytic Quarterly* first got started (1932) in the States, in making the London-based *International Journal of Psycho-Analysis* an obligatory subscription for all analysts. Most subscribers were already American, but Jones had gotten it passed that if you belonged to a member society of the international association then you had to subscribe; the *International Journal* remained, nonetheless, editorially a British publication.[26] Glover thought that the early analysts had generally been not too successful in their previous, ordinary professions, so that at contentious international meetings everybody was apt to be terribly "cock-at-the-hoop."

Glover and I talked about Miss Ella Sharpe, as we proceeded to discuss all the early British analysts in the Society Jones had succeeded in having created. She had first been a teacher at Nottingham, and had a lot of cultural interests before she took up analysis. She came to London around 1917, at a time when three psychological societies were in existence then. He mentioned in particular the Medico-Psychological Clinic in Brunswick Square[27] as a post-World War I "venture." Miss Sharpe was a student there, where she met James Glover. He took over the Clinic around 1918. He had had some analysis at that Clinic with a Miss Julia Turner; after being dissatisfied with what Jones called "the pseudo-analytic work in vogue"[28] at that Clinic, James Glover had gone to Abraham in Berlin. Edward Glover recalled that his brother ended up at the Clinic "by not recommending anything but psychoanalysis to patients."

(My notes record that Glover smiled at this proslytizing of his brother's; I felt rather startled, both by James Glover's missionary zeal as well as by Edward's evident pleasure even in 1965 at his brother's recommendations. By 1926 Ernst Simmel had started a psychoanalytic sanitarium called Tegelsee near Berlin, where Freud went to stay several times for operations; Simmel's idea was that everybody who worked there should have been analyzed, even the nurses and the janitor. And at Vera Schmidt's experimental psychoanalytic orphanage in Russia during the 1920s, which was attended by Stalin's son Vasily, "all the employees and teachers of the . . . pediatric facility were themselves to undergo analysis."[29] Neither the Simmel or the Schmidt project proved viable for long.) According to Jones's obituary of James Glover, "his first step" on returning from Berlin in 1921 "was to bring to a standstill the work of the Brunswick Square Clinic by refusing to prescribe any treatment other than psychoanalysis on proper Freudian lines. The members of the Executive Committee ultimately upheld him, and the upshot was that the clinic was finally closed."[30] Eventually James Glover passed the assets of the Brunswick Square Clinic along to Jones and the psychoanalytic society, which eventually set up its own clinic. In addition to Miss Sharpe, both Miss Mary Chadwick and Miss Nina Searl had become analysts through their association with James Glover's early Clinic.

Edward Glover remembered Miss Sharpe in Germany walking along with lillies in her bosom, holding them as if they were a child. She had been analyzed by Jones, and then went to Berlin to be treated by Sachs. It was Miss Sharpe who later invited Sachs to London in 1924 to lecture on technique. And she went back to Sachs as a student whenever she could, over summers for example. Glover thought she was a woman of "very fine feeling—a poetess *manqué*."[31] Literary work was her "forte," and he admired what she did in "applied psychoanalysis." (Freud assumed that psychoanalysis was a neutral system of knowledge that could be "applied" to problems outside of strictly clinical ones.) Miss Sharpe was known to her friends as "Brownie." Glover considered her a nice woman and "quite sound." He thought though that she was "a bit timid," and would not fight on scientific issues. (Glover was saying even more than that she had tried to stay out of the quarrel over Klein.) Glover wound up by characterizing Miss Sharpe as "a quiet, sweet kind of woman," which fit what others told me as well. (When I asked Sylvia Payne who was the best intuitively of the early British analysts, she immediately mentioned Miss Sharpe; evidently Jones had not liked her much and Dr. Payne, who considered Sharpe "a brilliant analyst," volunteered that she could be "tiresome.")

Miss Mary Chadwick dated from Miss Sharpe's period, but was not quite as old. Glover thought she might originally have been a secretary at the Brunswick Square Clinic. She was the first child analyst in England. It was difficult to get permission to travel to Germany in those days, although easier for a German to come to England. Abraham had arranged to get Miss Chadwick her visa; she had also been analyzed, like Miss Sharpe, by Sachs. Ultimately she became an associate member of the British Society in 1923. Glover remembered her as "a pleasant girl really," but when Mrs. Klein came over in 1926 she had "scooped the pool" of child analysis. Miss Chadwick was financially well off, and therefore could do as she liked in arranging her career. Glover said that Klein could "of course brook no opponent," so Miss Chadwick lost status. (Even Klein's own people implied how demanding she was; "not a modest person" was a standard evaluation.) Although Miss Chadwick was to go off from analysis and run a school for young women, she had first helped Ella Sharpe in bringing Sachs over to lecture. Glover insisted that in those days there was a serious lack of authoritative work on technique, and he still was complaining that by the 1960s analysts were continuing to spend more time on abstract theory than on how they approached clinical issues in practice.

Mrs. Joan Riviere was a different figure in the history of British psychoanalysis; no one would think of describing her, like some of the other women in the early Society were characterized to me, as a "very worthy bore." Joan Riviere was, Glover said, a "bright young girl" from Cambridge University (in fact she had not gone to college, but a couple of her relatives taught at Cambridge[32]. She had first been analyzed by Jones (she fell in love with him) and then later went to Freud in Vienna. He chose her to be one of his translators into English, and James Strachey told me that Freud had been fortunate here. (A Glossary Committee was set up in 1921 to decide, in Jones's office, on the English version of Freud's terms; the members consisted of Jones, Mrs. Riviere, James, and Alix Strachey. Jones had the earliest hand in key translating decisions; all the others on the Committee were nonmedical analysts, despite Bruno Bettelheim's later complaint about how scientistically Freud got translated into English.[33])

Was Mrs. Riviere a matriarch? No, but she was "authoritative"; she loved being "a power behind the throne," and succeeded in being just that under Jones's leadership. (Some analysts in London were shocked by James Strachey's lively official obituary of her in 1963:

> I really didn't know her very well. Perhaps I was rather afraid of her. A lot of people were. I often felt sure, for instance, that Ernest Jones was. And indeed she was a very formidable person.... She disapproved of many things in the modern world—including, I fancy, my distinctly leftish political views ... she also regretted my non-committal attitude to questions of psychoanalytic theory. Non-committal was a thing she herself could never be.[34]

Presumably by his having "non-committal" views Strachey was referring to his having been one of the moderates in the clash between Melanie Klein and Anna Freud.)

At one point Mrs. Riviere had tried to strike a bargain with Glover: "Now, as long as you are here, we don't need Jones." But Glover said he would not go along with conspiring with her. (After she had gone to be analyzed by Freud, he looked on her with favor.) She was in Glover's view an "*éminence grise*," and like Strachey Glover thought Jones was frightened of her. *Was she a nice woman?* "No, not a nice woman, but a handsome one with a male mind, if the distinction between male and female thinking means anything." Glover concluded his remarks on Mrs. Riviere by saying that she had later got "caught" in a transference with Mrs. Klein—although he qualified even this judgment by saying "largely." (Freud himself thought Mrs. Riviere under Klein's influence—Mrs. Riviere became a patient of hers—had become heretical, and said her views bore an "unfortunate similarity to Jung's, and, like his, is an important step toward making analysis unreal and impersonal."[35])

Miss Barbara Low was another notable early British analyst. From Glover's perspective she was a part of the Bloomsbury literary and artistic group, though historical experts might not place her there.

Her brother was Sir Sidney Low, an author and journalist, and she was David Eder's sister-in-law; like Eder she was Jewish. (Glover did tend to lump any intellectual, and nonmedical, practitioner of analysis under the heading of "Bloomsbury." It was only long afterwards that I realized Glover's mistakes on this score, but the whole intelligentsia in Britain—like Mrs. Riviere and the Stracheys—did tend to be socially secure, in contrast to the insecurities that the continental analysts brought with them.)

Glover was right in thinking that unlike in America, where the support for analysis came largely from medicine and psychiatry, in England there had been strong backing from cultural and academic sources. Glover specified that by "academic" he did not mean "dull," but was referring to great colleges like King's or Trinity at Cambridge University. Glover thought that on the one hand British intellectuals' pride in being free of prejudices and conventionality, along with their association with ancient centers of learning, helped to account for their receptivity to analysis. But on the other hand he felt that psychiatrists in England were unduly intimidated by the stellar cultural supporters of analysis, with their powerful social and political connections. (The most significant years, in Glover's opinion, that made up the shaping of the character of British analysis were the period from 1915 to 1922.)

Barbara Low had antedated Miss Sharpe in analysis, and wrote a preliminary textbook. Glover considered it unfortunate that she had been analyzed by Sachs. (According to Sylvia Payne, like almost all the other first people in British analysis Barbara Low had earlier been analyzed by Jones.) Glover said that he did not know what Sachs had done, but that whereas she had once been "a wild character" who would fight for a cause like "a tigress," after her analysis with Sachs she had become "soppy and sentimental." Glover conceded that Sachs had made her more "amenable." But he obviously admired the way she had been able to fight in the Society against Jones and "his people." In the end Glover thought she had "faded out" of British analysis (she died in 1955).

Adrian and Karin Stephen were both analysts who were correctly seen by Glover as "literary magnates" in London. Adrian was in Glover's mind "nothing" in particular, just Sir Leslie Stephen's son (which meant he was also the brother of Virginia Woolf and her sister Vanessa, both of whom rather patronized Adrian. His wife Karin also belittled him and even one of his daughters was dismissive about him. Yet a biography of Adrian has recently appeared.[36] As we shall see, Adrian Stephen—originally trained as a barrister—was prominent on governing committees at the time of the height of the controversy over Klein). Karin was the critic Clive Bell's sister-in-law because she was married to Vanessa Bell's brother Adrian, and Karin was a niece of Bertrand Russell's first wife. (Also, Karin's mother became the mistress and then the wife of the art dealer and historian Bernard Berenson.) Karin had given some influential lectures on psychoanalysis at Cambridge, which in 1933 came out as a book, *The Wish To Fall Ill*.[37] (Jones somehow once called her a "nonentity,"[38] but she was threatening enough that he felt he had to put restrictions on her lecturing in London.) Glover thought Karin was "a very good metaphysician"; she had in fact been trained professionally in philosophy. Bertrand Russell had said of her that he thought she had "more philosophical capacity than I have ever seen in a woman."[39]

Karin had a sad end, troubled by her deafness, and after her husband died of a brain tumor she herself later committed suicide. Glover's brother James had analyzed both Adrian and Karin. (According to Edward his brother had not yet learned that it was "difficult" to analyze married couples; Edward said that he himself had analyzed two couples, and that once it had been a big success but the other time a large failure.) It was reported that Karin had come to Edward for a short time over some troubles; he considered her "lovely." (Earlier she had also been analyzed by Clara Thompson in America, and then by Sylvia Payne, who, much to Karin's angry distress, considered her too "unstable" to be suitable as a training analyst for candidates.) Years later I learned from a daughter of the Stephens that Adrian had also been analyzed by Miss Sharpe; almost as a matter of course the daughter had been sent as a child for an analysis with Miss Nina Searl. Both Karin and Adrian felt that Jones had resented their social position, and they could never forgive him for having insisted that they both get medical degrees in order to become analysts.

(The reader can get a feel for Jones's human traits by how he described people in a letter to Brill which I think was about Karin Stephen and her husband Adrian:

> Mrs. —— is a qualified physician who took up medicine after starting her analysis. She was for four or five years in analysis with James Glover, who found her pretty unsatisfactory. The main difficulty appeared to be certain perversions which distorted her general perspective (that is of course, confidential). She had a very brilliant career at Cambridge along philosophical lines. I may add that she is extremely deaf, so it is doubtful how far she would be able to get in practice. She has, I believe, started practice but has not applied for membership of the Society. She is a daughter of Sir —— the famous writer, and is a quite trustworthy and respectable person. . . . She is married to a mild psychotic.[40]

Jones was commiting a slip when he described her as the daughter, as opposed to the daughter-in-law, of a famous writer. Even though Jones was reported to have "grievously insulted a long and imposing list of people," he could be unaware of his insults. He once wrote Brill: "Malice is not in my nature. . . ." Evidently "Jones's aggressiveness was not fully conscious. Anna Freud does not wish me to quote her remark of Jones hurting everyone he talked with at least a little bit. . . ."[41])

Dr. John Rickman was another intellectual, but one who Glover mistakenly associated with Bloomsbury; unlike the Stephens, who were part of Bloomsbury, Rickman was simply smart and well connected, as well as independent of Jones. Glover said he first met Rickman when he was in analysis with Ferenczi, but Rickman was earlier also analyzed by Freud. (One anecdote about Rickman's analysis with Freud is worth recording: Geoffrey Gorer said that once Rickman had shaved off a beard but it took ages for Freud to notice the change. According to Donald W. Winnicott, a friend of Rickman's, because of a distressing early childhood memory of Rickman's Freud had told him to "get out" of being an analyst.)

Rickman went on to play a great part in organizing the clinic associated with the British Psychoanalytic Institute. He also became a strong Kleinian, first going for an analysis to Mrs. Riviere and then to Mrs. Klein. Rickman had helped to bring together the eclectic Tavistock Clinic with the Psychoanalytic Institute, and then had a stroke. Although Rickman had been a successful editor of the *British Journal of Medical Psychology*, Glover thought his influence subsequently "faded." (When Glover also commented that "everyone's does after ten years or so," I felt he was thinking about himself as well.)

I had asked Glover about James Strachey, who obviously as Lytton's younger brother automatically belonged in the Bloomsbury category. (There is still little literature about Frank Ramsey, an extraordinary Cambridge logician and metaphysician, a friend of Ludwig Wittgenstein's and considered by James Strachey to be as brilliant as Bertrand Russell, who had been analyzed in Vienna by Theodor Reik and had written a book about psychoanalysis, but he died early.[42]) Since I had met Strachey, and saw what a bookishly distant person he was, I wondered whether he had actually practiced or, if he had, how he could have been at all good with patients. Glover replied that Strachey had indeed worked with patients, but mainly for the sake of training candidates. He had analyzed, for instance, Donald Winnicott, who then "finished up" with Mrs. Riviere. (Alix Strachey, like her husband a former patient of Freud's, seemed to me in better human contact, but she told me she had never seen the grocer from whom she had for years been ordering food over the phone. Evidently Alix did even less, as far as Glover knew, in the way of practicing. But when I visited the Stracheys in their isolated house at Marlow, outside London, a former patient of Alix's had just been to see her. After James's death in 1967 she seems to have gone to pieces.)

In Glover's view James Strachey was not a clinician, yet as an analyst "he could tackle any case." (Glover seems to have meant that Strachey could undertake so-called character cases, supposedly where symptoms are not a central problem.) Glover said that one did not send him hysterics or psychotics—after all, he "did not know medicine." (Unlike Adrian and Karin Stephen, neither Alix or James—who only spent some weeks before abandoning their medical studies—had had to become physicians; they had to be considered analytically qualified by Jones simply on the basis of their analyses with Freud. He sent Jones explicit instructions on this score.[43])

James Strachey had eventually given up therapeutic work since he "preferred his translating." Glover said that he had not seen either of the Stracheys for years. (He commented on them both having had physical troubles. The Second World War sent them to live in a country house that had belonged to Alix's mother; after her death the Stracheys moved there permanently in 1954.) Glover thought that perhaps Strachey's translations were just "too meticulous," which would fit his "obsessional character." He had heard of Strachey making a translation mistake "only twice," which Glover considered quite a record. (A generation later Strachey's work would be treated as an interpretation, as all translations must be. But I think that a puristic concern with correcting Strachey's translations tends to reinforce, rather than challenge, fundamentalist sorts of thinking. For if we start putting our scholarly resources into refining Strachey's *Standard Edition* of Freud's works, will there not be a tendency to slight the issue of the legitimate reservations that ought to be entertained about the substance of Freud's ideas? The recent effort to mount a return to the "true" Freud is bound, I suspect, to neglect the fair-minded criticisms of his concepts that ought to be considered.[44])

Dr. Lionel Penrose was a figure who again illustrates how hard it could be for Glover (as well as ourselves) to keep straight who was and who was not a member of the Bloomsbury intelligentsia. For Penrose was both a good friend of Rickman's and also once close to the Stracheys. Penrose's brother was a notable art critic. Although others spoke highly of Penrose as a geneticist, to Glover Penrose had been "sidetracked" into becoming a professor of genetics at the University of London. Glover was not sure that Penrose had been analyzed by Jones, but said that Penrose was very critical of him. (That summer I interviewed Penrose, and found that Freud had referred him in Vienna to be analyzed by Siegfried Bernfeld; part of Freud's power arose from the referrals he could send, and at the time Penrose came to Vienna Bernfeld was a special favorite of Freud's.[45])

Eric Hiller was a forgotten figure whom I only came across in the old membership lists of the British Society. Rickman had known him "quite well." Hiller was "a free-lancer" who tried to do publishing for psychoanalysis. He became closely involved with producing Jones's *International Journal*. According to Glover, Hiller was "a nice little man" who also did some clinical work on tobacco and other forms of addiction. Glover recalled all the "enormous, and petty, complications" associated with psychoanalytic (like other) publishing ventures. Hiller was not of any great significance to British psychoanalysis; he had "faded into the blue." When the "amateur" days of psychoanalysis came to an end, these kinds of people went with them.

In this connection Glover mentioned the Viennese A. J. Storfer as another "nice little man." "People" reported that Storfer was "oversensitive," a "paranoid" type, but Glover had been unable to see it.[46] He used to go to "pubs" with him. (Psychoanalysts, following Freud's lead, are extremely unlikely ever to drink much.) Storfer had started working at the psychoanalytic press in Vienna, which Freud had created as an independent entity. Storfer was in charge of a rather lavish collected edition of Freud's works; somehow he became "suspect" in Vienna's analytic circles (I believe because of lack of business sense), he quarrelled with them, and then disappeared from the movement. He ended up moving to the Far East (Shanghai) in the Nazi period, because visas were relatively easy to get for there, and died in Australia.

Dr. David Forsyth was another forgotten man in psychoanalysis, but he had been no minor figure. He was the first in England to get a permit to go to Freud after World War I. A man of "considerable talents," he was a London consultant. Glover thought that Freud had rated him highly. (According to Otto Rank's first wife, Forsyth had been such an important patient that she was asked by Freud to give a dinner party for him in Vienna.) But Forsyth felt that if he played a part in British psychoanalysis, then it should be a major one; and "this aim conflicted with Jones's view of things." Forsyth had come from medical societies where it was not unusual to aspire in the course of time to become president, but Jones stayed on in that office until his semi-retirement in 1944.

Forsyth had quarrelled with Jones, though not openly. Forsyth had a hospital background, so he went on with his medical work there, which "sickened" Jones since he himself had no such affiliations. Once Forsyth even got a hospital vacancy that Jones had wanted. Forsyth was extensively and successfully involved with academic medicine; earlier he had written on oral and respiratory "eroticism." (Under the circumstances it seemed to me remarkable how Jones, in his autobiography, could write about Forsyth's supposed personal jealousy of Jones.[47])

A number of people flitted on and off the British analytic scene, such as the famous psychiatrist Bernard Hart. Glover said that his own brother James had not been "a great fighter," but that he himself was. Once he had become a member of the British Society Jones would send Edward Glover off as an emissary to professional meetings that Jones himself could not attend. (Glover "published for the British Psychoanalytic Society a report on the work done by Ernest Jones and himself on a special committee of the British Medical Association by which psychoanalysis was granted specialty status."[48]) According to Glover, Hart was "obsessively sitting on the fence" about psychoanalysis. His famous 1912 book (*The Psychology of Insanity*[49]) went through numerous editions, and was still in print when I met Glover. That book had had a great influence on the British establishment, to which Hart belonged, but psychoanalysis had never, in Glover's day, won acceptance in those circles. Jones's "dictatorial methods" clashed with people like Hart and Forsyth.

To take another example, Dr. Emmanuel Miller was very keen on analysis; in order to get into the Society (Miller had once started to be analyzed by Jones, but walked out) one had to present a paper. Glover thought it was a good piece of work, but Jones "did not like Miller's ears" and therefore Miller got rejected. (It is amazing to me, now that I know of the abortive analysis with Jones, that Miller dared to put himself forward as a member of the Society.) Glover was still in touch with the erudite Miller in the 1960s, since they both were serving as editors of the *British Journal of Criminology*. (Sylvia Payne agreed with Glover's characterization of Jones's behavior as arbitrary about Miller. When I saw Miller himself he proudly mentioned in passing that he was the father of Jonathan Miller, who had recently helped create *Beyond the Fringe* and went on to be a famous medical journalist, opera producer, and man of letters.)

On the whole Jones felt more comfortable having female colleagues, or men without medical degrees; one of the contradictions in Jones was that, although he kept men out, fundamentally he could be subservient to women. As a Scot Glover seemed no threat to Jones's London position. (Jones himself was Welsh, and the sociology of marginality helps explain how such practitioners could be encouraged to take the risk of entering a new profession like psychoanalysis.) In fairness to Jones, Glover mentioned that "high-handedness" had not interfered with Jones's relationship with Dr. Thomas W. Mitchell, a general practitioner in Kent who had written *Problems in Psychopathology*. Jones invited him to come to London, but Mitchell did not want to get involved with "the hurly-burly" of London life, and resigned from the British Society in 1941. (In Geneva, Dr. Raymond de Saussure, prominent in the international psychoanalytic movement, told me that Jones had only wanted women around him, and had kept Hart and Mitchell out. Dr. Payne raised the suspicion, with regret, that some of the talented Viennese, like Ernst Kris, who came first with Freud to London, may have partly left for America because of Jones's autocratic ways.) Glover thought that these early people had done a great deal for psychoanalysis, even though they later dropped out; by then the organization had "a life of its own." All the early pioneers, including Freud himself, found that as the years passed the movement they had created became an entity in itself, one whose momentum could be beyond the control of those who had set it going in the first place.

3

The Controversial Discussions–I
"A New Weltanschauung"?

The one person I was absolutely obliged to discuss with Glover was Mrs. Melanie Klein (1882–1960). Her name came up again and again with others I talked with in London. At one point Glover told me he was the same "age level" as she, but when I checked later it turned out he was 6 years her junior. If I provide here relatively little discussion of Glover's substantive objections to Klein's ideas, this is because he did not emphasize these points in conversation with me. He did give me a copy of an extensive article of his attacking Klein's concepts, which appeared both as a separate pamphlet and in a slightly abbreviated form in the first volume of *The Psychoanalytic Study of the Child*.[1] Perhaps it was a failing in me as an interviewer that I did not pursue investigating the full bases for Glover's opposition to Klein, but with Glover and other analysts I was able fairly easily to detect some standard critiques of Klein's work. His essay on her ideas was a coherent indictment, mainly devoted to distinguishing her writings from those of Freud; Glover's mature reaction to her was utterly negative. It may be that Glover assumed that I understood the basic theoretical issues involved, but mainly lacked an appreciation of the personal clashes that were involved.

The reader is asked to remember, in connection with the phenomena of Kleinianism, the idealism of the early analysts. Freud had his mission, what he called "the cause," and he was willing to stake his life on the achievements of his work; he was holding out the hope of transforming human nature, by means of psychoanalysis, from within. As Freud confidently wrote in his polemic against Adler and Jung, "Men are strong so long as they represent a strong idea; they become powerless when they oppose it."[2] Freud felt that his ideas, including theories that may now seem almost theological, were the most precious part of what he had to contribute to the world. And his intolerances in imposing his vision were an essential constituent of his success in implementing it within intellectual history. Had he been less sure of himself, others might have been unlikely to have been as attracted, and his intransigence meant that the world has acknowledged his originality.

In behalf of the movement Freud founded he pursued those renegades, or fallen angels, such as Adler and Jung. In the 1920s he was trapped by the success of his own ideology, in that Abraham and Jones seized on Rank's innovations in order to prove the analogies between his work and the famous pre-World War I heretics. (Glover remained proud that he and his brother had been among the first to assail Rank.) Much as Freud wanted to keep Rank within the movement, the "cause" was strong enough as an autonomous being to succeed in coming between the intense personal tie linking Freud and Rank.[3] Glover's critique of Klein was able tellingly to remind people of the similarities between her own position and that proposed by Rank, who was already excluded from psychoanalysis by the late 1920s. In hindsight, Rank and Klein were among others at the time who were trying to ensure that mothering got fully incorporated into psychoanalytic thinking.

Klein thought of herself puristically as more Freudian than Freud; she claimed that the Oedipus complex started in the first months of the infant's life, and that she was taking literally Freud's hypothesis of the importance of a death instinct. She was elaborating on the anxieties associated with aggression. But Glover was able to accuse her of advancing "a new *Weltanschauung*," one that began with "a mystical interpretation of life immediately after birth." She had, Glover maintained, "projected into biological science . . . moral values," and her approach rested "on faith rather than science."[4] Her most original ideas were concerned with phenomena that were so developmentally early in an infant's life as to be in principle largely incapable of verification. But the heat about the issues between Glover and Klein can be related to the idealistic motivations all the early analysts shared, which necessarily implied hatred for anyone guilty of betraying "the cause" Freud had initiated.

How did Melanie Klein become so important in Great Britain? The British analysts had a realistic "sense of inferiority" in the early 1920s. During the period 1920–1925 they were looked down upon as "a low-grade" Society by the continental analysts. The British were therefore receptive to Klein because they felt that they did not have to feel "inferior" any longer. When Glover first went to the meetings of the Society in London they were "starved" for ideas. There was just Jones and J. C. Flügel, who became a prolific author,[5] and someone else might give an "unimaginative" paper on dreams. Jones was jealous of what Berlin and Budapest, as centers in analysis, already had; the British were then such a "poor Society, like the French until recently." (Jacques Lacan was like Jones in single-handedly creating psychoanalysis in France, but unlike Jones Lacan was full of his own theories and not at all adept at organizational politics; in 1963, because of his ideas and practices, Lacan could only have remained in the IPA if he had accepted being no longer a training analyst. In New York City Karen Horney would also not allow herself to be demoted.) Glover remained insistent that Jones had "made" the British Society.

Glover thought that the most obvious reason for Jones's inviting Klein to lecture in 1925 was to help build up the British Society; then in 1926 she decided to settle in England. (Like Anna Freud, Melanie Klein had had no formal higher education as a scientist.) By 1931 Klein was already very important in London analysis, although the conflict between her own perspective and the traditional Freudian one was still "under cover." Glover was said by others to have been influenced by her early work and, although I did not know this when I first interviewed him, he did maintain that many of her ideas from her initial period were "perfectly sound" and that she had been "quite a good stimulus." (As late as November 1933, Glover was writing Jelliffe in behalf of Klein to find out about reviews of her *The Psychoanalysis of Children*.) However, she started to construct elaborate theories about the early psychology of child development from the first few years of life, and this is where she "went wrong." (In my opinion, then and now, Klein's project of aiming at the discovery and cure of psychosis in children was preposterous. It is misguided to have such confidence in the power of any psychoanalytic procedure. Mrs. Klein herself rarely treated psychotics, and stopped analyzing children as early as 1946–1947. In talking with me Glover did not, like other London physicians then, object to her discussing psychosis because she was not medically trained. British analysts remain, I think, too flippant about the concept of psychosis.)

In general Glover thought that up until 1930 Freud's ideas had been so powerful and authoritative that the discipline had been kept controlled; from then on, however, Glover thought that things had gone to being "all at sixes and sevens." And it was after 1930, as far as Glover could reconstruct it, that Klein's ambitiousness inaugurated a new period in the history of British analysis. (Klein's self-involvement can be well illustrated by an anecdote in a 1925 letter from Alix Strachey, then in Berlin, to her husband James in London about a performance of Mozart's *The Magic Flute* that Alix went to with Klein:

> I arrived at the Operahouse at 7.14, &, to my astonishment, saw Melanie already at the trysting place. It then turned out that I'd very fortunately made her believe the opera began at 7.0, so that she had arrived at five minutes past, & instead of being hopelessly late (as I had expected) was nice & early. So tho' morally disgraced, she had saved herself from actual annihilation. But not for long. She was in a flood of conversation from the moment we met till the moment the lights went out—all about her plans for social life during the winter. Then, after a momentary pause, just as a hush fell upon the audience & the conductor raised his stick, she turned to me & took a fresh start.

Melanie was so struck with the divine music that she could not help bringing it right back to herself in concluding that she must "take up her piano practice again."[6] One of Klein's followers sounds right in emphasizing to me that Mrs. Klein had felt that she never received the recognition she was entitled to, and that she had had little patience for anyone who did not agree about her work's importance.)

Sometime in the course of the 1930s Glover convinced himself (while Freud was doing so too) that Klein was a "deviationist," leading a new schism like Adler, Jung, and Rank before her. (Glover took a relatively benign view of a so-called troublemaker like Wilhelm Reich, partly because Glover had witnessed Jones's harsh interrogation of Reich in London. Glover complained that the public was too apt to see schisms within psychoanalysis.) While Freud kept his views private, Anna Freud ultimately expressed them to colleagues in the British Society.[7]

Glover maintained that Mrs. Klein had formed an alliance with Joan Riviere, who in his opinion was "quite a good woman." (Glover was kinder about Riviere than Sylvia Payne, who told me that although Riviere was "brilliant" and "charming," "everybody had trouble getting on with her." Riviere was "not at all" a good analyst, and too "obsessional"; John Bowlby was with her as a patient, and wanted another analyst, but Jones would not let him change. Payne considered Bowlby "a fighter.") Although Mrs. Klein had herself become an analyst before training was "carefully scrutinized," she could then begin to build up a group around her in London. Thanks to Jones's backing she was able to become a training analyst. As an individual he could swing in the 1920s an amount of influence for Klein that would be hard to imagine in the mid-1960s, by which time the membership of the Society was much broader.

Was it generally known that Melanie Klein had analyzed Jones's own child? I brought up this question more or less out of the blue, in the course of discussing Klein; the moment I did so Glover had trouble with his hearing aid, and he paused to put in another battery. He explained that he had been going deaf for the last few years, and that hearing problems were particularly difficult for an aging analyst. In answer to my specific question, he finally said "no," it was not generally known that she had analyzed Jones's child. (I took Glover's delayed response to mean that he was not eager to fight, or to carry on unnecessary grudges. This is at odds with Klein's biographer's view that

Glover was guilty of spreading "scurrilous stories about Klein."[8] For the Columbia Oral History project, with a tape recorder in front of him, Glover did not mention Klein's analysis of Jones's child.) At a later interview it turned out that Glover was certain that Mrs. Klein had analyzed two, and perhaps three, of Jones's children. (The toys Mrs. Klein had used in her first child analysis in England—with Jones's child—were preserved, I found out, as relics in the British Psychoanalytic Society. Later I came across evidence that Mrs. Klein had also analyzed Jones's wife, Katherine.)

Glover was opposed to what he called "the dangers of tolerance" in psychoanalysis. He knew that some people said that since analysis was a science, it could afford to let different ideas compete, but he felt that this line of reasoning ignored, or denied, the powerful role of "suggestion." (Glover was also alluding to this point by his 1931 paper on "inexact interpretations.") It could take "twenty years" to correct a mistake in analytic teaching. Mrs. Klein had "piped down" when the Viennese came over to England in 1938; until then she had been talking about Freud's ideas being "passé." Glover was convinced that originally Klein's system was conceived as a substitute for Freud's. (Other reputable analysts disagreed with Glover here; on the contrary, they felt Mrs. Klein had never really had a system until she began to feel threatened by the arrival of Anna Freud and the Viennese. In this view Glover's public attack on her work had finally driven her to systematize her insights, and to attract loyal followers of her own; Klein had already withdrawn when Glover entered into her dread of enemies.)

Glover was distressed that Klein's ideas seemed to be lasting even longer than he would have thought her "mistakes" could prevail. At first she was "ignored" by the Americans, but he had detected that her works had begun to "creep" into their bibliographies. (By now that would be even much more the case.) Such a gradual change made "no sense" to him "whatever"; "either you believe something or you do not." It was to him as clear-cut as that. He had been worried all along about the dangers of suggestibility. When he was an officer on behalf of the British Society, he passed on to the Kleinians people he did not "care too much about." But he had sent those he thought would make good Freudians, the ones he saw as promising, to Freudian analysts. Glover did not want the British Society "overrun by transference reactions." (Candidates do tend to absorb the theoretical views of their training analysts, and it is only human for them, like other patients, to develop emotional "transferences" to those they are professionally dependent on.) Glover did concede, without any prompting from me, that through such training referrals he had been engaging in "politics," and "bad politics at that."

Glover was a mild-mannered man who in print can sound truculent. As I mentioned at the outset, Sylvia Payne agreed with me when I said to her that I would never have believed that of all people Glover could have precipitated such a fierce struggle in the British Society. She shook her head in emphatic agreement. (Payne was about 86 when I saw her, but I was impressed by her balance and insight. A large painting of her once hung prominently at the British Psychoanalytic Society.) Independence and toleration are key values in the best of British culture; according to these beliefs, it ought not to be necessary to make an enemy of people you differ from. It turned out that Payne had privately written about Glover to Klein in 1942:

> I am not such a blind fool as to deny that E. G. is hostile to you, & you make no attempt to disguise the fact that you are hostile to him & regard him as a personal enemy. Of course the situation is partly the outcome of the unconscious of the people concerned, but I do not think that you will deny that unfortunate circumstances have played into the present situation and precipitated an actual situation which need not necessarily have occurred.
>
> I have known from the first day I met E. G. that he feared and defended himself against & was jealous of the successful intellectual, i.e. rival woman. It [sic] happened to be meeting in circumstances which were somewhat unusual. This particular unconscious attitude obviously was going to make cooperation hard but not impossible as long as one's own unconscious did not respond.
>
> I do not agree with you that he has for many years been *conspiring* for power. He has of course worked for his position and wanted to have it, & it is a pity that he did not have a *limited* tenure of office as President a good many years ago before these dissentions

became so marked. He is afraid of power & expects to have it taken from him all the time, so he trusts no one. At the same time he is now consciously doing all he can to keep what he has had, & in his alarm he is more likely to become unscrupulous. He appears to me to make such *obviously* gross psychological blunders that I cannot fear his methods very much. He has in many ways a right to expect to replace Jones for a time anyhow. I do not believe it is sound or right for you to feel that his wish is to destroy Ps.An., I do not believe he wishes to destroy the *whole* of your work. I cannot accept the proposition that it is right to speak as if psychoanalysis and your contribution to Ps.An. (which I never deny) are one & the same thing. I think that to do so is equivalent to regarding the *part* as the same as the whole. I am sure you injure your own position by giving this *impression*. I am fully aware of the difficulty in keeping in touch with the unconscious & the ease with which we can slide into superficialities, & I know it is the most important problem of all. I believe however that you tend to increase the tendency rather than diminish it in the Society by ignoring the unconscious work, which is done by workers who are not so profound & have not the insight which you have.

The point is that there are parts in Glover which you ignore. He can and has acknowledged himself in the wrong & has apologized for a projection. He wanted at the beginning of the war period to be absolutely fair to everyone & if he thought he was in any way acceptable to you I believe you would see a change of conduct.

You must see he is also being driven by Melitta, & that brings us back to the tragedy of the personal aspect of the situation. I am not whitewashing E. G. I know him too well to attempt to do so. I am only saying he is not all black. He regards me more as an enemy & a rival than anything else . . .

I know that we understand one another, & that you know I am *terribly* anxious for your work to receive its proper recognition & that we should be able to work freely & openly. I think that proper representation of different opinions should be on all representative bodies, & I am sure that offices have been held much too long in the past.[9]

Payne's letter was a model of diplomacy and even-handedness. Payne was laying quiet blame on both Glover and Klein, at the same time she was identifying with Klein's difficulties in dealing with Glover. Payne was being rather outspoken in telling Klein that there was not, in Payne's view, an identity between Klein's work and psychoanalysis as a whole. And Payne spoke up for Glover's intentions to be fair, as well as his capacity for self-criticism; Payne was suggesting that Klein might have handled the problem with Glover in a better way. At the same time Payne was expressing her genuine appreciation for what Klein had added; and in her concluding sentence about "proper representation of different opinions" on all of the Society's committees, as well as her conviction that the officers of the Society should change more often, Payne was offering Klein the kind of political support within psychoanalysis that would have been most gratifying to Klein.

A key issue, which I think Sylvia Payne both accurately and tactfully described, was that Melanie Klein's daughter, Dr. Melitta Schmideberg, was herself in analysis with Glover during the period preceding the worst of the controversy. Nobody at the Society had a harsher or more uncharitable view of Klein than her own daughter. In 1942 Mrs. Klein used in a letter the word "illness"[10] to account for Melitta's accusativeness. Mrs. Klein suffered terribly under the cruel public attack from her daughter; the more Mrs. Klein felt misunderstood, the angrier she got. It was no wonder that in her later writings she developed an increasing need to justify the mother and blame the child. Glover openly painted Klein's approach as one of "mother justification," and *"a matriarchal variant of the doctrine of Original Sin."*[11]

In 1944 Mrs. Klein wrote to Winnicott of Glover: "he is crooked and unscrupulous . . . I think he is very pathological."[12] (A prominent Kleinian suggested to me that clinically Glover "must" have done something pretty "shocking" to Melitta.) Klein's biographer, as recently as 1986, tried to argue that "Glover, in his deep resentment of Klein, exploited Melitta to wound her mother in the cruelest possible way." Even further, it has been hinted that there might have been an "affair" between Glover and Melitta, one bit of so-called evidence being that someone recalled "seeing Glover and Melitta openly holding hands at an international congress."[13] (Glover was such an old-fashioned gentleman that I would interpret any such hand-holding as an aspect of his Victorian courtliness rather than being a sign of any erotic intentions.)

All these early analysts appealed too readily to psychological interpretations of unconscious motivation; and Sylvia Payne, in a 1966 letter to Anna Freud marked "private and confidential,"[14] did observe: "Edward Glover is a very able man, & has a first class mind for the grasp of theory, as his brother James had also, but neither had a stabilised emotional life. Both have suffered great tragedy in their private lives. Neither had enough psychoanalysis to stabilise them, but they could grasp and understand new ideas at once. This was a characteristic of many of Jones' [sic] first chosen colleagues." It would seem to be a besetting sin of psychoanalysts to think that such stabilization can come from more analysis, and that emotional conflicts are a sign of inadequate analyses. (Within intellectual history there is the old problem in Plato's theory of who is to guard the guardians.)

Glover's own comments to me about both Melanie Klein and her daughter were more cautious and reserved than some of the literature has been. He said that Abraham's daughter had told him that her father did not really like Melanie Klein, but Glover honestly maintained that he thought Abraham had in fact "admired" her. Melitta had said to Glover that Melanie had "pinched" her ideas from Abraham, but Glover said no, she had an "original" mind of her own. (When Melanie Klein's older son died in an accident, Melitta said that it was a suicide although her mother supposedly denied it; Melitta was unremitting. The play *Mrs. Klein* illustrated Mrs. Klein's disbelief in the occurrence of so-called accidents as great as any hard-lined Marxist.) And in Melitta's view her mother had a "hold" over Jones because of her analysis of his family members, but Glover said he was "not sure" that was so.

I had one memorable interview with Melitta Schmideberg: she seemed to me an extraordinarily difficult person. Her mother's diagnosis of an "illness" would seem to me more accurate than seeing in her merely "eccentric behavior."[15] Melitta insisted on demanding from me an answer to her question of who would ultimately publish my material. (I may have underestimated how difficult a time she was having getting her own views in print.) She also rather angrily maintained that psychoanalysis had "horrible" therapeutic results. Although she talked with me about many things, and gave me some of her recent papers before I left, I cannot get out of my mind the picture of a small woman sitting in a large chair in a room darkened by thick curtains, and the memory also stays that throughout the interview she was sucking on something in her mouth that [I think] caused a little white drool to come down one side of her chin. It was frightening to see someone in her state, as she referred to her mother throughout the interview as "Mrs. Klein." I do not believe I ever have had an anxiety attack like I experienced after interviewing her; I had absolutely no hostile or suspicious feelings toward her before our meeting, but she treated me in a verbally assaultive way.

(In 1942 Melitta had publicly referred to "a Member in a leading position and official capacity trying seriously to diagnose me as a paranoiac and to persuade my husband that we should leave the country because I had dared to protest against certain intrigues and organized attacks."[16] In a 1971 article Melitta wrote that Jones had

> asked my husband whether he would not like to emigrate to the U.S. . . . When he refused, Jones asked me to see him, and pointed out in a fatherly manner that I was working too hard, and should stop my training analysis with Dr. Glover. This was very unusual advice in a Society in which everybody was urged to have more and deeper analysis. Dr. Jones also tried to help me by explaining my relations in terms of paranoid attitudes . . . the letter of mine on which he based his diagnosis of "paranoid" had actually been drafted for me by Edward Glover. Ever since I have been wary of diagnoses given by colleagues to each other.[17]

More than a couple of people who had known Melitta socially told me that they considered her paranoid; one professor at the London School of Economics said she was "straight out of a horror movie." The editors of *The Freud–Klein Controversies* maintain that "many of those present felt that Jones was unable to control Melitta,"[18] but it remains unclear to me what on earth he was supposed to do about her.)

I told Glover, when I next saw him, that I had interviewed Melitta; he cautiously asked me how it had went, and although perhaps disappointed did not seem at all surprised when I indicated that things had not gone well. If I were to sum her up now, the nicest way of putting it would be that she was mad as a hatter—which does not mean, of course, that some of what she said was not valid enough. (Oddly, she had once seen as a London patient, after he was first analyzed by Theodor Reik in Vienna, no less a personage than the great historian Sir Lewis Namier; it is a worrisome sign of the extent of the power of human vanity that analytic patients so often do not seem able to size up the nature of the analyst to whom they are confiding their most intimate troubles.)

Evidently Melitta had early on seen her mother as a rival of Freud. Glover said that Melanie had told "someone" that after Jesus Christ she was the most important person who had ever lived. (Melanie does seem to have been extraordinarily egotistical; that performance of *The Magic Flute* leading her to speak of taking up "piano practice again" would seem to have been par for the course.) Melitta, a physican and an analyst, was being both a challenger to her mother and also helping Glover to lead a palace revolution in the British Society. (Melitta had been originally trained on the continent by Eitingon and Horney, and in England had gone back into analysis with Miss Sharpe, who could not bear her and was relieved and thankful that after a year she left when she decided to go to a man instead, and chose Glover. It has been suggested that Melitta went into analysis with Glover "in order to deal with her dependence on her mother,"[19] but I do not know the evidence for that idea.) In retrospect Glover thought that the turmoil in the Society was fed by "dragons," women who wanted men to do what they bid; he had in mind, I think, Melitta behind him, and Mrs. Riviere in back of Jones. In a 1944 letter to Jones, Glover referred to "a woman ridden Society (your favoured hypothesis.)"[20]

Sylvia Payne told me in no uncertain terms that she thought Jones had been "a fool" about Melitta and Glover. (In another connection, discussing a harsh and tactless letter from Jones to former Ambassador William C. Bullitt, someone who knew Bullitt observed of Jones: "The man is a fool!") At the height of the Controversial Discussions Jones was technically still President of the Society, but at the worst of the quarrel over Klein's ideas he was living in the country and Glover functioned at his deputy in leading the Society in its proceedings. Nevertheless, at a meeting of the Training Committee, and in the presence of Payne, Klein, and Rickman, Jones had once said to Glover, "Why do you permit Schmideberg to say such things publicly against her mother?" Payne was horrified that Jones would bring something like that up, and in such company, since Melitta was already a full member of the Society and her analysis with Glover had not been for training purposes; for Melitta ever to refer to her analysis with Glover as for "training" would have been an excuse for its not being for personal therapeutic purposes. Jones's remark was absolutely no business of the Committee. (In Payne's view Melitta was a "devil," and Payne thought that Glover had "taken over" some of Melitta's aggressions. Dr. Clifford Scott also thought that Melitta had "probably stirred Edward up.")

Payne then confronted Jones after the Training Committee meeting, and asked him point blank why he had said that to Glover. (She thought it was perfect for making Glover more intransigent.) Jones "weakly" replied, "Mrs. Riviere had said I should say so." As Payne wrote to Mrs. Klein in 1942,

> I agree that the attitude taken by G. at the last meeting seems to indicate that he has definitely adopted a certain policy with regard to you and intends to carry it out unscrupulously. This is of course what I have striven to prevent for a very long time. I have never been in his confidence, but of course have known the conflict which was going on. The only hope was that the better side of his nature would succeed in controlling the "persecuted" side. He is not a strong man & is always aggressive when driven to take action. What has crystallised out & made him consciously & openly organise this line of policy is of course the fear that he will not be president, & will lose other positions. It seems to me from his point of view to be idiotic as the line of attack launched via the Schmidebergs alienates people who might otherwise be friendly.
>
> His hostility to you received an initial drive from which it has *never* recovered owing to Jones' [sic] grave error of judgement in bringing up his relation to Melitta before the training committee. The affair should have been dealt with privately, but there again Jones was not strong enough. However it is no good now spending time over regrets.[21]

(This harmless use of the words "relations" and "affair" led Klein's biographer to suggest some possible erotic impropriety.)

Payne wrote to Anna Freud in 1966, "I guess that you will agree with me that Jones made a number of mistakes, which is not surprising considering the way he had been treated in England in the past . . . the . . . situation might not have happened if Jones had had more insight, and had not been so afraid of the war." Jones was staying at his cottage outside of London because of the fear of invasion. Payne also wrote Anna that Payne thought that Glover's resignation "could have been avoided if Jones had said the right thing."[22] (At the time I was interviewing Glover none of this private correspondence was yet available.)

Melitta had been, according to Glover, the first person to "counter" her mother's ideas. Presumably he meant to do his best by her, and saw how she had been emotionally damaged. (She appears as a child in one of her mother's early case histories.) But it is still obscure how Glover allowed himself to make her grievances into such a campaign against her mother. Melitta was not, Glover said to me, "a very tactful person," which I would say was a great understatement. During the controversy Anna Freud deemed Melitta "too asocial" for her "to cooperate with."[23] (I am presuming that Melitta cannot have been as obviously difficult in the late 1930s as when I saw her in 1965; but her presentations were sometimes so rapid that others could not always follow her, and more than one person shuddered at how horrible it was to witness Melitta's critique of her mother in public. By the time I saw Melitta she had lost contact with her surviving brother for years.) Melitta had once helped her mother, at an international Congress, criticize Anna Freud's work; at the time Freud complained in a letter that he thought Klein and her daughter had both been unjust.

In the 1920s an issue between Melanie Klein and Anna Freud was whether play technique with children, as Mrs. Klein held, could be considered an exact equivalent of an adult's free associations. Also, Anna Freud then thought that children need a preparatory phase for analysis, since they were still tied to their parents, and therefore could not be expected to establish the emotional bonds of "transference" the way adults do. Melanie was outspoken and doctrinaire about using the same technique with children as with adults; she self-righteously thought she could ignore completely the family dynamics of the child, and reach directly to the child's unconscious conflicts. And her interpretations could be extravagant. (It would be mistaken, however, to underestimate just how therapeutically ambitious about children Anna Freud remained to the end of her life.[24])

Glover realized later on, after Melitta left London to live in New York City for over ten years, that she had not been able to get along professionally there anymore than she had managed in England. (It turns out that on March 8, 1946, Jones had written Brill about Melitta, "I hope Dr. Schmideberg will stay in America. She has an excellent flair, probably because of personal reasons, for delinquents and is very intelligent. But she was a great nuisance in the Society and perhaps may find more scope in New York for her quarrelsomeness.") Glover acknowledged that she had now turned against not only psychoanalysis, but he thought she was against psychiatrists as well. (Sylvia Payne said that if Melitta were finally against psychoanalysis, "so much the better for analysis.") Glover remarked that it was "easy" to get support for such antipsychiatric sorts of thinking in London. *Was she as tactless then (in the 1940s) as now?* Yes, but she had "courage" too, more than others would have had. She had been "introduced" to psychoanalysis by her mother, and then when she went "violently" against her mother she transferred her animosity against Melanie to both psychiatry and psychoanalysis.

Melitta was, Glover said, his only "supporter" at the time; the others were "too timid." But in print he was able to cite lots of other analysts who took his side. (A 1942 list exists, I think with Glover's handwritten corrections, breaking down the Society's membership into four possible camps: Klein, Glover, Freud, and Doubtful.) He conceded, without any prompting from me, that Melitta had pursued her course for her own separate motives. "A cunning little thing," he once muttered about her under his breath, and I put in brackets in my notes: "I'll bet." (This was not a medical indiscretion on Glover's part, since he had had loads of contact with Melitta outside the analysis itself.) For his own reasons Glover had been seduced into Melitta's apparently paranoid delusions about her mother; but he never quite conceded as much in talking with me.

Melitta had, Glover felt, been a "good little daughter" in imitating Melanie but she "lacked her mother's imagination." Somehow Glover had the idea that Melitta's husband, Walter, who was also an analyst, had been a "favorite" of Freud's; although Walter Schmideberg was Viennese and a friend of the Freud family, I do not think it can ever have been much more than a social relationship. (A letter of Glover's to Anna Freud indicates, while writing Walter's obituary in the mid-1950s, Glover's hesitancy about Walter's position vis-à-vis the Freud family. Walter had reminisced about Freud as a supervisor of one of Walter's cases during the Controversial Discussions.[25]) According to Glover, Walter was a protégé of Eitingon's, and claimed to have himself "built" the Clinic at the Berlin Psychoanalytic Institute. In any event Walter publicly backed up his wife during the fight within the British Society, which is what Payne was referring to as an "idiotic" move from Glover's point of view since the spectacle alienated neutral-minded people. (Walter referred to what he called "Kleinism." To call someone then a "Kleinite" was intended to be derogatory, rather like "Trotskyites" were distinguished by Stalinists from "Trotskyists.")

Glover objected to what he considered the "undisciplined" character of Melanie Klein's mind. He said that, despite the way Klein chose to put it, Freud had never "discovered" the death instinct but rather suggested it as a philosophic postulate. (Klein's ideas about aggression and inborn envy were tied to the death instinct side of Freud's dualistic theory; the sexual side of Freud's thinking came earlier, and has received both more publicity and more clinical acceptance.) Both Alix and James Strachey, for example, thought that Melanie Klein was merely going in the direction Freud would have himself, if he had lived and "had his health." (But they were appalled at how seriously she came to take her every word.) Most people I met in London thought that even though Mrs. Klein had not at all been a scientist, nonetheless she was very original and creative.

Glover readily said he thought that as a therapist Klein was "probably a good one." Almost everyone I spoke with among London analysts agreed on this important point. She was, Glover thought, "a woman of hunches," and in retrospect I wonder whether he did not in some sense envy her capacities as a healer. (Payne thought admiringly that Klein had the talents of a "medium.") Glover told me he was "dubious" about how Klein had gotten her therapeutic results, since he suspected they were probably the result of "suggestion." (Analysts preferred instead to think of their successes as the outcome of rational interpretive "insight," which would supposedly be more long-lasting and also distinguish their work from that of alternative rapport psychotherapies.)

Glover saw that the way to get "power" was by training analytic candidates, and he realized that Mrs. Klein had an immense suggestible influence over her trainees. Even people of independent minds were influenced by her; he cited her sway over Jones and Mrs. Riviere, as well as those he considered even more autonomous and responsible, such as Sylvia Payne.

One 1940 letter of James Strachey to Glover deserves to be quoted here:

> I should rather like you to know (for your personal information) that—if it comes to a show-down—I'm very strongly in favour of a compromise at all costs. The trouble seems to me to be with extremism, on both sides. My own view is that Mrs. K. has made some highly important contributions to PA, but that it's absurd to make out (a) that they cover the whole subject or (b) that their validity is axiomatic. On the other hand I think it's equally ludicrous for Miss F. to maintain that PA is a Game Reserve belonging to the F. family and that Mrs. K.'s ideas are totally subversive.
>
> These attitudes on both sides are of course purely religious and the very antithesis of science. They are also (on both sides) infused by, I believe, a desire to dominate the situation and in particular the future—which is why both sides lay so much stress on the training of candidates....
>
> In fact I feel like Mercutio about it. Why should these wretched fascists and (bloody foreigners) communists invade our peaceful compromising island?[26]

Strachey's point of view did not persuade Glover to the approach of placing a pox on both houses. But I think that what Strachey had to say about training analyses was right to the point, and a key to Glover's willingness to fight. Nowadays in France some of the most far-seeing analysts are going so far as to propose abolishing the institution of a training analysis. The idea of training analysis was in the first place Jung's, and I believe that he came up with it out of dissatisfaction with Freud as an unanalyzed leader of the movement; the proposal was beaten back, with the help of Victor Tausk and Otto Rank, at the Budapest Congress in 1918, and went through at an international meeting only after Freud had already fallen ill with cancer of the jaw. It is now heralded as an implication of Lacan's admitted genius to question the requirement of training analyses, but no one seems to remember that Glover was calling attention to this issue over fifty years ago.

In Glover's reconstructing the tale of the Klein controversy, at one point he said that the conflict between her and traditional Freudianism had come out in the "open" between 1931 and 1938, but later he specified 1931 and 1936. In his 1945 summary article Glover had mentioned an "open split" in the Society developing after the 1935 discussion of a paper of Klein's. And he wrote that "the first signs of an open breach occurred in the summer of 1939, when as the result of differences in training the Training Committee began to consider whether it would not be advisable for Kleinian and Freudian candidates to be trained separately." He was in no doubt that "the transferences and countertransferences developing during training analysis tend to give rise in the candidate to an emotional conviction of the soundness of the training analyst's theories."[27]

There were enthusiastic Kleinians, convinced Freudians, and then the compromisers. Glover claimed to me that he had come out "in opposition" to Klein between 1928 and 1931. But there is good reason to doubt the reliability of his dates, since there was a natural tendency for him retrospectively to exaggerate how soon he started to have his substantial reservations about her work. (A favorable review by him of one of her books appeared as late as 1933, and gets cited by Kleinian literature in the 1970s.) General agreement exists that the Kleinians had already formed a distinct group before World War II.[28] While the Viennese might have thought that in their eyes they were VIPs who had come to a provincial Society, apparently it never occurred to any of the British analysts in the 1930s that London was not the center of the universe.

At the outset of World War II Jones, whose second wife was Jewish, expected an invasion and moved to the countryside (this was the fear of the war that Payne in writing Anna Freud had reproached Jones for); most of the Kleinians had also temporarily left London. That meant that Glover, as Jones's longstanding deputy, was left to preside in London over psychoanalytic meetings. (The reader will recall all the offices Glover then held, including being Chairman of the Training Committee, Scientific Secretary, Director of the Society's Clinic, Director of Research, and also Honorary Secretary of the International Psychoanalytic Association.) Whatever Glover's titles he was also in effect the acting President. The newly arrived refugees from the continent were, as aliens, unlikely to be able to get permission to leave the London areas. For a time then Glover was able to lead an ideologically compatible group of analysts; he was proud to have presided over "a Freudian" Society. The war had temporarily put an end to the quarrelling; some analysts had gone into military service, besides others who had left London because of the bombing. By late 1941, however, it was clear, as analysts were returning to London, that some formal confrontation between the conflicting forces within the British Society was inevitable.

By 1942 analysts started coming back to London. The division in the Society that had existed before the outbreak of the war was still intact, so the arguments began again as analysts returned. The fight lasted about eighteen months; lots of articles were to be published in the journals, which ostensibly were purely scientific papers but were in fact a part of the controversy. In late 1943 a draft report of the Training Committee, authored by Strachey although the Committee was elected by the Society itself, proposed that the principal contenders not be permitted to act as training analysts—a slap at Glover, Anna Freud, and Klein, but only Glover and Anna Freud resigned from the Committee. The maintenance of the status quo could only be supportive of Klein. (Lest anyone think oral history intrinsically less reliable than the written record, a published article on the history of the psychoanalytic movement in Britain by Mellita Schmideberg that appeared in 1971 wholly ignored the intense eighteen months of discussion that Glover and others talked to me about. On the other hand she is the only person to have referred to the power Glover had by virtue of just how often he was a source of referrals. "Edward Glover once stated in a discussion that he saw and referred in initial consultation one-third of all London patients who were being analysed, and had a follow-up on two-thirds. There was an uneasy silence."[29])

The thick of the fight had gone on despite the fact that there were those reluctant to come out in the open. According to Eva Rosenfeld, an old friend of Anna Freud's who had dared to go to Melanie Klein for an analysis, even though it hurt her standing with Freud himself, Melitta would say "terrible things" about her mother, opposing her point by point, and Glover would back her up. Since there were more declared Kleinians than embattled Freudians, Glover concluded that Klein's supporters were "going to win." And that is partly why he decided to "cut adrift" and leave the Society entirely. Few wanted Glover to resign; it was quite personal, so even some who approved of his efforts decided not to go with him.

Glover had, according to Sylvia Payne, gone to her before quitting. She was a down-to-earth woman who had helped Glover run the Society during the war. (He never said anything to me that was remotely critical of her.) Although she had not aspired to be President of the Society, she did not think that "Edward" had been much good as head of the organization. (The editors of *The Freud–Klein Controversies* remark that Glover was "a good administrator, he helped Jones in his negotiations with the British Medical Association. . . ."[30]) Just before his resignation he had come to her to ask that she say that Klein was "getting all the people in training." According to her version she could not say what was untrue, and she refused. "Nobody was going to give everything in Klein's hands; Edward was wrong." Glover "knew," according to Payne, that her candidates and those of Miss Sharpe added up to more than Mrs. Klein's. (But from Glover's point of view it was not only a question of numbers, since it was Mrs. Klein who had the new ideas. Further, she was such a good therapist that there were lots who wanted to go to her for training analyses. And after World War II

Glover was able to illustrate, in a letter to Anna Freud, how Miss Sharpe, though distressed about how Rickman could do in one of Miss Sharpe's candidates, would be unwilling to fight in behalf of her student. The peacemakers like Payne, in Glover's view, could be no match for the committed partisans in behalf of Klein.)

It seems to me impossible clearly to distinguish the ideological struggle from the clash of personalities. These were intellectuals for whom ideas mattered in the fiercest possible ways; allegiances were based not just on friendships but on long-lasting therapeutic transferences. And it seems natural that people, even when idealistically motivated, also struggle for power. In advancing themselves they were also simultaneously forwarding a cause they believed in. Yet as long-standing as the differences were, with Glover's final decision to resign the quarrel apparently disappeared. His position, and the respect his writings and career had earned, had meant that his views had been able to carry a special amount of weight; without him, and following the withdrawal of Anna Freud and the Viennese into a separate training system, the Society has been able to endure under a new arrangement for over half a century now.

Before resigning, however, Glover had put all his objections in writing to what had happened within the British Society. First there was a contribution he made to the Training Committee discussion just before quitting:

> Mr. Strachey's approach to the problems with which the Training Committee is faced was evidently influenced by two factors, his concern that teaching methods should not infringe scientific traditions at any point and his interest in the technique of psychoanalysis. In his view "the essential criterion of whether a person is fit to conduct a training analysis is not whether his views of aetiology or theory are true but whether his technique is valid." His practical recommendation is that before touching on the political problems of training, i.e. who should teach and what he should teach, we should decide what are the essentials of a valid psychoanalytic technique. With Mr. Strachey's general approach I am of course in entire sympathy; and I believe also that an investiga-

tion of technique, in particular of the technique and content of interpretation, would bring to light many important divergences of outlook and method bearing on our present controversies.

But I do not agree that the training problem is one that can be solved by investigations of technique alone.

To Glover Strachey had artificially isolated technique as an entity of its own.

And this not simply because, in my view, the technique of the teacher is very considerably influenced by his theories but because our practical problem is not concerned solely with technique. There are four main factors in the analytic situation, the analyst, the technique, the transference, and the analysand. To measure the technique without at the same time observing the other factors in the training situation, viz. the training analyst, the transference and the candidate would in my opinion be an error in method. It seems to me therefore that Mr. Strachey has not fully appreciated the exact nature of the impasse in which the Committee finds itself. And so, before we discuss his practical recommendations in detail I would like to summarise briefly my 15 years' experience as a member of this Training Committee.

My first conclusion is that for all scientific and practical purposes, the training system of this Society has already broken down. And my main recommendation is that the Committee should report this fact to the Society. I have my own theories as to the cause of this breakdown; and though I do not wish to become involved in a theoretical discussion, I would like to offer briefly my favourite explanation. It is simply this: *so far, it has not been possible to eliminate adequately the vitiating factors of transference and countertransference arising during analytic training*. In theory, of course, one of the aims of the "training analysis" is to resolve the candidate's transferences even more thoroughly than is done in the case of, say, a neurotic patient. As far as the training analyst's countertransferences are concerned it is merely assumed that he will be able to resolve these himself.

Abuses in training would remain the central principle behind Glover's resignation. He continued:

Now we know from clinical experience that the practical test of resolution of a transference does not differ from the test of resolution of a symptom, namely, that it should not be capable of reactivation under stress. And this brings me to my second conclusion, namely, that whereas, with reasonable luck, the neurotic patient may not experience stresses liable to reactivate his symptoms, the candidate both during and after analysis works under professional conditions calculated not only to prevent resolution of his transferences but to promote their reactivation. These professional stresses tend to go unobserved partly because they have not the dramatic quality of neurotic stresses, but mainly I think because we turn a blind eye to them. I am not prepared to say whether this blind eye is turned voluntarily or whether it is a myopia of unconscious origin. What I can say is this: never in my experience of committee work or of teaching institutions have I come across a committee that was so obviously hampered and intimidated by what might be called their "unrealistic idealisations" or "pedagogic perfectionism."

Glover was objecting to what he saw as utopianism:

It is true, of course, that this form of defensive timidity is not confined to Training Committees. Nevertheless it is a fact that in the work of the Training Committee the cult of perfectionism has gone far to prepare the ground for our present stalemate. At any rate I could go so far as to say that the professional trainee—so long as he continues in active work and so long as his training analyst remains in active work—has little opportunity of emancipating himself from the transference situation. Although his analysis may be longer than that of a patient and although it is actually brought to an end in the same way as that of a patient, he does not, as the ordinary patient does, resume an independent existence. The analysis may stop but the candidate remains in an extended or displaced analytic situation. He cannot even speak at an ordinary meeting except under the shadow of his former transference.

I do not suggest that this is a complete account of our main training problem; nor, as I have said, do I wish to become involved more than is necessary in a theoretical discussion. My immediate aim is a purely practical one. I am even ready to agree that for most therapeutic purposes, the candidate's "training transferences" may have been well enough analysed in the past. Even his reactions to professional contacts with colleagues in the Society were on most occasions satisfactory enough—though, let it be said, by no means so good as the reactions of most unanalysed scientists in other societies. In short, under ordinary conditions, the stresses peculiar to analytic life used not to lead to violent eruption of transference reactions. It is true that minor manifestations were plentiful enough. No objective observer of discussions of scientific meetings of the Society could fail to note the existence of training allegiances, even of the phenomena of postponed obedience. But so long as no major scientific divergences existed in the Society the most that could be said of these allegiances was that they gave rise to monotony in discussion and to a low level of spontaneous research. When, however, major divergences arose regarding the validity of Mrs. Klein's views, a situation of stress developed that increased existing training transferences and reactivated old transferences. On this occasion I shall not attempt to give personal illustrations; I shall content myself rather with the blunt assertion that for some years past transference eruptions have occurred so powerful that it not only makes scientific discussion impossible but reduces analytic training to an unscientific level. Moreover I believe that unless we admit this fact and recognise that the difficulty is not confined to the reactions of the candidate but depends also on the reactions of his training analyst, there is little chance of re-establishing scientific standards of training.

Glover's calmness may have helped infuriate his critics:

In earlier days I used to think that these sources of emotional bias might be reduced by a balanced curriculum of instruction, in lectures, seminars, in analytic controls and later in Society discussions. But this I can see was a naïve hope. There is little evidence that the curriculum brings about correction of bias except in those candidates who have a temperamental inclination to eclecticism or in candidates whose analysts have kept aloof from controversy or have no strong feelings on differences of opinion within the Society. Such candidates are certainly in the minority.

As I have indicated the problem is not confined to the reactions produced in candidates. At every point of organisation

THE CONTROVERSIAL DISCUSSIONS—I "A NEW *WELTANSCHAUUNG*"?

> including even the initial selection of candidates difficulties arise. To whom, for instance, is the candidate to be allocated for training analysis? If the rota of training analysts includes, as it does, a number of analysts who differ on important points of theory and practice, the responsibility of the Training Committee is a heavy one. For it is morally certain that the candidate's future opinions, allegiances and professional life will be determined by that first choice. The same applies though no doubt to a lesser extent to the choice of control analysts, to the organisation of lecture courses and to seminars. Nor does the matter stop there. Although postgraduate training is not compulsory—a good deal of unobtrusive and unorganised postgraduate training goes on, e.g. secondary analysis of associate members and members, private controls, and private group discussions. The immediate effect of these activities is to increase the cleavages in the Society, and this in turn affects, sooner or later, the training situation. For the training analysts of the future will in the natural course of events be chosen from amongst analysts whose training allegiances are at present being formed—and in the meantime a number will be chosen from those unofficial postgraduate trainees who will inevitably bring their allegiances with them. This is only natural. Firmly convinced that their views are correct and that their techniques are justified by their views, they are bound to feel that their teaching is entirely legitimate. To cut a long story short this is in my opinion the present situation of training in the Society. For all scientific purposes our training system has broken down.

This incisive critique is how Glover earned his reputation as a troublemaker.

> The obvious question is: can this situation be put to rights? If so, how can we set about it? Here again a distinction must be drawn between principles and practice. In principle, of course, the remedy should lie in more thorough training analyses, more thorough resolution of training transferences, and more thorough analysis of the identifications with and introjections of the analyst which the candidate builds up. In practice, however, there is, as I have suggested, little sign of these radical changes, still less that the influence of varied controls counteracts the original bias. We must

face the fact that so long as important divergences exist in our Society, the immediate aims of training are bound to be influenced by the more distant aim of securing converts to any given set of views. And this in turn is bound to affect the selection of members of the Training Committee, the appointment of training analysts, and the advancement of members in the Society. It seems to me quite obvious that the logical end of such a situation is a fight for control of the psycho-analytic Society.

James Strachey had thought so, too. Glover went on:

No doubt, so long as there exists a solid group of training analysts who are opposed to extremist views or who do not countenance the teaching of controversial views as a natural or essential part of technical training, this end can be delayed. But in my experience such groups are too indifferent to take effective action to counter or even to modify extremism. They do not appear to be coherent enough or organised enough to withstand the influence of more enthusiastic groups.

The "Middle Group" of compromisers was not, in Glover's view, up to its task, as exemplified by Strachey's whole draft report:

Nevertheless we might well consider whether the situation could be improved by increasing the numbers of training analysts, control analysts, seminar leaders and lecturers who do not hold extreme or controversial opinions; possibly even by excluding from teaching activities those whose extreme views handicap their teaching capacity. I thought once that extremists might be prevailed on not to obtrude their personal convictions in their training activities and I still think that this ideal could be attained by lecturers, possibly even by seminar leaders. But I now admit that it is unreasonable to expect the training analysis to follow these more balanced lines. And since the training analysis is the Achilles heal of our system there is no escaping the fact that modifications in training can only be effectively secured through selection of training analysts. The only other alternative I can think of is to abolish the designation of training analyst, to return, for a time at any rate, to our previous system of accepting candidates from amongst those analysed by *any* recognized member. This would no doubt reduce extremism for a time at any rate. A training committee could still function for interviewing the candidate's *analyst* before acceptance of the candidate and for providing a variety of pedagogic lectures and seminars. The analyst would, however, select the candidate's "controls" from among the general list of *members*.

Finally, what course should be followed if neither of these expedients is adopted? It seems to me that two alternatives exist. Either the Society adjudicates on the respective validity of opposing views and prohibits the teaching of views that are held to be either invalid or controversial; or the Training Committee organizes two or more systems of training wherby candidates can be trained exclusively in any given system. However absurd such a system might appear to a casual observer, it is the only one that would prevent for a time official splitting of the Society. I came to this conclusion with regret. For a long time I held the view that candidates should have sufficient gumption to see through the idiosyncracies of their teachers. Evidently this is too much to expect.

As for the teachers, I find it hard to abandon the view that these at least should have sufficient gumption not to make controversial views an essential and binding part of their instruction. It follows therefore that in my opinion the main flaw in our training system has been the selection of teachers who are strictly speaking unqualified to teach that most impressionable creature—the student in training.

Glover was clearly writing with the future in mind. But in the heat of the moment little attention got paid to his words themselves; they did not even succeed in being wholly accurately transcribed years later when *The Freud–Klein Controversies 1941–45* came out as a book. (And they got printed there—without a proper date—alongside a series of other memoranda on technique.) The high point of the controversy had been Glover's resignation from the Training Committee, since it was almost immediately matched by Anna Freud's own withdrawal; Glover had gone further, however, since he had also quit the Society itself.

With all the thunder and lightning around Glover, the sequence of events has been fouled up, and nobody has emphasized that Glover left for reasons that were different from those of Anna Freud. Anna Freud's biographer confused what happened; first Glover resigned from the Training Committee and the Society, then Anna withdrew from the Training Committee. Despite Anna Freud's biographer's account, she did not leave first.[31] Glover's reasons for leaving had to do with his fundamental objections to what had happened to the training of candidates; of course, he had been objecting also (like Anna Freud) to Klein's theories in general. Glover maintained that he would have been content had none of the principals in the Controversy continued to train candidates. Anna Freud, following Glover's resignation, withdrew from the Training Committee when she realized that she and her work were being considered one of the "extremes" in the situation; it seemed to her an insult.

Glover's letter to Payne, dated January 24, 1944, recapitulated what we have discussed:

> It is now almost 2 years since I first contemplated severing my connection with the British Psycho-analytic Society. For many years—in fact from 1933—I had formed the impression that sooner or later the scientific divergencies in the Society and particularly in the Training Committee would become more and more acute. But I did not think of resigning until after the Blitz, when an originally scientific discussion on "The Relations of the P.A. Society to the Public" became politically organised. This political development coincided with the return to participation in Society affairs of some members who for one reason or another had been absent for some time previously. It then became clear to me that the Society could no longer claim the status of a scientific society; also that it was unlikely to remain a purely Freudian society. In fact it had been less and less Freudian since 1933–34 when Mrs. Klein first adumbrated theories belonging to what I have called elsewhere her "second phase."
>
> The subsequent course of events is familiar to you: a) the organization of the "Controversial series of Discussions" intended to examine the doctrines held and taught by Mrs. Klein and her adherents, b) the appointment of a committee to examine the

Society's system of electing office bearers, c) the mandate to the Training Committee to report on the effect of current controversies on the training situation.

All these activities were sufficiently far advanced by the end of 1943 to permit an accurate estimate of future tendencies and developments in the Society; and, as you know, following the Annual Meeting of 1943 I decided to resign my office and membership, and was induced to postpone the decision only on urgent representations from certain members of the Society. I said then, however, that I would not delay longer than Christmas 1943.

The present situation, as I read it, is as follows: a) The Controversial series of Discussions will end in smoke. Indeed it is already pointless to continue them. The Klein group will continue to maintain that their views are either strictly Freudian or legitimate, not to say valuable, extensions of Freud's work. The "old middle group" will hedge but end by saying there is no ground for a split. Only the Viennese Freudians and a few isolated members will continue to maintain that the Klein views are non-analytical; and these will be outvoted by a combination of the Klein group with whatever younger groups are interested less in the present controversies than in the future administration of the Society, so the outcome is a foregone conclusion.

But quite apart from those political orientations, there is, in my view, no scientific justification for continuing the series. The new Kleinian metapsychology that has already been presented to us is not only fundamentally opposed to Freudian metapsychology but can be adduced in substantiation of any possible clinical theory that the supporters may choose to bring forward.

My reading of the situation is confirmed by the activities of the "Constitutional Committee" and of the Training Committee. The former will produce a majority report in which the importance of scientific divergencies will be discounted and the troubles of the Society attributed to its mode of electing office bearers!

The Training Committee will produce either an unrealistic "head in the clouds" document suggesting that there is no real dilemma before the Society or a majority report suggesting that the trouble can be eliminated by a change of spirit in the members electing the Committee. It is, in my view, unlikely that the Training Committee will report to the Society the salient facts, viz. that the Committee has been for a long time at a practical deadlock and that for the past year it has sanctioned in effect the existence, as it were under one umbrella, of at least two entirely different systems of training. It will certainly not recommend either the resignation from the training staff of any existing members, or the abolition for an indefinite period of the Training Analyst system, thereby leaving training analyses to be conducted by any qualified member of the Society.

In addition to these three mains reasons for my resignation, it is my impression, from a study of recent events, that the Society is about to develop new orientations in the near future. E.g. a) it is likely to make a closer move towards general psychiatry on the lines already observed in America, b) it is likely to spend a good deal of energies on the technique of static rather than of dynamic psychology.

So, talking it all over, I see no point in delaying my resignation longer. Indeed, if I delayed until the Annual Meeting, it might be more likely to encourage others to follow my example. These are matters which everyone should decide for himself or herself. Personally I think it is desirable that a new Freudian society should sooner or later be formed: indeed I think it is very likely that one will be formed. But not all members are in such an independent position as myself and I do not wish to bias them in any way. Indeed I'm not at all sure that I could shoulder the burden of developing a new society.

Anyhow I wish my resignation to take effect from the 25th January, i.e. the day after the meeting of the Training Committee called to consider its draft report to the Society. In this way the comments on the Draft which I have sent by separate post will still be in order as part of the Training Committee deliberations, and therefore can be minuted as such.

Any practical points arising in the process of handing over will, I think, be easy to deal with.

As if enough had not already been put down on paper, Sylvia Payne wanted still further clarification from Glover. From his perspective the Society had become politicized; but he did not want to be viewed as someone who had bent on being a wrecker:

THE CONTROVERSIAL DISCUSSIONS—I "A NEW *WELTANSCHAUUNG*"? 75

> Feb. 1, 1944
>
> To come back to your letter: You say in it that we worked in cooperation until the troubles in the Society became acute, and that thereafter our aims became opposed to each other, in that I "worked for a split" and you "worked for compromise." On the second part of this statement it is naturally not my concern to make any personal comment. I will content myself with saying that scientific compromise must be distinguished from administrative conciliation; also that compromise on matters of principle often ends by accelerating the cleavage it is intended to prevent—as indeed has been the result in this instance.

(Fifty years later Dr. Clifford Yorke would quietly echo exactly Glover's point.[32])

> On the other hand your suggestion that I "worked for a split" (although limited as to its time reference) might easily give rise to a false impression. I should like therefore to state categorically that I have never worked for a split, have never asked anyone to split, have refused to split when urged to do so and have consistently refused to be a party to movements behind the scenes such as have frequently occurred in the Society since 1928. I have now simply exercised the privilege of withdrawing from the Society (a) because its general tendency and training has become unscientific and (b) because it is becoming less and less Freudian and has therefore lapsed from its original aims.
>
> It is of course true that I have criticized the Klein deviation with increasing vigour and plainness ever since 1934 when the Klein party adopted the theory of a "central depressive position" (together with all that this theory connotes). But this criticism, so far from constituting "working for a split," is a legitimate exercise of scientific criticism. When, shortly after the publication of Rank's "Das Trauma de Geburt," the late James Glover and myself prepared a comprehensive adverse criticism of his Birth Theory of Neurosogenesis, no one suggested that we were working for a split, although in fact we attacked the Birth Theory at a time when many analysts had swallowed it whole. Incidentally it may make the present issue more plain if I point out that Mrs. Klein's latest theories, although differing in content from those of Rank, consti-

tute a deviation from psycho-analysis of the same order. The implications are identical and the theories are unsound for precisely the same reasons as were those of Rank. The resemblance between the two deviations is indeed remarkable.

May I further point out that during what I have called the "first phase" of Mrs. Klein's theorising (i.e. prior to 1934) I went out of my way to find a common basis for some of her views and classical Freudian teaching. Anyone who attended Psycho-analytical Congresses was perfectly aware that even her early views were not accepted by any branch of the psycho-analytic Association except the British Society and, for that matter, not even by the whole of the British Society. At the Oxford Congress I devoted a paper to this task of compromise and was roundly taxed with the fact by many of our then European colleagues. But already during that "first phase" I was profoundly disturbed by two manifestations that developed in the Society (a) the blanketing of scientific discussion in the Society, where acceptance or non-acceptance of Mrs. Klein's views became a sort of religious "test." (b) the policy of the Training Committee. May I therefore end this letter with some further comment on the Training situation as it has developed from 1928 to the present day.

I have always held that the power to influence the future of psycho-analysis lies, not in the scientific discussions of the Society, but in the policy of the Training Committee. The operation of training transferences and counter-transferences is the decisive factor. When differences of opinion become acute, these transferences automatically lower the level of training from a scientific to a quasi-religious plane. Unfortunately this fact was never openly admitted in the Training Committee. Instead, lip service to the myth of the "trained (and therefore unbiased) analyst" developed to a degree that was, in my opinion, little short of conscious hypocrisy. The result of this policy could not be indefinitely delayed; already before the War, the Committee was driven to consider the possibility of having two distinct systems of training and during the war period has openly countenanced two distinct and opposed systems. Candidates who wish a Kleinian training are given Kleinian analysts and controls. Candidates preferring a purely Freudian training are given Freudian analysts and controls. Those who have no particular preference are given potluck. Yet their future views and professional careers will be finally determined by this haphazard allocation. Even so, until the last few years I held out in the Training Committee against a split. But I see now that the position is an impossible one not only for candidates but for psycho-analysis.

And so, when it became clear from its Draft Report that the Committee was still prepared to pretend that this real problem is "an unreal dilemma" I could only conclude that there was no prospect of scientific progress in the Society itself. For if the training is unscientific, what hope is there of establishing scientific standards amongst members whose entry to the Society depends on their conforming to the regulations of the Training Committee. Better by far to scrap the whole system and start again.

P.S. Since writing this I hear that Miss Freud has resigned from the Training Committee. I need hardly say that although her decision was taken independently of any action of mine, I am not at all surprised: The phantastic stress laid by Mr. Strachey's Draft Report on the alleged capacity of training analysts to promote objectivity in their candidates is in such glaring contradiction to the facts of the present situation! As I said in my "Comment": if this were really the case candidates would already be more advanced than their training analysts and so be in a position to analyse their training analysts with some benefit to the latter.

The letter writing still did not stop between the British Society and Glover. In the fall of 1943 Glover had publicly criticized army psychiatrists and their approach to selection boards. Several members of the Society (including Adrian Stephen) felt that they were under attack, and after Glover resigned a resolution was unanimously passed in the British Society asking Glover to send a statement to the medical press affirming that his position had been personal and "did not represent any expressed or implied attitude of the British Psychoanalytic Society as a whole."

Adrian Stephen was exulant to his sister Vanessa at the upshot—Glover had been "driven out," and once Payne succeeded Jones as president (Jones going into the "gilded" cage of "past president") Stephen could claim "complete victory": "It has all been great fun. . . ."

Stephen was unhappy, though, about "that miserable James Strachey, lickspittle that he is" being against Stephen: "I think because his practice depends on the goodwill of Jones and Glover...."[33]

Glover, at substantial length, had a fine time puncturing the position the Society was asking him to take on the issue of army psychiatrists. How would medical journals respond to his declaring that his views were only his own, and not the Society from which he had already resigned? For years he had been accustomed to expressing his views publicly, and was perfectly prepared for any public controversies that might follow. "I cannot help thinking that in its older and more robust days the Society would never have allowed itself to be dragged by a small minority of members into the present ludicrous and somewhat humiliating position." By May the Society tried at last to put an end to the painful situation by, belatedly, passing a resolution thanking Glover for his past services to "the science and movement of psycho-analysis." Glover thanked them, adding two comments. His services "though not longer at the disposal of the British Society and Institute" were "still devoted to the advancement of Freudian psycho-analysis," and that he regarded it as his "greatest service to the *science* of psycho-analysis in this country" his "repudiation not only of the pseudo-scientific theories which the Society has seen fit to endorse but also of the system of training it has now sanctioned." It would be hard to imagine a more unhappy breach, one that because of Glover's international stature would become widely known abroad; Freud's daughter's resignation from the Training Committee of course added to the scandal. This distressing state of affairs helps in itself to explain how the mythology associated with the history of the British Society has been driven to assign him to the outer darkness of oblivion.

4

The Controversial Discussions–II
"Double-barrelled Training"

At the time I knew him Glover was able to acknowledge that he had been in error in his estimation of the future of Klein's strength. (Anna Freud's party, who today still feel an oppressive Kleinian atmosphere in England, might disagree with Glover's mid-1960s hindsight. And more than one theorist within the general psychoanalytic movement would be inclined to think that the British Society was unusually overrun with Kleinian ideas at odds with those of Freud.) I had asked Glover, trying to search for similarities between orthodox psychoanalytic thinking and Klein, *Don't you think there are analogies between the ideas of Ruth Mack Brunswick on the pre-oedipal phases and Melanie Klein's own system?* Yes, Ruth Brunswick had a great deal of "freedom" in her thinking, although neither she nor Melanie would probably have recognized the similarities. (One of Klein's central contributions was to put her finger on the significance of "pre-genital" levels of development, which Ruth Brunswick, a great personal favorite of Freud's, had talked about as "pre-oedipal"; so had Otto Rank.[1] The mother as a positive source of emotional development was a relatively late addition in psychoanalysis. Jung had raised it earlier, but few of the Freudians followed the intellectual history of the pre-World War quarrels. When Anna Freud wrote about children separated from their mothers during World War II giving up symptomatology once they reestablished surrogate maternal bonds, this was considered an advance in analytic thinking.)

Klein's own emphasis on early aspects of personality growth seemed to Glover and Anna Freud as reminiscent of the way earlier psychoanalytic heretics had tried to get away from the centrality of the Oedipus complex. What struck traditionalists as offensive in the work of Rank, also an early proponent of the role of mothering in the history of psychoanalysis, was somehow acceptable when articulated by Ruth Brunswick, who was like an adopted daughter of Freud's; she tactfully phrased her points in terms of Freud's oedipal thinking, showing that the Oedipus complex simply had an earlier "pre-history." Glover, however, had long been proud of how early and successfully he and his brother had combatted Rank's birth trauma as a betrayal of the purity of Freud's message, without Glover following some of the more subtle continental innovations.

Almost from the beginning Jones's own enthusiasm about Klein was not endorsed by Freud. In 1925 Freud let Jones know that "Melanie Klein's works have been received with much skepticism and opposition here in Vienna. As you know, I myself don't have much of an opinion on pedagogical matters."[2] Freud was being discreet with Jones, who in turn was defending Klein's orthodoxy on grounds that "prophylactic child analysis" was "the logical outcome of psychoanalysis."[3] By 1927 Freud was being more outspoken; he wrote Jones that "Mrs. Klein's view of the behavior of the ego-ideal in children seems quite impossible to me and is in contradiction to all my postulates." One might think that was pretty strong language on Freud's part, but he was forced to spell out what he meant. Freud could accept that Mrs. Klein "makes children more mature than we used to think" as "in agreement with my ideas." But Mrs. Klein was presenting "the superego of children as being . . . independent as that of adults, while Anna seems to me right in stressing that the child's superego is still under the direct influence of his parents."[4]

Freud also bobbed and weaved to Jones about Klein's work, but Freud could not tolerate criticisms of Anna's contribution or Jones's allegation that Anna had been insufficiently analyzed. (It has to remain an open question whether Jones suspected that Freud had analyzed Anna himself, but it was an almost unbelievably insulting ploy on Jones's part to cast doubt on the extent of Anna's maturity.) In the meantime Klein was saying in public that Anna was "avoiding the Oedipus complex on principle." Freud was distressed that Mrs. Riviere was following Klein's line of thinking: "Naturally I criticize her for denying half the facts. . . . This makes her viewpoint 'heretical,' contains an unfortunate similarity to Jung's, and, like his, is an important step toward making analysis unreal and impersonal. . . . All our apostates always grasped part of the truth and wanted to declare it as the whole truth." In 1929 Freud had reiterated that "the more I learn of these things, the more I believe that Melanie Klein is on the wrong track and Anna is on the right one." In *Civilization and Its Discontents* Freud could defer in passing to Klein's work; he did not cite people often, and was eager to hold onto his following in England. The "injustice" of Klein and Melitta toward Anna had been, Freud wrote Jones, "set right" by Jones's "kindness." But Freud repeated to Jones, "I am of the opinion that your society followed Mrs. Klein on a wrong path"; at the same time Freud qualified his indictment by saying he was "unfamiliar with just that sphere of observations [child analysis] which she draws upon and hence have no right to a firm conviction."[5] Someone like Payne, who was regarded by most in British analysis as a sober onlooker, was convinced that there could be no doubt that Klein was "awfully good" with patients, even though Payne thought her deficient in theory, and said she had largely adopted it from her pupils. The early stages of development, in Payne's mind, were formulated by the Kleinians in "too adult" terms; Glover termed this "adulterization."

For myself, I cannot understand how theoretical ideas should ever have overwhelmed the significance of therapeutic concepts in practice. Throughout the 1991 *The Freud–Klein Controversies, 1941–45*, which take up almost 1000 pages, almost no clinical material whatever appears. One of the few clinical examples has to do with a Kleinian mentioning a girl of 16 months who played a favorite game with her parents: picking "small imaginary bits off a brown embossed leather screen in the dining-room, carrying these pretended bits of food across the room in her finger and thumb and putting them into the mouth of father and mother alternately." The analyst felt justified in treating this as the girl's feeding her parents "with symbolic faeces."[6] To compound how theory-ridden Kleinianism could be, I met one leading Kleinian who talked about analyses that were supposed to last, as a matter of principle, for ten years, without acknowledging the negative aspects of such a massive invasion of another person's privacy. If research, which was proposed as the justification of such analyses, requires guinea pigs, then patients deserve to be told beforehand. I never heard Glover talk about patients in such sectarian terms. Dogmatism may inspire faithful disciples, and can have a curative impact of its own, but still I find ideological intolerance distasteful, and not good for therapy.

Glover himself had a doctrinaire side, but I thought him more reasonable than others that I met, even though he had been at the center of the controversy during World War II. (He has been accused of being the one "who did most to stir things up at the British Society," and that is the way it looks from the outside. But I doubt it would be fair to refer to "the persecutory violence of Glover's threats."[7]) In spite of all his differences with Jones, for example, Glover said that "to the end of his days" he would insist that Jones had been a good President of the Society. But Glover felt that, when it came to Klein, Jones had been "a bloody fool" in losing his disciplinary hold of "those damn homosexual women." (There was no heat behind Glover's words. Kleinianism can be looked on as a movement of feminine protest, Glover explained, since it emphasized the significance of the mother and breast envy, and downplayed Freud's own concentration on the father and castration anxiety. I believe Freud could not conceive of either mothers or daughters being bad, but this blind spot of idealization of women may have been built on an unconscious devaluation of them.) Glover said that Freud's was "a man-made psychology," and "intelligent women ended up violently opposing him"; this was "the sexual tie between them."

After the conflict in the Society was over a book[8] came out containing a series of papers that represented Klein's side of the controversy; Glover (rightly I think) thought that both sides should be on record. *Who led the Kleinian cause?* Dr. Paula Heimann, Dr. Susan Isaacs, and Joan Riviere were the most prominent, and "gave" Klein "a theoretical base." (Paula Heimann, no longer a Kleinian, complained to me that she had been in analysis with Mrs. Klein from 1942–1944, and that Mrs. Klein had had no compunction since she was "dependent on idealizations" in asking her analysands for public support. Dr. Clifford Scott maintained that there was a strategy on Klein's part throughout the Controvérsial Discussions, for example, about who would speak when.)

Who led the battle against Klein? Glover himself, and Melitta. (Glover was leaving out Rickman among the Kleinians, and even more strikingly had ignored someone like Barbara Low as an opponent of Klein.) The "moderates" included Payne, Adrian Stephen, Ella Sharpe, and James Strachey. (We have had examples of Stephen's so-called moderation.) Jones himself was trying to be a peacemaker, although he leaned a bit to Klein's side. As for Anna Freud, despite her part in the controversy she always gave off the decided impression of being self-effacing or, as Dr. Charles Rycroft once put it, "retreating into the limelight."[9] She did in 1942 remind the Society how a 1927 text of hers had been censored: "I resented it very much in time past, not when this Society criticized my little book on the psychoanalysis of children, but, I resented it when the Society refused to have it printed in England."[10] (In fact I think Anna Freud, known in the profession as "Miss Freud," must have been more shocked than even others at the rough-and-tumble of debate, to which she was unused, throughout the Controversial Discussions.)

To Eva Rosenfeld, a foreigner relatively new to England, Jones and Glover looked like "deadly enemies." Glover told me that Jones had said of Abraham that he was "divinely normal," and Jones had once used that expression to characterize Glover, but Glover was sure that later Jones would have withdrawn that label about Glover. I asked about what position Dr. Marjorie Brierley had taken, since I knew that she had been trained by Glover and that he thought well of her. (She had collaborated with Glover over a 1940 survey on technique that many saw as an opening shot against Klein.) Glover said that Brierley had opposed both himself and Klein, which he thought "pretty good going." (Glover seemed to take a genuine satisfaction in the controversy, without losing a sense of detachment. If he can look scholastic in having fallen back on quotations from Freud for his critique, the Kleinians took pleasure in citing against him his earlier articles approving of Klein. In the end it was considered noteworthy that Brierley had resolutely stayed in the Society rather than leave with Glover. She had suggested, like Paula Heimann, that Klein became an overidealized object for her followers.)

Glover had a Scottish independence of mind, and this was part of his having resigned from the Society without trying to lead a secessionist movement. He had his psychoanalytic contacts abroad, to whom he sent notices explaining his decision; he was willing organizationally to step outside the history of British psychoanalysis. For all the factionalism he had not tried to lead a splinter group, creating a formal schism. (Both Miss Sharpe and Miss Searl could not stand the ideological civil war, and were considered "victims" of it.) Before long Dr. Douglas Bryan left the Society. "Perhaps a couple" of others had gone, too, although Glover claimed not to have encouraged anyone else to leave. (On this point he was flatly contradicted by Jones's pupil Elizabeth Zetzel; she told me that Glover had sent a letter around explaining his resignation, supposedly trying to take others over the side with him. Richard Wright, in *The God That Failed*, was shocked at being similarly accused when he left the Communist Party.[11] Not even Melitta Schmideberg resigned with Glover.)

Most British analysts comprised the "middle group," those who wanted peace and "no more fighting." Glover thought that if it were a "scientific" dispute such reasoning "could not count." Payne had been a leader of the peacemakers; they wanted eclectically to combine elements from every viewpoint, and as so-called Independents disliked "washing any more dirty linen in public." Glover felt, when I met with him, that the conflict had been "muted by not resolved." He had thought, when he resigned in 1944, that the Middle Group of "independents" would be sterile and lose their power. By the mid-1960s, however, he had come to believe that both poles, that of the orthodox Freudians and the Kleinians, might be going to wither away. (Young analysts, however, were maintaining then that Anna Freud's group and that of Melanie Klein were still well-heeled financially, and that being caught in the middle could mean a financial sacrifice. One

Independent maintained that he could expect referrals neither from Miss Freud's group nor from Mrs. Klein's.)

When Glover quit the Society it was partly because he did not think it was "proper" to have students being trained in three divergent schools —Freudian, Kleinian, and the Independents. All along he had thought that "controversial issues" should not be introduced into the course of psychoanalytic training. (Freud once made exactly the same point in an unpublished letter to Wilhelm Reich about his own original ideas.) Glover said that there was nothing wrong with "the principle" of training analyses, but that "the practice" of it fell far short of anything ideal. (An essential accusation of Glover's had been that the Kleinians were gaining power by means of the system of training candidates.)

Glover quietly insisted to me that the issue over Mrs. Klein could not have ever been "to exclude" her. The controversy had "fizzled out" into nothing, and his resignation had ensured that it only "petered out." He maintained that he went when he found that Payne's compromise was to have separate training groups, "B" for Anna Freud's people and "A" for everyone else. (I regret now that I did not think to ask Glover point blank whether or not he had been offended that the constitution of the Society had been changed so that if the presidency were ever offered to him, it would only be held for a period of three years, unlike Jones's prior continuous tenure. Glover was caustic though about the way analysts "rotate" offices nowadays, as opposed to earlier "when to hold an office meant something." Freud shared Glover's point of view; in 1925 he wrote Sandor Rado: "The Americans transfer the democratic principle from politics into science. Everyone has to be president once, no one may remain president, no one may distinguish himself from the others, and thus they all learn and produce nothing, one and all."[12]) Bitter feelings linger on after such a dispute; after Glover had resigned from the Society, Adrian Stephen had said to him, "now that we have gotten rid of you we can get down to scientific work." But Glover felt that that was "just what the British Society had not proceeded to do." (As early as 1942 Adrian and Karin had telegrammed their agreement with Klein: "Glover behaving like a lunatic. People are realising dangerous for him to stay in power."[13])

Sylvia Payne's compromise has endured until now.* Anna Freud had resigned (along with Glover) from the Training Committee, and she was tempted to leave the Society too. (They both temporarily became honorary members of the Swiss Psychoanalytic Society; Switzerland was a country of neutrals.) Payne, according to Glover, "talked Anna out of" resigning from the British Society, convincing her to stay. Payne presented Anna with her own separate training set-up (the "B" group) within the British Society. Anna "could scarcely refuse," since it gave her everything that she wanted, and Anna could not go completely against Jones, and damage his Society, since he had gotten her, her father, and others out of Vienna. (Freud decided to go to England in 1938, which was the worst possible place to bring Anna, given her old struggle with Klein. Meanwhile Klein blamed Jones for having caused Klein the trouble that went with the arrival of the Viennese contingent of analysts. Jones wrote at the time to Klein trying to mollify her about Anna: "She is certainly a tough, perhaps indigestible morsel. She has probably gone as far in analysis as she can and she has no pioneering originality." The same day he wrote to Anna Freud that Klein "has neither a scientific nor an orderly mind, and is also in many ways neurotic."[14] This was run-of-the-mill for Jones's capacity for double-dealing; he liked to characterize himself as a psychoanalytic diplomat. He later dedicated his biography of Freud to Anna: "True Daughter of an Immortal Sire.")

Anna Freud was relieved that her students would be trained uncontaminated by Klein's ideas. Although Anna later outwardly mellowed somewhat about Klein, as was the politic course to take, at the outset she would not have anything to do with her; she would not compete at the British Society but kept mostly out. The arrangement was that the rest of the analytic candidates, the "A" group, would be exposed to ideas from a variety of analytic sources. Glover readily conceded that Payne was "the only person" who could have held the

---

*Dr. Payne mentioned to me with some heat how money donated around the time of Freud's centenary in 1956 for the subsidizing of training analyses in general had come under the influence of a committee of only members of the "B" (Anna Freud) group.

Society together. He thought her "a bit timid fundamentally," since she was "all for peace," but he knew she was "quite a bright woman." (He said she had been analyzed by his brother at the Brunswick Square Clinic, and knew she had gone elsewhere for treatment, but he did not seem to realize she had been to Sachs.) "Only to some extent" had Payne persuaded Anna Freud not to resign, for "on her own" Anna did not want to be responsible for splitting the Society.

As Glover saw it, Anna Freud and her supporters as guests in England had not wanted to "cause too much trouble"; therefore they had, in his way of thinking, "only sat on the fence." Glover himself had been more anti-Klein than pro-Anna Freud. He used to say to Anna, "I'll give you three years to decide if you will be free and independent, and quite moral." In the end he thought she had come to be "quite satisfied" with her own clinic at Hampstead. (Anna Freud and Dorothy Burlingham together founded the Hampstead Child Therapy Clinic in 1947; they started a training course, in 1951 they bought 12 Maresfield Gardens for the purposes of a clinic, and finally in 1956 they opened the additional premises for the clinic at 21 Maresfield Gardens. Anna and Dorothy then headed a relatively small staff, who aimed to specialize in the children, mainly between the ages of 4 and 7, who got referred there.) Melanie Klein and Anna Freud, whose disagreements about child analysis had gone back to the 1920s, had never become involved in any "open confrontation" at the Society.

But Anna had, however, "wanted the support" of Glover for her clinic for children. (He did not mention to me that Jones, as President of the International Psycho-Analytic Association, had proceeded to appoint Anna, with her approval, to replace Glover as Secretary, an office she had held before him. Evidently Anna felt that that way she could, as a member of the IPA Executive, help protect Glover and tame Jones.) Glover had thought that even his backing Anna in her venture at Hampstead would not solve the problem within the Society. He was not ready "to support a new group." He told her in effect, "Either come out openly against Klein, or else just sit down and be quiet." Anna and he knew how much Jones had backed Klein. But by the mid-1960s the "average member" of the British Society, he thought, knew little about all these earlier matters.

Anna Freud's files fill out the story of events following Glover's resignation. As late as April 29, 1947, Adrian Stephen (who had succeeded Glover as Secretary of the British Society) was writing to Anna to object to the announcement that Glover was scheduled to be one of the speakers at a Conference of European Psychoanalysts to be held in Amsterdam in May, 1947.

> I am rather surprised at this because surely the meeting is for the members of the various Societies and Dr. Glover has resigned. I have heard the rumour that he had somehow or other joined the Swiss Society but if that is true I can scarcely believe that the Swiss are in possession of all the facts connected with his resignation. I wonder whether you, as Secretary to the International Association, can do anything about it. Surely before electing him the Swiss should have communicated with the British Society and found out what their views were. One may or may not agree with his scientific views—that is a question of evidence and argument—but it is hardly very courteous to us to assume that Dr. Glover's account of the differences is true without making any enquiries. In my own opinion it would not be very difficult to show that the main difference was purely a question of power politics in which he did not act very scrupulously.

Anna Freud did not save a copy of her reply, but Stephen's letter of May 2nd indicates she had defended the propriety of Glover appearing at the Amsterdam meetings; Stephen wanted to pursue the point:

> Thank you for explaining the situation with regard to Glover. Of course, if he is an Honorary member of the Swiss Society, nothing can be done to prevent his appearance at Amsterdam, and there is no more to be said unless, indeed, he was elected after the trouble in England. If that was so I still think the Swiss and any other Society that elected him should have made some official enquiry into the circumstances of his departure from our Society.

(Glover had obviously only gone to the Swiss Society after planning to resign from the British group, so Stephen's objection to Glover speaking in Amsterdam still stood.)

Evidently Anna had raised the contentious issue of Rene Laforgue, who had run into trouble with the French Society because of the charge of wartime collaboration with the Nazis; Laforgue had in fact also helped Anna's brother Oliver escape from France. Stephen wrote:

> I do not agree that Laforgue might have no difficulty in lecturing over here as a guest. Many of us know that there has been trouble with the French Society and I am sure that we would ask them before inviting him officially.
>
> I absolutely agree with you that it was a pity that Glover preferred to resign rather than to stand to his guns but *if* his grounds for resignation had been purely scientific I feel certain that he would have done so.

Someone as genuinely distinguished as Donald W. Winnicott joined in protesting against Glover's speaking on the Amsterdam program. He wrote to Anna Freud on April 7, 1947:

> From my point of view this is a big snub to the British Psychoanalytic Society, and I am wondering what you feel about it. Have you time to let me know?
>
> My own conviction is to feel a distaste for the conference, for the Dutch made rather a special point of getting the British Society over, and they could have easily avoided this annoying back-slap.
>
> Perhaps they do not know the circumstances under which Dr. Glover resigned?

Anna continued to run interference for Glover, and promptly replied to Winnicott on April 11.

> Concerning Dr. Glover:—He has been well known and well liked by the members of the various Branch Societies on the continent who think of him as one of the leading people in the International Society and have always liked his scientific contributions. What is known on the continent, of course, is that he left the British Society of his own free will because of his disagreement with the theories of Mrs. Klein. I am sure that his invitation to Amsterdam is not meant as a move against the British Society, merely as an

unwillingness to take part in what the people on the continent will consider a local difference of opinion. I am very sorry that you feel so strongly about it. His paper, so far as I know, will not be of a controversial character.

Winnicott replied on April 15:

> It was good of you to answer my letter. I see where the difference between our points of view lies. From your point of view Dr. Glover left the British Society because of his disagreement with the theories of Mrs. Klein, and your attitude towards this matter is, therefore, quite consistent. From my point of view Dr. Glover left because of something much more complex, so that it was a great relief to me when he went, although I should not in the least have minded a scientific disagreement with Mrs. Klein's or anyone else's theories. So there it has to be.

(When I met Winnicott in 1965 he was regretful that Glover had ever left the British Society. By then it had been considered established about Klein that "any disagreement with her theories came to be considered as evidence of disloyalty to her and thus some of her previous supporters . . . were dropped and withdrew from membership of the group."[15] These people included Heimann, Winnicott, Rickman, and Scott.)

Behind the scenes Jones had raised his own vengeful objections, as President of the IPA, to Glover's becoming a member of the Swiss Society. Glover had, within a few days of resigning from the British Society, sent a copy of his letter to Payne along with a separate letter to Jones.

Jan. 28, 1944

Dear Ernest,

> I think you ought to see the enclosed which explains itself.
>   Looking back on the situation, I see that there was a good deal of intelligent anticipation behind your suggestion that the Society should go out of operation for the duration of the war. But I don't believe it would have made any difference in the long run.

> Anyway it's an auld song now.
> I wonder how much we fundamentallly agree. On one thing, I think, certainly that it was a woman ridden society (your favoured hypothesis).
> Apart from that I have on unalloyed feeling of satisfaction:— we made a good team together until the Klein imbroglio developed. Without being oversententious, I stuck to the professional tradition of loyalty to you as First in Command and didn't mind taking any raps on that score. I'd do the same again.

For years Jones had presided as Chair, with Glover at his left hand. Jones "invariably opened the discussion and so set its tone. . . . Glover followed up before there was discussion from the floor."[16]

By December 1944, Glover was struggling to hold onto his office as Secretary of the IPA. He wrote to Jones, addressing him formally now as "Dear Dr. Jones."

> First of all I should like to make it clear that I am writing this letter to you in your capacity as President of the International Psychoanalytic Association, of which body I was re-appointed Secretary at the last Congress. The issue I am about to raise comes exclusively within the scope of the Association and of no other body. I feel sure that on reading farther you will agree that this is a strictly proper reservation.
> As President till July 1944 of the British Psycho-analytic Society you are of course aware that in January of this year, I resigned my branch membership and branch offices. I did so on the scientific grounds which were set out with the then Business Secretary of the Society in a correspondence, copies of which you have already acknowledged receiving from me. One of the main reasons was the fact that the British P-A Society is no longer a Freudian Society and is officially committed to teaching psychoanalytic candidates the Klein System of Child Psychology as part of psycho-analysis, whereas in fact it constitutes a deviation from psycho-analysis.
> You will also recall that I did not at any time resign my membership of the International Psycho-analytic Association or of the post

of Secretary to that body, appointment to which is made by the International Congress only. Nor would it have been proper for me to do so since (a) the Association exists for the advancement of Freudian psycho-analysis (b) I am a Freudian psycho-analyst.

Shortly after my resignation from the British P-A Society I heard from indirect and unofficial sources that you had "appointed" Anna Freud as Secretary of the International Association. This has since been confirmed in the International Bulletin. But owing to war circumstances and the impracticability of getting together a quorum of the International Council, I delayed bringing the position before that Council which is the only proper body to deal with it. I understand however that recently Princess Marie of Greece has arrived in this country and since there is no longer any obstacle to calling a meeting *I wish now formally to request you as President to convene a meeting of the Council of the International Psychoanalytic Association to consider inter-alia the situation that has now arisen.*

(Princess Marie was a consistent ally of Anna Freud.) Glover went on:

I will not attempt at this juncture to present any of the considerations which make this course essential and urgent. I would merely point out that a number of important precedents have been established (some of them during my own tenure of office as Secretary) governing situations of a similar kind. Actually the original statutes laying down the relation between Branch membership of the International have been modified both by resolution and by precedent. I mention this point in order to indicate that the present situation can not be dealt with by invoking the original statutes but in terms of the modifications and precedents since established.

Yours faithfully,

Edward Glover

P.S. As a matter of form and to keep the Council informed, as is my duty as Secretary, I have sent a copy of this letter to all the other members of the International Council.

In the short run Glover was knocking his head against a stone wall, and Jones just dug in his presidential heels. As his biographer comments, Jones replied "disingenuously" to Glover, "I send at last the official reply to your letter but must add my surprise that you are not yet tired of psychoanalytic politics." Jones's letter

> then plunged into undisguised polemic. "Your request that I convene a meeting of the Council for a certain purpose raises at once the matter of your capacity to do so. . . . I do not see how you have any locus standi in the Association. The Congress of course ratified your election and it would not occur to any one that a non member could hold any official position so that your resignation of membership automatically included that of officer."[17]

As early as January, 1942, Jones had said he was willing to accept the inevitability of a less autocratically run British Society; he wrote to Anna Freud then that

> Dr. Glover seems inclined to adopt a defiant attitude and insists that the present regime continue. . . . I am very dissatisfied with the present unproductive activities of the Society, for which I hold Dr. Glover partly, though by no means wholly, to blame. By nature I believe in aristocratic leadership, but I think there are occasions, and I wonder if this is not one, where it is more successful to exert that leadership indirectly instead of overtly. Thus I am inclined to the solution of reducing the reponsibility of officials, making their policies or decisions more a matter of business meetings, and having the officials re-elected annually. . . .[18]

(In 1930 Jones had thought Brill was being unwise in adopted fixed rules for the New York Society: "we are wise enough not to tie ourselves to having any rules at all. That gives the executive body [i.e., Jones himself] the power of doing what it likes."[19])

By the spring of 1946 Jones was once again being "aristocratic," and wrote Anna (on stationary of the Institute that still listed Glover as an officer):

> I really do not find the Glover case so simple. My memory coincides with yours very definitely that such matters were left in the

hands of the President, and the confusion probably arises from the fact that the term Central Executive for the first 15 or 20 years referred to the President only and then gradually got extended to the Council. It was never made sufficiently clear when the transference took place. More important, however, is the fact that the Congress when debating the matter was very anxious that the permit would not be given just in cases like the present one. Otherwise the precedent would be set for any dissident members perhaps strongly disapproved of by the local Society (I am thinking especially of America) to claim this privilege, in which case it would lead to a quarrel either between him and the president or between the latter and the local Society. The instruction was therefore definitely given to restrict such permits to people where there is no local Society . . . or to former members of the Association who were not eligible for membership of the local Society . . . I feel therefore that I am being asked to do something definitely illegal and contrary to the expressed wishes of the Congress. Clearly it is a matter that should be submitted again to the next Congress who might wish to extend or to clarify their previous resolution. It is not, therefore, a question of my refusing anything in my power.

Anna (who, it will be remembered, had been appointed Secretary of the IPA by Jones, replacing Glover) proposed that the Swiss could list Glover provisionally as a member; but Jones tried to stop that by writing Anna on May 1st: "I do not see how any Society can ask to have published in the Official Bulletin the fact that they have committed an illegal act. Such an act should be suppressed rather than advertised." As Secretary of the IPA Anna went ahead anyway and listed Glover as a member of the Swiss Society—with the qualification stipulating "confirmation of the Central Executive Not Confirmed.").

Even by March 21, 1947, when Anna could announce that she would not be resigning from the British Society, since a *modus vivendi* had been worked out for her group with Sylvia Payne, and that she herself wanted to be only an honorary member of the Swiss Society, rather than a full member, Jones was still dragging his presidential heels about Glover's Swiss credentials. According to Anna, Glover needed ratification by either the President or the whole Central

Executive, and since she, Princess Marie Bonaparte, and Philipp Sarasin (all on the Central Executive) were in agreement in favor of Glover, she proposed to Jones that the matter be settled privately. But in the end it was only in 1949, when Jones vacated the Presidency of the IPA, that Glover could securely become a full member of the Swiss Society.

The correspondence between Anna and Glover bears not only on his standing within the Swiss Society, but on her negotiations with Payne. On April 11, 1946, Glover wrote Anna:

> I . . . heard with considerable interest of Ernest Jones's refusal to recognize my membership of the Swiss Society. Sarasin didn't mention it in his letter to me and I have already subscribed my "dues" as Ordinary Member. Do you know anything of the story?

Glover had also reported on the British Society's "rapprochement" with the then-eclectic Tavistock Clinic (both Adler and Jung had once been invited to speak there), which Glover claimed had "practically abandoned individual treatment." Glover's P.S. to this letter bears on Glover's general assessment of what was happening:

> Many years ago (about 1925) I prophesied to Flugel that in the course of a generation or so PA would be officially watered down in this country by analysts themselves. It appears that this stage has duly arrived somewhat earlier than I expected.

From the beginning of 1946 Glover was writing to Anna to inquire about how her negotiations were going with Payne. Anna seems to have regularly consulted with Glover about the proposals that Payne put forward. (He must have been pleased when asked to back her up with a letter to the Home Office in behalf of her application for naturalization.) Anna shared with Glover their joint problem about becoming members of the Swiss Society. She wrote him on April 19, 1946:

> I knew that Jones had raised difficulties about our Swiss membership but I did not know that he had refused outright. Sarasin cor-

responded with him about it. According to the statutes of the International Jones thinks that he has the final right of decision and Sarasin thinks he has not. I suppose they will have to fight it out.

That spring she and Glover were having occasional lunches together, when they could discuss any training proposals that Payne might put forward.

In May Glover was advising Anna about "sticking to your price. It should be in a form that *makes clear that there are differences in principle at stake and that you are in fact standing up for your side.*" In June Glover advised her:

> Don't be under any illusions as to the motives of Payne and now Jones. They are concerned merely to establish unity to the public. When there was no official disunity, both of them were ready enough to plan pushing your Group into a pedagogic sub-group of the Society, leaving the Training open to the Kleinians.

Glover was still getting requests for training, but said he had "nothing to offer."

> I have just heard of a possibility that sufficient funds could be donated to ensure running a new clinic. But I am doing nothing until I see what is going to be the upshot of these negotiations. I realize now that if I had not been so busy with so many commitments I would not have been content with a breakaway but would have started a new clinic straightaway.

Anna had left it up to Payne and the British Society to come up with something that would suit her. Glover remarked:

> I hadn't realized that you had abandoned the policy of putting a plan before the Society and letting *them* decide. It seems to me (a) that if you go and speak in favor of your proposal and get your group to *vote* for it, you are in effect *making an application* to allow Freudian teaching in the Society and (b) unless it is made crystal clear what the plan is about, the fact that it is carried (as I've no doubt it will be) will represent only the plastering up of an official façade of unity.

Glover wanted to be sure Anna knew exactly what she was getting into.

> (a) is it agreed *beforehand** that *training analysts recommended by your group* will be accepted by the T.C. on your recommendation? Otherwise you walk into a *cul-de-sac* (b) is it agreed that *existing* trainees of your group are taken over?
>
> *"beforehand" indicates my distrust of their integrity!

Payne had the burden (as the new President of the British Society) of making arrangements with Anna for the proposed separate training track. It required at least as much diplomatic tact as when Payne dealt with Mrs. Klein during the Controversial Discussions. Payne wrote Anna on January 2, 1946, trying to clear away any possible misunderstandings:

> This is a private letter as it is better at this moment that we should deal with the training problem privately before making official statements.
>
> Adrian Stephen tells me that you read something into my official letter which is not the meaning intended by me and I want to make this clear to start with. The sentence was at the end of the letter, and I think the phrase was "rather than by promoting isolation and rivalry." I must point out to start with that the phrase cannot be taken from the whole sentence. I did not mean that the approach which you made to us was with the *intent* to promote isolation etc., on the contrary I have *said* to the Board that the intent was to make contact again. What I meant was that regarded from the outside the establishment of an alternative method of training did ... promote the idea of fundamental differences and therefore of separation and rivalry. The point in my mind being that the established curriculum is *fundamentally based on Freud's accepted teaching* and differences can only creep in (as they always must if people are free to think for themselves) at certain places.
>
> The second problem of the staff was obviously going to arouse endless dispute if dealt with under the first scheme and therefore it seemed wise to make new propositions. I think the next step is

for you, I & Adrian to meet and have a private talk to see if we can put forward something which is less difficult to put into practice. I feel that a way ought to be found and that you will gain and not lose by taking the goodwill of those whom you have had friendship with for granted.

Will you let me know whether you will meet us both. It is better that this meeting should not include others.

The application of a candidate (being analyzed by a member of Anna Freud's group) to the British Society moved Payne to write again to Anna: "I think we must now come to an agreement about the procedure and endeavor to find a plan which will recognize the training committee's responsibility and authority and at the same time give you sufficient freedom to use methods of teaching which you believe in." Anna's influenza had delayed the meeting between her, Payne, and Adrian Stephen. They evidently met at the end of April, which enabled Payne to come up with "a rough draft" of a proposed letter. Payne thought it was "essential to include some of the *details* as a general principle would alienate many of the uncertain people whose chief aim is to guard against domination by anyone." Anna made some changes in the draft that Payne was very pleased with. Anna was now willing to stand once again for the Training Committee.

While Glover was regularly in touch with Anna about her negotiations with Payne in behalf of the British Society, Payne was bearing the brunt of working out the exact terms that would satisfy Anna. As Payne wrote Anna on June 7, 1946:

The difficulty was first that the Board wanted it put in general principles and I agree that this is right as long as the present situation is understood. I could not make a great point of putting in your name without stimulating the kind of opposition which I am particularly anxious not to do. As a matter of fact I do not think that this will be misconstrued any more than the whole principle of double training will be misconstrued. This is that some people will think that you only will teach sound Freudian principles. I know that you will realise that this idea is hard for many of us to contemplate as it is not true, and of course I know that you personally and others with direct knowledge do not hold that view, but you must accept that the recognition of two methods will be liable to be interpreted in these terms.

The Training Committee had come to the decision that "recent theoretical developments should be taught in the third year *only*," which presumably would appease Anna's wanting her people to be uncontaminated by Kleinian ideas. "Freud's works only" would be the subject of the first two years.

Glover was kept informed by Anna as developments unfolded; he wrote on June 25th:

> My staircase thinking is becoming interminable!
> But—
> If there is a case for separate *theoretical* courses (as well as practical) for *child* analysts why not for *adult* analysts also? In other words, why is the early theoretical training of adults not Freudian pure and simple (or until the last year).
> If there is a case for separate courses why not an allocation of seats ½ and ½ on the Training *Committee*. This would govern appointments of training analysts, selection and allocation of candidates.
> If Jones enters into this agreement, it would be logical to take full part in Society proceedings. Council, Training Committee, and meetings.

Glover was clearly cautioning Anna about proceeding to the agreement with Payne, and was suggesting provisos that might well, at this late stage in the negotiations, have sunk the plan. (The three groups got equally represented on all Society bodies.)

> If this goes through, you sell yourself to Payne & Jones for the next ten years and for what? To satisfy their urgent need to present a united front to the public—i.e. to cover essential differences. . . . If they pass it, will you accept on the spot or reserve your decision.

By late June Payne had gotten the Society's agreement to the new arrangement. Glover wrote Anna on June 28th:

As it was a foregone conclusion that the proposals would be accepted, I think the appointment of an editorial committee can be regarded as a tactical victory. The next step is obviously to gain as much ground in the Committee as possible. Although I don't believe that a double-barrelled training will prevent the Klein group keeping training power (unless "allocation" etc. is settled favorably for your group). I have a certain grim satisfaction in knowing that my resignation has forced the Society to take some practical steps to cover up an *actual* split. I feel sure the ultimate aims of Dr. Payne's drive for "official unity" was to offset extra-mural realization that a split had occurred.

By late July Glover was telling Anna:

I think you are right to conserve your energies for there is lots to be done. About resigning it seems to me that it started a chain of events going which would otherwise have been stillborn. However we shall see.

In the fall Glover was reporting to Anna about how the Training Committee was being unfair to a candidate, and since Miss Sharpe "characteristically" did not "stand up" for her trainee he failed to qualify. "This sort of thing makes me feel glad I cut clear of the whole gallery." Glover had been approached by someone ready to found and maintain for some years either a small model nursery school or a school for "slightly difficult (i.e. not *too* abnormal children"—"in both cases where parents can be helped"). Glover met with Anna about the project, which was to be "a model experimental unit." (It is unclear, but possible, that this contact ultimately benefited Anna's Hampstead Clinic.)

Glover had been playing a central part in the Institute for the Study and Treatment of Delinquency, and its clinical affiliate, the Portman Clinic, ever since the 1930s. The ISTD had been first founded in 1931 by Dr. Grace Pailthorpe, a psychoanalyst who had been trained by Jones; earlier she had been a surgeon who served on the front lines during World War I, and later, after she left the ISTD, she became a remarkable surrealist artist. The idea behind the ISTD was that there had to be a better way of dealing with criminals than incarcerating them in prisons. By early in 1932 the new organization Pailthorpe had founded was coming under Glover's protective wing, and the history of the ISTD credits him with having put "the new society on a sound footing. . . ." Glover was considered to be the ISTD's "*de facto* founder."[20]

The ISTD had both humanitarian as well as research and scientific aims. A public appeal was advertised in the *Manchester Guardian*, and a couple of other papers printed it as well; it was signed by, among others, Alfred Adler, Havelock Ellis, Freud, Glover, Jones, C. G. Jung, Otto Rank, and H. G. Wells, but despite this publicity the statement brought it no more than £10. Crime and delinquency were to be the central objects of the organization's investigative and clinical work, and other illustrious names, such as the anthropologist Bronislaw Malinowski, were associated with the organization. A Clinic was started in 1933, and the therapists who worked there, an assortment of different analysts, did so without payment. In 1948 the clinical facility was taken over by the National Health Service, but continued as the Portman Clinic.

In 1950 the *British Journal of Delinquency* (later renamed the *British Journal of Criminology*) started, and its founding editors were Glover, Emmanuel Miller, and Hermann Mannheim. These three men were quite different from one another, yet somehow managed to function together. Miller was a lovely, amiable, and generous polymath; as a child psychiatrist he was interested in problems of guidance and how behavioral difficulties could lead to delinquency. (Miller's wife was a distinguished writer.) Miller's own family had originally come from Germany in the 1860s, and he spotted Mannheim (a student of Max Weber) as a German refugee. Mannheim was a Prussian, a former judge of appeal who was wounded by the loss of status involved in the despised Nazi "rabble" having come to power.

Glover was the Freudian, and he sometimes seemed narrowly intolerant of dissent, but he also made valuable and provocative contributions to empirical criminology. For example, he wrote a pamphlet on prostitution that acknowledged that prostitutes were earning money at their trade, but also inquired into their mind-set toward fathers and men in general. Glover was a stimulant for others to do research into the motivation of offenders, and workers started to come up with confirmation of some of Glover's suggestions.

One key to the success of Glover at the ISTD was its general secretary, Eve Saville, who worked there for thirty years. It was almost a family situation between her as an older sister to the three siblings—Glover, Miller, and Mannheim, all of whom came to defer to her. For example, she would not let any of them see the financial accounts. Eve Saville wrote that from the first she found it "delightfully easy to get on with the twinkly" Edward Glover.[21] She proposed:

> It might be thought that the three members of the Editorial Board—Scottish psychoanalyst, Jewish child psychiatrist, German judge/criminologist—were strange bed-fellows. In a sense they were, but it was this very diversity which made them such an effective and unusual triumvirate; it was astonishing how harmoniously they worked together and how easily differing points of view became reconciled, with an extra dimension added to the matter under discussion. . . . Although they worked as a team of equals, Dr. Glover was tacitly regarded as *primus inter pares*; it was always he who presided in any external negotiations and whom it was safe to consult in any emergency.[22]

Editorial board meetings were bound to be sources of controversy. It is striking from the point of view of intellectual history that when Eve Saville died in 1986, her obituary in the *Times* was more extensive than what Glover had received in 1972.

Unlike what had happened among the analysts, Glover succeeded in cooperatively getting on at the ISTD and the Portman Clinic. He was the capable administrator he had always been, chairing meetings, organizing minutes, raising funds, writing introductions for annual reports, and overseeing the programs of conferences. Probation officers, as well as magistrates, medical superintendants, and consultant psychiatrists, needed to be trained in an enlightened way. Oddly enough he was functioning in the context of a multidisciplinary enterprise, bringing psychiatry into contact with sociology, and expanding the ISTD sphere of interest. Social science was slow to get started in Britain, and for years was looked on as only the realm of Fabian socialist do-gooders like Sidney and Beatrice Webb. (Upper-class prejudices slowed down the acceptance of modern social science in Britain.) Glover's being a representative of Freudian psychoanalysis fitted in with the broader concerns of the organization as a whole. The ISTD was "very much a place of applied psychodynamic ideas, including the practice of group therapy, with many other intellectual standpoints and disciplines playing their part. In view of Glover's ruthless orthodoxy at other times this liberality of outlook is impressive."[23]

Unknown to historians of psychoanalysis, who are only apt to appreciate Glover as a contestant over Klein, he was not only an important and successful clinician but also a pioneer in the field of forensic psychiatry.[24] The idea from the 1930s that crime is a disease capable of being cured may seem now dated, as an aspect of a tendency to psychopathologize everything, but so would Cesare Lombroso's old conviction that the "criminal type" was "a species apart." Glover was part of a movement to bring more humanity into criminal law; the original ideal was to create treatment centers that would help prevent crime. He was co-founder of the British Society of Criminology. Glover did manage to help toward reducing the incidence of flogging and capital punishment, and also he worked toward improving prison conditions. In combatting cruelty to children his early socialist idealism had found an outlet. He hoped that psychopaths were malleable, and thought parents were the real problem. He knew how hard rehabilitation could be, and tried above all to promote more study and research.

> He has written about alcoholism, drug addictions, the psychopathology of flogging, the diagnosis and treatment of delinquents, about the social, legal, and clinical aspects of sexual perversions, recidivism, the M'Naghten rules, the prevention of violence, the treatment and classification of psychopaths.[25]

Glover's role was often behind the scenes, but he testified in the late 1950s before the Wolfendon commission when homosexuality was first being decriminalized. Despite the loss in 1948 of its clinical *raison d'etre* and its main fund-raising potential, the ISTD managed to survive and in fact flourish. The ISTD has now become the Centre for Crime and Justice Studies at King's College in London, which has a bust of Glover done in his last year by a sculptor (Peter Lambda) who was the son of Hungarian analysts and who also did a remarkable bust of Freud in his own last months of life.

But we must return to the earlier problem of Glover's struggle to maintain his standing within the International Psychoanalytic Association following his resignation from the British Society. After the Spring 1947 Amsterdam Congress, Glover sent some impressions to Anna Freud, since they hadn't "really" had the "leisure" to talk together there.

> (1) What unmitigated rubbish the Kleinian acolytes do talk. *Scott*—pretentious and harebrained: *Winnicott* as moonshiny as ever: *Stephen*: silly: trying to be clear and just exposing his muddleness. *Bowlby* bumptuous and hollow. Yet I suppose the others couldn't be expected to realize this through the barrier of language.
> (2) The Dutch seemed to me to be sound enough.
> (3) The political rapprochement of your group with the Society is bound to obscure the issue. Better out than in.
> (4) I'm glad I gave that paper: somebody must keep the issue alive: otherwise it will go by default.

Glover's paper on "Basic Mental Concepts" appeared not only in the *Psychoanalytic Quarterly* but also in a small booklet published by Imago Publishing Company in London.[26] Although Anna Freud had predicted his presentation would not be "controversial," in its Imago form he took some swipes at Kleinianism. Glover's approach was abstract and conceptual, but he was trying to establish the impossibility of squaring Klein's postulation of early stages within Freud's own metapsychology. But Glover had vetted an uncorrected proof of the Congress paper with Anna, as well as her ally Ernst Kris; Glover thought that Kris was working along similar lines with Heinz Hartmann. "Hartmann's concept of the conflict-free sphere seemed to be the classical wing's effort to describe development outside the realm of early phantasy."[27]

Glover's standing with American psychoanalysis had only advanced thanks to the way he had conducted himself over the struggles with Kleinianism in Britain. For when in 1947 he was "unofficially approached to take over the Directorship of the New York Training Institute at a guaranteed salary from it and from private practice of 7,500–9,000 [pounds]," he turned to Anna for advice. He wanted her to say whether he would be of more use to "Freudian analysis" in London or the U.S., and if she would feel it as a loss to psychoanalysis in Britain were he to leave. "To make the answer easier I should add," he wrote, "that my *inclination* is to stay here."

Glover continued to consult with Anna (and Lawrence Kubie) about revisions to the bylaws of the IPA. At the same time Glover wanted to know from her what she thought of some of the younger members of her group, so he would have some idea of the "order of priority" she held them since he had extra cases to dispose of. Before the Zurich IPA Congress in the summer of 1949 Glover asked Anna for help in certifying his Swiss credentials. The American Psychoanalytic Association had instructed its delegates to support the recognition of Glover's membership in the Swiss Society. As we have noted, once Jones was no longer president Glover's problem evaporated, and he was promptly appointed chairman of the Committee of Research of the IPA; members included Edward Bibring, Anna Freud, Maxwell Gitelson, Heinz Hartmann, Jeanne Lampl-de Groot, Philipp Sarasin, Gregory Zilboorg, among others. (Unfortunately this committee proved no more successful than earlier such efforts.)

When an irreverent (but in retrospect path-breaking) biography of Freud by an American freelance journalist, Helen Walker Puner,[28] came out, Glover wrote a blistering attack on it for *The Listener*. But first he lent Anna Freud a copy of the book, and in response to his request for help she wrote by hand a two-page list of her objections. The commercial success of the Puner book, which had not been based on any archival research, was to be one of the last straws in breaking the Freud family's commitment to obeying Freud's injunction against authorizing an official biography of him. Although Jones's three-volume study of Freud starts off with a number of objections to Puner's conjectures, it is not generally recognized what an accomplishment for the time Puner had made. Glover's review was held up because of the fear of the law of libel (in Britain the truth could be a libel at law). Even though Glover substituted an "expurgated version," it continued to be held up until it was too late. (Glover said it was his "first and only rejection" of a review. Glover considered himself an "addicted" book reviewer.)

Naturally there were clinical matters (including Diana Churchill) that Glover wrote Anna about, and training issues also came up, given Glover's reputation and international standing. But Glover also did what he could on a more personal level, for example, trying to find work for her oldest brother Martin. When Glover gave broadcasts, he notified Anna in advance. He was particularly active in the year of Freud's centenary (1956), and even Jones wrote Anna in admiration of one of Glover's efforts. Glover and Anna stayed in contact until his death, although much of it was concerned with the passing away of mutual acquaintances of theirs.

The whole question of the Controversial Discussions came up once again in 1966, when Sylvia Payne wrote Anna (in a letter marked "private and confidential"). (Anna did not destroy the letter, nor those by some others written in confidence to her.) Payne had heard that the Board and Council of the British Society had given permission for the full minutes of the Controversial Discussions to be published in the Scientific Bulletin of the British Society. Evidently Anna had agreed to collaborate if Payne would write an introduction. Payne said she had studied "the documents recording these meetings & Dr. Glover's resignation most seriously," and that she knew "a great deal more about the causes of his resignation" than got revealed in print. But she could not see that "the Society would benefit in any respect by this publication. On the contrary it would only draw members' attention to unsolved problems in the past rather than those of the present day."

Payne clearly considered Glover the central person in connection with the project of publishing the proceedings of the Controversial Discussions. In my interviewing, Payne seemed to me harder on

Glover than he on her, but it seems unlikely whether by that time Anna Freud was still close enough to Glover for her to have consulted with him. Payne reminisced to Anna that "after the first meeting of the Society at which Melanie Klein expounded her ideas, Dr. Glover drove me home, and I asked him what he thought. To my surprise he said that some of her contributions were the most important since Freud, but we were not ready for them." It is unlikely that Payne, even though 85½ years old, did not realize how Anna might react to hearing anything favorable written about Klein. But Payne went on to recount about Glover:

> Subsequently Melitta Schmideberg went to him for analysis and his attitude changed completely. She was an impossible person to analyze. Ella Sharpe had her for a year and said she could do nothing with her. I am telling you these facts because I am sure that they played some part in preventing Glover take [sic] over leadership in a stable fashion.

Payne also brought up the issue of the Presidency of the Society:

> When Jones resigned the committee formed to consider the future consisted of the men returned from war work, Adrian Stephen, Rickman, Gillespie, Bowlby, Glover & I. It was voted that the President should serve for three years instead of for ever, like Jones. Glover could not deal with this, and it precipitated his resignation.

Payne wondered who might have suggested publication: "I think you will agree that differences of interpretation will not be solved by resurrecting an incident like Glover's resignation." (Even at that advanced age Payne could type such a letter, though she apologized to Anna about it since to people of that generation a handwritten note was more usual among old acquaintances.)

Ten days later Payne again wrote Anna, this time by hand. She had now "seen copies of the controversial 1943 discussions, and the fact that [they] concern the development of controversial theory and avoid personal conflicts makes me change my opinion about their publication." The only copies she had had before were "of the meetings concerned with Glover's resignation. . . ." Payne did not think she was the correct person to write an introduction, given that her age made it difficult for her to judge "the developments which have taken place in the theories connected with pregenital levels." (Pregenitality meant those phases before the development of the classic Oedipus complex.) Payne felt she should add: "I have no idea what present-day therapeutic results are," but she hoped that Anna would contribute to the project. It would not be until almost ten years after Anna's death in 1982 that the proceedings of the Controversial Discussions finally appeared as a book. Ever since then they have become a standard text connected with what has made British psychoanalysis so distinctive.

5

Freud in Exile and Technique

Glover had once described himself to me as "one of Freud's grandsons" in the profession, so it was natural for me to inquire: *What was your personal contact with Freud like?* Glover had first seen Freud in Berlin in 1922 at an International Psychoanalytic Congress, which turned out, because of Freud's illness, to be the last one he ever attended. Glover had asked Abraham to introduce him to Freud. Glover thought that in those days there had been a "Sunday-school atmosphere" within analysis. He reminded me of the traditional continental "worship" of professorships; being a professor "*was*" rather something in Europe, but not in Britain where it was typical to be more "cynical" about professors. While the word "professor" when applied to Freud had a "worshipful tone," Glover had already acquired in Glasgow a "skeptical habit" of arguing with professors.

Yet Glover freely admitted that "for a while" he had swallowed the reverential continental spirit. He read his first psychoanalytic articles in German in the *Zeitschrift*—there would be one by Freud, another by Ferenczi, and a "metaphysical" piece by Alexander. (Glover's distaste for Alexander became unremitting. Alexander in the late 1930s had expressed his own reservations about the impact of training analyses, rather like Glover's. But Alexander had, as we shall see, opposed Glover's being recognized as a full member of the Swiss Society, on the grounds that freedom to discuss differences was an essential component of a psychoanalytic society; the inference was that Glover should not have resigned from the British Society. Eissler's interview with Alexander was to have remained sealed until 2056, but can now be studied.) Glover thought that at first he did not discriminate enough between the papers that he read.

What was Freud preoccupied with during the period 1938–1939 that he lived in London? Glover's chief impression was that Freud had "retired." He saw Freud sitting in his back garden at Maresfield Gardens in Hampstead, "wearing a Harris tweed suit and a soft hat, with the *Times* folded in his hands." Freud seemed a "visitor with no local connections," and "not very sure what was going to happen." Of course Freud still worked and had analytic patients. (It seems to me that commentators too often underestimate Freud's medical reasons for having chosen to remain in Vienna so long, well after the Nazi threat to Austria was apparent; under the care of new doctors, who were intimidated by his fame, he went downhill pretty fast in London.)

Glover was present at two formal meetings with Freud, mostly connected with the *International Journal of Psycho-Analysis*. Freud obviously had very painful troubles with his jaw. Once when Glover saw him Freud had just undergone another corrective operation on his jaw. Freud said to Glover: "I can't write," and was unsure how much more he was going to be able to do. Glover thought Freud did not succeed in doing much more. "Freud did not play any part in local psychoanalytic activities." Freud's mind seemed still "active," but he could not "rise to fresh activity." (Freud worked on manuscripts in London, saw *Moses and Monotheism* published, and still kept up his letter writing.) Freud had physically shrunk a lot by his London period. Glover thought he had been, when younger, "a well-shaped man." To Glover Freud remained "a very great man with a very good head."

What were those meetings like with Freud in connection with the International Journal? Glover said he had not noticed much, except Freud's habit of listening, letting everyone express his opinion, and then at the end "butting in." Glover remarked that what Freud had to say was accepted by everyone as final.

Glover emphasized that really he had only been in social contact with Freud. He had not felt inclined to invade Freud's privacy, or to press him on psychoanalytic issues. The problem of talking with Freud was aggravated, Glover felt, by the fact that in Vienna people never pressed him much. A theoretician like Otto Fenichel, for example, might publicly say: "'Professor said this,' and then 'Professor said that,' which was contradictory." Glover would think to himself: But why not ask Freud how he reconciles the two positions? (In 1935 Fenichel and Glover had engaged in a sharp public debate. Fenichel was a Marxist who objected to the simplicity of Glover's assumption that groups display the same neuroses as individuals. Fenichel thought the crucial issue was under what social conditions unconscious aggressions get released. Fenichel endorsed Glover's 1933 recommendation that diplomats undergo analyses so sadism would be better controlled, but doubted that war could be avoided. Glover retorted that Fenichel was attempting "to pull socialism's chestnuts from the fire," and that Fenichel's politics were likely to end up distorting psychoanalytic principles.[1])

Was seeing Freud like visiting a royal monarch? "It might well be." *Was the circle around Freud like a court?* "Yes," there was "a semi-religious atmosphere" around Freud. (Professor Kazanjian from Harvard, who worked on a new dental plate for Freud in 1931, afterwards wrote in a memoir that there had been a "cult" around him.) Very few people would "stand up" to Freud; Glover claimed that Freud did not mind criticism, but that it was the loyal students who had created the situation of awe. (It seemed remarkable to me that Glover did not appear to realize to what extent Jones in Britain had tried to model himself on Freud's authoritative kind of leadership.)

Abraham's widow was still alive, and she, for example, had that "worshipful attitude" toward "Professor" Freud. Glover thought that the atmosphere of a "movement" or a "cause" had not been good for psychoanalysis, and he preferred for it to be a science. (But the way he attacked Puner, for example, was emotionally colored by her willingness to be challenging about Freud. Once Glover became convinced that Klein represented a "deviation," her goose was cooked as far as he was concerned. He was similarly tough on others—Jung, Horney, Rado, Hartmann, Alexander, and so on.) I raised the issue of someone like the Viennese analyst Paul Federn's religiosity toward Freud, with some concrete examples of his reverence to illustrate my points. Glover claimed that Freud had not cultivated that sort of piety, but that his disciples had simply reacted to him that way. (I think now that Freud must have been far more complicit in what had happened than Glover seemed to imply.) Glover suggested that Freud had to have had his "suspicions" about his apostles, since he very rarely quoted them. (Glover must also have been thinking of his own experience with supporters in the British Society.)

I tried to probe again about the adulation surrounding Freud. Glover maintained that Freud "could not have been fooled." Then Glover corrected himself; Freud had been "taken in" at least in the cases of Rank, Jung, and Adler. *Why had Freud wanted Jung so badly as a follower?* Freud had a desire for someone outside the Viennese Jewish crowd, and, Glover exclaimed, Freud was mistaken! *Was Freud so wrong if his quest for Jung represented an implicit denigration of the Viennese group around him?* Glover agreed with my point.

Freud was "human," Glover said, "that was the great thing about him." He claimed that when he heard Freud's disciples saying "the Professor says such and such," Glover was moved to ask, "Which Professor do you mean?" Abraham, who Glover thought was "self-analyzed" like Freud himself (few of the earliest analysts had themselves been analyzed), was about as good as anyone at "standing up to Freud." (But Helene Deutsch, who had also like Glover been analyzed by Abraham—after her being with Freud—and retained a high opinion of Abraham, told me she was "traumatized" at discovering from reading the Freud–Abraham correspondence how childish Abraham's attitude toward Freud had been. There was so little give-and-take between the two men.) Glover readily admitted the presence of the continental "religious" flavor around Freud; he thought that it does not cut against psychoanalysis but only against "religiosity." (For all Glover's own polemics he did not seem to admit that he too shared in that religion-like passion; he was not alone in that as an early analyst.) The British Society, otherwise "handicapped," had a geographic advantage in being at a distance, and Glover mentioned that he thought that the Americans may have had even more objectivity than the British.

Even though Glover had mainly seen Freud as a distant observer, I asked a few questions about Freud's relationship with his wife. *Was Freud impatient with "Frau Professor"?* Professor and she were "very different personalities." He was rather Victorian (like Glover himself); on the basis of their love letters, any "decent" girl nowadays would consider him "square." Frau Professor "ruled the roost" at home. (Melitta Schmideberg used to visit with her husband on Sundays; Freud's wife "gave me little pieces of motherly advice. She told me how important it was to water flowers every day at the same time. . . . Suddenly I was struck by this Victorian stress on regularity."[2]) Freud's wife was indulgent to his work, but then the whole family revolved around that. "Freud did not know he was alive—any decent family would have given him a lot of trouble." (No matter how ironic or cleverly phrased Glover's formulations about Freud's family life, I think Glover was also forgetting his own earlier point about the special social status of professional men on the continent.)

In London Glover had not wanted to interrupt Freud too much by asking to see him, and Freud was so sick that Glover said he did not want to push him intellectually. A handwritten letter of Glover's to Freud, dated November 6, 1938, has survived:

Dear Professor Freud,

Herewith the first draft of my Congress paper. It was later shortened and really starts on p. 4.

The part on "ego-nucleation," "synthesis," "splitting" and "dissociation" is contained on pages 12 to 21 (particularly 18–21).

On reading it over I see that it is very scrappy and gives no idea of the clinical observations on which it was based. But I hope to write a clinical paper on the subject later. I enclose also an earlier paper on classification written many years ago. It was at this time that I was first impressed by the concept of ego-nucleation and synthesis. It is very schematic and exaggerates for purposes of making my points clear.

Your sincerely,
Edward Glover

P.S. I should be glad if you would accept the copy of the classification article. Perhaps you would give the paper to Anna to return to me when you are finished—as it is my only corrected copy.

EG

This contemporary evidence would seem to imply that Glover dealt with Freud as fully in possession of his faculties.

In those days the "tradition" within the field was that Freud was "perfect." Only after Freud's death did Glover discover about "Freud's neurosis," his fears of death, and so on. (Glover had learned about this side of Freud from his letters as well as Jones's biography.) Glover thought that Freud's own personal difficulties bore on the problem of training analytic candidates, and whether they needed to be "normal." (I would have thought that the question was not so much "whether" they need to be normal, but rather "how much," and what the concept of "normality" in psychological life can amount to.) Glover agreed with me about the telling significance of the fact that Freud had not been analyzed; it had to entail a lack of self-knowledge. Like others who have tried to understand Freud's intimate relationship with his friend Wilhelm Fliess, Glover thought that Freud had needed this early isolation, which is why he dramatized it; Freud required a blank uncomprehending screen in Fliess, in order to proceed with his own "self-analysis." (I now think that any such picture of Freud's friendship with Fliess is much too closely allied with a parallel to the model of the analytical situation. Freud's involvement with Fliess, a man of many wild ideas, was so strange as to require a variety of interpretative explanations.)

In talking about Freud's personality we seemed naturally to slide into discussing Anna as well. Although he did not make the point explicitly, Glover implied that she had identified with her father's attitude toward living in Britain. She is still "careful," Glover pointed out, "to this very day," in how she conducts herself. She was granted "asylum," and hence felt that she should not interfere with local affairs. So since she did not like the way the British Society was going, she built up "her own show" in Hampstead.

Glover regretted that Anna had not done more in Britain; he felt that she could have led "a standard Freudian" movement. But such an attempt would have taken much time and effort, more than Glover himself was prepared to put in. That was why she had founded her own clinic. (By the end of her life she was bitter that she failed to succeed in getting IPA accreditation for her students in child analysis independently of the British Society.) She succeeded in attracting some good people there, Glover thought, without impinging on the functioning of the British Society. When Glover resigned in 1944, Anna still had an opportunity to do something about the Society; after a while, though, she had "lost her chance."

What about Freud's relation to Anna? In a "funny way" Freud was a "patriarch." Frau Professor catered to him. Freud was "a childish lover," and she probably equally so; "therefore it was a successful marriage." Freud was "always being attended to." Anna is very like him—for example, in her freedom and spontaneity in public exposition. He pointed out, as I had already observed myself, that she could be unusually lucid and connected in speaking at meetings. It reminded Glover of how Freud delivered his lectures at Clark University in 1909. (Freud would walk with Ferenczi beforehand, deciding what he should best talk about. Freud never liked using prepared notes, and, according to Theodor Reik, Freud advised other analysts against the practice of reading their papers in public; Freud thought it undermined the capacity of the audience to identify with the speaker. But I cannot think of a single psychoanalytic meeting I ever attended, aside from "Miss Freud's" presentations at her own clinic, where the analysts present did not ignore Freud's advice.)

Glover did not think, whatever the resemblances between Freud and Anna, that she had anything like his "penetration." It was "clear" she had "sacrificed her life for him." Glover considered her a "nice" woman, though a bit "too hieratic," too much "the high priestess." She repeated her father's kind of authority over his following, although she had "nothing like his brain." Glover remembered that she dressed like "a peasant"; of course, he said, her grandfather was "almost a peasant." (Anna did dress almost outrageously unstylishly.[3] The reader will remember Glover's description of his own "peasant" background.)

When Glover used to take Anna out to lunch he said he liked to watch a nondrinker try to drink; after a fraction of a glass of sherry, he remarked, Anna could be "flushed for hours" afterwards. (He was exaggerating here, but I thought I knew what he meant.)

What about Freud's having analyzed Anna? There is such a thing as a "friendly, intra-familial analysis." It is very different from "an aggressive matter of setting children right." Abraham had done "a lot" for his daughter Hilda. But it is "quite hopeless" to analyze your own children, and Glover would not recommend it to others. After I talked with Glover so much about Anna, it was a matter of course for me to inquire: *What about Freud's sons? What were they like?* Martin had not been "a great success" in working for the psychoanalytic press in Vienna. In Britain he had a "commercial job in the Midlands" at one point; although Glover tried to help him, it was hard to get Martin a job because of his age. In the 1960s Martin had a "tobacco business" (a shop?) near the British Museum. "Ernst, though, did pretty well here" as an architect. Freud's relations to his sons looked to Glover like a set of pretty "classical neurotic symptoms."

I did not spend much time with Glover talking about Freud's family, since that was not an area he could be an expert on, but Freud's surrogate family in the movement he founded inevitably came into focus. And so issues connected with psychoanalytic training tended to be central in all my interviewing, since Glover had been in such a senior position during the formative years of British analysis. Originally the training "system" had been a straightforwardly informal one; after someone had been in analysis for some time, and the issue of becoming an analyst came up, Glover would send the potential candidate around to see Jones and Flügel. Evidently that was all there was to it; nothing further (outside of presenting a paper) was necessary to becoming an analyst. In his own experience his brother James had been already known to Jones before his being analyzed, and it was taken for granted that when he himself came back from Abraham in Berlin that he would become an associate member of the Society.

Then, thanks to Eitingon and the International Training Commission, a "fairly rigid" distinction arose between training analysts and regular ones. Later this system was made more "fluid"; it was finally left to each individual branch of the IPA to set up its own conditions for training. At least in Britain it was accepted that anyone could train candidates, provided that the candidate was considered qualified. Once the concept of a separate group of "training analysts" (as in North America) gets introduced, there has to follow a fairly extensive system of bureaucracy. In principle Glover thought that the Americans had the most "rigid" training arrangements, and the figure of "twelve years" was somehow what he had in mind. But he was aware that there was some doubt whether, whatever the theory, American practices could be that "stringent."

Glover was, I think, being realistic when he pointed out that once a training committee exists, then it becomes "a decisive matter to which analyst you send someone." The problem is that the candidate takes over "all the analyst's views," or eventually "challenges" his ideas, or somehow "compromises" between these alternatives. It is in any case "natural" to adopt some of one's analyst's opinions. (It was understood between us that Glover was maintaining that this process also goes on at an unconscious level.) In addition to the role of transferences, and how candidates can transpose problems from their past onto the analyst, Glover thought that old-fashioned "egoism" also plays a part; for it is hard not to be "compelled to think that those five or six years were worthwhile." (It had not yet at the time I saw Glover come home to me how expensive, in terms of lost earning hours, psychoanalytic training can be, for example, to a qualified psychiatrist.) Glover thought that "control" analysts, who supervise a candidate's early cases, could help to check some of these difficulties. (But we know now that supervised analyses have problems of their own.[4])

Out of his long experience Glover was concerned about the "manipulation" of training analyses. He thought it was "an unsettled question" whether transferences, mobilized in the treatment setting, are ever really liquidated. In the case of patients who come only for therapy this can be "O.K., provided they are able to carry on their lives despite the presence of irrational feelings toward their former analysts." (Other senior analysts I met wondered whether, when such emotions lasted a long time, they should not be considered as more or less realistic.) Glover thought it was an open question whether analysts themselves can manage with undissolved transferences without suffering from the consequences of a subtle form of indoctrination.

The "central defect," he thought, of the psychoanalytic training system is its "ideals." When he got started in the profession there was the concept of "the fully analyzed analyst. It is a myth!" There was too much "perfectionism" surrounding the training of analysts, and uncertainty combined with inferiority bred such "make-believe." (He was making these general points independently of the trouble over Klein, but they harked back to his critique of Strachey's draft Training Committee report.) There can be no final answer to the problem of training, or therapy. "A fallible analyst cannot adopt an infallible technique for a fallible patient." (Many of the most eminent British analysts I met considered their North American colleagues naïve about the possibility of evolving a neutral or scientific technique. I wonder now how relevant this still is in an era when psychopharmacology has been so much more successful, encouraging new forms of naiveté. Old World culture seemed more secure then about acknowledging the inevitably artistic component in a psychotherapist's work.)

"All the analyst can do is his best." (Glover's realism here seemed to me then, and now, wholly admirable, but I wonder how it squared with some of the published declarations of his own against Jung, who was early on insistent about the more subjective sides of an analyst's approach. Glover oddly enough skipped discussing Jung's own critique of authoritarianism in psychoanalytic treatment, or Jung's special contribution to the uses of short-term treatment.[5]) In keeping with Glover's skepticism about how objective many psychoanalytic principles really were, he thought that a committee of selected analysts could in a short time outline important projects of research inquiry, but the big "if" in such a proposal "would be the choice of the people for the committee." (If Glover thought that that was the case, what does it mean for our understanding of what kind of science psychoanalysis can be understood to be? I found that whatever the published versions of the theory of psychoanalytic technique might sound like, the first question an analyst in private would want to know about someone in treatment was who was the analyst. Disagreements in any field are, of course, perfectly legitimate, and can sometimes reflect a high degree of sophistication; historiography is not, for example, in any way impoverished by the multiple interpretations of the coming of the French Revolution.)

The instance of J. C. Flügel illustrated Glover's thesis about the vagaries of psychoanalytic reputations. Flügel had come from a comfortably well-off German family; he had become an assistant to Sir Cyril Burt at University College in London. (In the 1970s it was discovered that Burt, who had once been listed as a full member of the British Society, was guilty of having fabricated some of the experimental evidence for which he had won fame.) Glover was not sure Flügel had been analyzed by anyone, but thought if he were then the likelihood was that Jones had done it. (Sylvia Payne confirmed independently that Jones had indeed analyzed Flügel.) Glover had always recommended in lectures Flügel's book *One Hundred Years of Psychology*. Flügel was both "highly intelligent" as well as "amiable"; Glover remembered especially his early paper on Henry VIII's married life. But Flügel seemed to Glover a "disappointed man" in that he did not get the academic accolade of a regular professorship. (Yet the title "professor" appeared before his name on the membership roster of the Society.)

Flügel had "a foot in both camps," the Freudian and the Kleinian, though Glover thought this had "hurt" Flügel's work. By around 1926, when Klein had settled in London, Flügel had "faded out" of the analytic picture. For years he was "regarded as no good," until the Klein group arose and then Flügel was needed as "a compromise trainer." (Dr. Willi Hoffer said to me that he himself was in the 1960s the compromise author of obituaries.) According to Glover, Flügel was "calm, reflective, and a metaphysically minded man." Although Flügel had attempted to "straddle" the barrier between academic psychology and analysis, Glover thought it just as well to be a "100 percent analyst." Glover had brought Flügel's name up in the context of the politics of training analyses; while he was out of fashion "he had not gotten any cases," until the time came when the Middle Group felt it needed him for training purposes. Of course, in those days there were not that many candidates, approximately a dozen or so at a time, as Glover recalled it.

Glover raised the issue of whether personal difficulties should exclude a person from training, or whether people should be accepted assuming that a training analysis will help to overcome problems that might exist. Glover thought there were "advantages" to an analyst in being neurotic, or at least in being "a neurotic of a certain type." (Presumably Glover had in mind how personal suffering can be an asset in understanding another's troubles; his position was sufficiently unusual that I wish I had asked Glover to explore more of what he meant here, with specific illustrations of difficulties in therapists that might suit certain categories of patients. In his Columbia Oral History Interview Glover had said that in the handling of schizophrenia, a schizophrenic analyst could be useful.) Glover did not think one should be too "puristic" about accepting candidates. He was specifically inclined to suspect the so-called normal candidate, on the grounds that such a person is apt to be "too well defended," and therefore incapable of being needy enough to make a breakthrough into deep insight. As far as training goes Glover did not think analysis was any better off than at the end of World War I.

Glover was still very interested in the problem of "inexact interpretations," the subject of one of his famous early articles; his concern with the possibilities of suggestion had not pleased Melanie Klein, since the implication was that good therapeutic results, including her own, might be the result of factors other than genuinely rational insight. Glover asked again how it was after all that people got well in the old days of analysis, when we supposedly know so much more today. (I think now it is more an open question just how successful the early analysts—or anybody else—were therapeutically.) In thinking through various technical issues, Glover noted that Freud himself on occasion had advised departures like "active therapy," in contrast to the more standard passive-sounding approach that he usually recommended; and Freud had taken a long time in making up his mind about the innovations first proposed by Ferenczi and Rank. Ferenczi had then "retreated" from his new position for awhile, and Rank "went off on his own" and left analysis; but then Ferenczi supposedly had ended up with "a love therapy," which also would divide him from traditional analysis. Freud, however, thought that in most cases the "classical" technique was good enough, and to Glover that seemed most sensible.

Glover then raised what he called "the great issue of elasticity." He felt that there was nothing wrong in principle with the traditional analytic situation, but only in the "rigidity" of its application. (Glover's use of the concept of elasticity seems to me now almost a theological one. How can one make such a secure distinction between a "principle" and its "application"? And does one have a right, based on a philosophy of so-called elasticity, to criticize dogmatically advocates of different techniques altogether, such as Jung or even Alexander?) Implicitly Glover could acknowledge the presence of difficulties in the classic psychoanalytic approach. Analysis is, for example, "a one-sided situation"; "the patient opens up while the analyst stays apart." Interpretations by the analyst are perhaps rightly taken as "a criticism," since they do imply that the patient "does not know what he or she is talking about." With hysterics in particular Glover said that one has to be careful of using "illustrative material" given the "power of their fantasies."

According to Glover the whole first generation of analysts, including Freud himself, was "rigid in principle but elastic in practice." (This bit of reasoning seemed to me in itself admirable, yet I do not see how Glover did not realize how it could be used to justify almost anything in technique, including hypocrisy.) Psychoanalytic "formalists," from which Glover sought to distance himself, only reveal their "inferiority complex." Excessive formalism was only one problem, and the analytic therapist can err in the other direction, in "making it too easy for the patient." (Freud had argued that without the incentive provided by suffering the patient would have no need to seek further insight.)

But Glover still felt that "most of the troubles" that he saw as a senior consultant were due to "rigidities in technique." (He is not the only analyst who had done a lot of consulting to have made the same point privately, yet failed, I think, to make it an adequate part of their public statements.) Glover had had a huge London consulting practice, which no doubt had given him the independence to leave the British

Society. (If Glover had not had such a secure position as a practitioner, his leaving the Society could have been enough to ruin him professionally. It is easy to underestimate an analyst's need to maintain his clinical practice in enforcing professional conformity. This can be largely an unconscious sort of pressure, but Jung had complained that after his break with Freud, analysts loyal to Freud had almost wrecked his clinical practice.)

As an expert in therapeutic technique Glover said he was distressed by how analysts could prefer to dodge their patients' hostilities, and that negative transferences could easily pile up. Furthermore, failures in analysis, or so-called negative therapeutic reactions, could prove "refractory." (The term "negative therapeutic reaction" was devised to help account for patients who got worse in analytic treatment, supposedly out of the pressure of their guilt feelings blocking the prospect of analytic progress; I wonder now whether the whole concept is not a piece of double-think, designed to let the therapist off too lightly. As one senior analyst once told me, when confronted with a so-called negative therapeutic reaction he always asks, "Whose"?) Glover felt that if you are going to fail therapeutically "it is better to tell the patient." Analysts are "too defensive" about this part of their work. (I am reminded of a similarly self-critical comment that Sylvia Payne made in connection with a candidate for psychoanalytic training who was dismissed for immoral conduct: "Patients are completely at one's mercy, one's victims." The psychoanalysts I met had high standards for themselves. It would be less than honest for me not to add that Payne commented in passing that Glover had been better in theory than practice, and had been "not a bit good with patients." She had been even harsher about Riviere, but I now regret not having asked her and others more about Glover's clinical skills. His technical approach sounds promising to me. Maybe it would be best to put the patient first, not technique. Yet a teacher strives to do more than offer an example, and Freud's creation of a technique is what made it possible to found a school. Glover surely succeeded with such highly intelligent students like Brierley and Kubie; his busy practice helps confirm that others certainly thought that "basically" Glover "was a good clinician."[6] Payne herself wrote almost nothing, in contrast to

Glover's remarkable output; I wonder how she would have evaluated Freud's own clinical results. If Glover's therapeutic range was less than it might ideally have been, he did consistently maintain that therapeutic success was unable to establish the validity of a theory.)

Glover mentioned that analysts were then writing about new kinds of "characterological cases" in their practice, in contrast to the rather florid kind of symptomatology described in Freud's earliest papers. Glover said that he, like others, no longer found glaring cases of hysteria anymore. (I should have pressed him about how diagnoses have changed over the years, and raised the possibility that alterations in clinical practice may partly reflect different terminological uses.) Glover was repeatedly insistent that whatever the presenting clinical problem might be, interpretations by the analyst may have a suggestive impact. The big problem of technique, he felt, was not to find "a stock formula" but to work out a "variation" on a standardized interpretation. He regretted the tendency to adopt stereotypes in therapy. Whatever the defects in analytic practice, he reminded me that traditional psychiatrists ignore transferences; even if analysts do not succeed in handling transferences perfectly, at least they are aware of the general concept and its implications.

It seemed to me striking that Freud himself had written so little on technique, and in particular I asked Glover about Freud's never having written on the analyst's countertransferences. Glover agreed, and thought that perhaps he did not write much on technique in order not to "lay down the law" too much. The "accent" on countertransference came into the field after Freud's death. Now analysts have gone "to the other extreme," and they are "always" writing about countertransference. Perhaps Freud had had the attitude: "Well, I'm all right, Jack!" The troubles were supposedly the patient's, not his. Freud pointed out the logic of the existence of countertransference, but he never developed the concept. He used to get "impatient," though, as an analyst; Glover said he would always remember a story of Alix Strachey's about how Freud would "bang his hand" on the top of the couch, implying that she should "produce!" (She seems to have gone to Glover for a time. Smiley Blanton confirmed how Freud could express his impatience that way.)

Even though so many of the early analysts were patients of Freud's, Glover pointed out that there were two kinds of pupils of Freud's, direct ones with personal ties to him, and those who were not personally involved with him but who, out of intellectual commitment, wanted to carry on his work. For all of them, though, Glover thought that in the early days there had been "a virtuous ritualism." It was considered "high treason" to commit certain technical offenses—for example, failing to analyze negative transferences. On the other hand, Glover felt that without interpreting a patient's anger there was a danger of mere "transference cures," built only on positive feelings toward the analyst. (These are supposedly only temporary recoveries.) Glover himself thought he was "too priggish" in his early technical articles. (It is hard not to think of his Presbyterian background; he said that as a youth he was "a little prig and have remained so. . . ."[7])

What do you think about using a couch or not? Once upon a time the couch was an "acid test" of whether it was really a proper analysis. If you did not use a couch then you were "not an analyst." (I have wondered whether or for how long Jung had used a couch; he wrote persuasively about the authoritarian implications of a couch, but in his consulting room at Küsnacht there was scarcely any room for a couch. If Freud had not objected to Jung's reliance on face-to-face contact, it might mean that the couch only became a standard feature of analysis after the creation of the Berlin Institute.) Glover held that certain hysterical women, for example, or patients having paranoid tendencies, may be scared of lying down. Glover thought that the correct attitude should be "all right, in the meantime, sit up." Glover still felt that the couch is "the most easy way" of producing a good situation. (That logically still leaves open the question of where the analyst's chair might best be positioned; Dr. Martin Grotjahn in Los Angeles in the 1960s, for example, used to place his chair so that patients on the couch could easily turn to their side and see him; I have seen the same thing in Japan recently.) Erik Erikson had interestingly raised the issue of whether the traditional analyst's anonymity does not amount to a form of sensory deprivation, with consequences of disorientation, and indoctrination, which might be predictable.[8] Orthodoxy is one way of handling doubts and fears. An analyst sympathetic to Otto Rank has wisely pointed out, "not *all* the reactions of the patient to the analyst are projections that originate in the patient's mind; some are induced by the contrived, unnatural way in which the situation is set up."[9]

As long ago as 1934 Jung had expressed his disapproval of artificial rigidity in therapeutic technique; speaking of the analyst's analysis, he wrote:

> Freud seconded the requirement, obviously because he could not escape the conviction that the patient should be confronted by a doctor and not by a technique. It is certainly very laudable in a doctor to try to be as objective and impersonal as possible and to refrain from meddling with the psychology of his patient like an overzealous saviour. But if this attitude is carried to artificial lengths it has unfortunate consequences. The doctor will find that he cannot overstep the bounds of naturalness with impunity. Otherwise he would be setting a bad example to his patient, who certainly did not get ill from an excess of naturalness. Besides it would be dangerous to underestimate the patients if one imagined that they were all too stupid to notice the artifices of the doctor, his security measures and his little game of prestige.[10]

(One of Jung's final letters to Freud had frontally contained a set of such reproaches to Freud.[11])

Like others I met in London then, Glover never made any mention of Jung's clinical recommendations. But, in concentrating on Freud, he maintained that he did not think much of Freud's early practice of putting his hand on a patient's head to encourage associations; Glover considered it "a great pity" that Freud failed to write more on technique. He had had such great experience in the course of devising psychoanalysis. Of course he wrote some important papers on technique. But the upshot has been that the "perfectionist" system of thought still operates; for example, there was plenty of gossip among analysts about so-and-so not "analyzing the negative." (I think now that an analyst's whole being, his existence as a person, as well as the specifics of what he says or does, is far more decisive than anything I once understood. Marie Bonaparte once quoted Freud as saying to her about the role of an analyst: "more important that what one does is what one is."[12] Such an observation, if valid, has to put in perspective all possible manuals about technique, at the same time not implying that "anything goes." James Strachey said that favorite lines of Freud's were those of Mephistopheles in Goethe's *Faust*: "After all, the best of what you know may not be told to boys."[13])

How come Freud said he could not bear to be looked at all day, and that that was a personal reason for his using the couch set-up? Glover simply said that he himself "did not find that the case" in his own clinical experience. *Then why would a person mind being gazed at?* It must be a "residue" of "sensitiveness to examination," stemming from an infantile conflict. A child inspects the parents, and parents keep children under observation; there is a sensitivity on both sides. Being touchy about infantile inspection would lead one to think about the role of guilt feelings. (In a sense here Glover was helping me try to psychoanalyze Freud himself, or at any rate to account for Freud's special preferences.)

At first, Glover said, he thinks he would have been sensitive himself. If one feels inspection is hostile, there will be bound to be a "strain." One can be afraid of being looked at if inspection implies criticism. Perhaps Freud was also "avoiding intimacy." (Glover was thinking out loud in response to my questions.) Since Freud had both male and female patients, his avoidance cannot be pinned down to one or the other. He may have been defensive about his relationships with other people; it was either hostile or libidinal attack that he was afraid of. Much of the time Freud got off very easily because of the passive attitude of his own followers. Josef Breuer was, Glover claimed, someone consciously afraid of libidinal contact in his clinical practice. (Here Glover was accepting what I later found out to be a myth about Breuer's contact with the early patient "Anna O."[14])

Glover concluded this line of reasoning by proposing that Freud was "probably afraid of libidinal contact"; after all, he stood up to hostility "very well"—look how he behaved against the criticism of the external world. Alternatively, one might propose that Freud was narcissistically sensitive to attack—afraid patients would find his weak places. He was generally well defended; if he gave way to hostility it would be damaging to his theory, and if he could not stand up to attack it would weaken his conviction. There was a good deal of "reserve" in Freud. Notice how few people he quotes. He does not "put himself at the mercy of his followers," only when he is going to exploit their ideas. Of course, "followers cannot be trusted very far." (Here I have in my notes: "clearly Glover is speaking" about himself.) In his lifetime Freud was thought to be a "faultless God"; it was the equivalent to the myth of the perfectly analyzed analyst. "We are human, thank God."

Glover seemed to have a practical sense of what kind of patients it was wise to refer to which analysts. Dr. Marjorie Briererly amounted to, he felt, a specialist in "intellectual, inhibited women with slightly bisexual constitutions." Dr. Estelle Cole was, he once remarked, like a child, "a cough drop," and "a jolly good analyst." (She had resigned her membership in the Society in 1927, according to Jones for "neurotic reasons.")

Glover knew much about European analysts as well. Hermine von Hug-Hellmuth's *A Young Girl's Diary* was he said "a great scandal," a fake. It was subsequently withdrawn from publication in England; it simply represented everything that was known at the time about female sexuality. Dr. Felix Boehm had "spent his whole life" writing about homosexuality, and Dr. Jeno Harnick ended up "paranoid." Glover added that he thought Dr. Sandor Rado was paranoid, too, "even if not diagnostically so." (As a group I found that analysts were too free in using diagnostic terms about people they disapproved of; by 1965 Rado had long since become a psychoanalytic heretic, but he remained extraordinarily brilliant, charming, and original. Rado analyzed a range of people like Benjamin Spock, Mary McCarthy, and Leonard Bernstein, in addition to analysts like Hartmann, Fenichel, Spitz, and Wilhelm Reich.[15]) Glover said he had heard good reports about Erik H. Erikson; former patients had "the highest opinion" of him. What was wrong with Erikson's concept of identity is only, Glover thought, that it caught on so; Erikson had not, Glover rightly pointed out, intended to trace it to infancy. (Erikson's ego psychology did start with earliest childhood.)

Despite all the generosity and personal mildness I saw in Glover, every now and then I detected signs of his public capacity to be embattled. He early on expressed surprise at the rapprochement between Freudians and Jungians in Britain, and when I expressed some enthusiasm about the idea his quick disapproval reminded me I had temporarily forgotten all that Glover had written. (He was, I think, correct in sensing similarities between Klein's work and that of Jung.) Glover once cited the name of an eminent figure in British intellectual life, Dr. W. H. R. Rivers (who treated Siegried Sassoon and Wilfred Owen); Glover had never met Rivers, but Glover said of him reproachfully that Rivers could not "go all the way" as far as psychoanalysis. ("Jones, Edward Glover, John Rickman, and other pioneer analysts vehemently opposed the work of such people as Rivers, who they saw as purloiners of Freud's ideas, without being true disciples. It was this intransigent view held by Jones and his followers that helped to maintain the longstanding isolation of psychoanalysis from the mainstream of British psychiatry."[16]) In connection with the greatest heretic of all, Jung, both Glover and I were aware of Freud's ambition to have a non-Jew as leader of the movement. But then Glover claimed that no one would "bother" about the apostasy of a Jung "if he came along now." (I had my doubts when Glover made this claim and, as I continue to encounter fanaticism in psychoanalysis, I still have my reservations.)

Glover said that he had never been very satisfied with the name "psychoanalysis," which tied practitioners to a certain technique, but he had not been able "to think of a better one." When the Jungians "left" they had had to pick the name "analytical psychology," which showed to Glover that psychoanalysis was probably as good a label as one could have. He thought it well that the Jungians had their separate name and a distinct group. He claimed that the way Professor H. J. Eysenck's ideas were "tolerated today" showed that the Jung situation would never be repeated, but then Glover later said that Eysenck was not a clinician but essentially a laboratory psychologist using some very old ideas into which he put new life. (But if Eysenck was an academic psychologist, and his ideas not anything like analysis, how did that illustrate that the excommunication of Jung could not happen again? Such a point only occurred to me after I had looked through my notes with care.) Glover remained proud of the fact that when Ferenczi and Rank had been "carried away with their enthusiasm," he and his brother James had "stood fast" in combatting their approach for the sake of traditional analysis.

When I knew Glover he was convinced, despite his once having functioned as a defender of the faith, that the state of psychoanalytic theory was "just a God-awful mix-up." He had already published a critique of Heinz Hartmann's ego psychology, at a time when Hartmann was the unquestioned Prime Minister of analysis, whose ideas were considered sacrosanct.[17] (Glover thought Hartmann was an armchair metaphysician rather than a true clinician.) Glover had been asked by the *International Journal of Psycho-Analysis* to write an essay on Dr. Edith Jacobson's work, in a period when her ideas were very fashionable; but his views were so critical that they refused to publish what he had written. Glover had already put into print a negative essay about Franz Alexander's contribution,[18] and Glover still did not think much of the label "neo-Freudian." (Nor did anyone commonly associated with the so-called neo-Freudian school, like Erich Fromm, much like the term.)

In all his views Glover seemed to me a curious combination of boldness and conformism. For instance, on the one hand he maintained that he thought that the recent tendency of psychoanalytic congresses to be devoted to a single topic was a mistake; he was willing to concede that such a focus might be good for any one clinical problem, but felt that a Congress should stimulate ideas across the board if it was going to be good for analysis as a whole. Yet if Glover could stand back and reject much of what he saw around him in contemporary analysis, he could be startlingly credulous about other issues. I remember starting off one interview by asking him what he thought about Freud's *Totem and Taboo*, even though to be sure it was reconstructed anthropology. I had been floored by Glover's complete lack of curiosity about what Freud might have been doing with his most speculative sorts of flights of fancy. (For one thing it now seems established that in *Totem and Taboo* Freud was dealing in part with his difficulties with Jung.)

Whatever I may have failed to explore adequately with Glover, I found his exchanges lively and interesting. He had his contradictions, as anyone who is worth talking to inevitably does. Despite the flashes of intolerance he showed as part of his participating in some of the famous controversies within psychoanalysis, and however unattractive may have been his implicit conviction that the truth was in danger of being betrayed, Glover had at the same time a touchingly religious quest for purity. He, as part of the London psychoanalytic world, represented a kind of intellectual liveliness not to be found in most cities then. (I presume that someone as eminent and genuinely distinguished an analyst as the American Dr. Lawrence S. Kubie thought so, too, and that that helps explain how he came to Glover for an analysis.) I think that the presence of two rival orthodoxies in Britain, Kleinian and Freudian, had the residue, whatever the various disadvantages, of ensuring that received wisdom is less likely to go unchallenged. For Glover, as for myself, Freud can be a model encouraging us to think for ourselves, and I believe it ought never to be the case that being independent means one can be safely abused as "antianalytic." The traditional Marxist epithet for traitors was "counter-revolutionary," but the continued use of such polemical epithets can do no service to what giants like Freud and Marx have contributed to the life of the mind.

6

Star Pupil: Dr. Lawrence S. Kubie

Kubie became one of psychoanalysis's most distinguished thinkers. He is now known for having authored books like *Neurotic Distortion of the Creative Process* and *Practical and Theoretical Aspects of Psychoanalysis*; unofficially Kubie may sometimes be remembered as Tennessee Williams's analyst, but in addition to hundreds of Kubie's papers a volume of his selected essays got posthumously published.[1] It is no accident that as a student of Glover's Kubie was to publish in 1973 the best biographical account of Glover that we have.[2] Earlier, in 1969, Glover had published an essay in Kubie's honor for the *Journal of Nervous and Mental Diseases*[3]; Kubie had been editor-in-chief of that journal from 1960–1967. Glover's own piece on Kubie became the finest we have on Kubie so far; but Kubie himself, born in New York in 1896, died in 1973, not long after Glover himself. Kubie has been characterized by one fair-minded historian of American psychoanalysis as among that country's "powerful and imperious personalities":

> Kubie was brilliant, gracious, and had mastered a raging temper, sparked by boyhood fights with a brother who was a year older. This early pugnacity later was "sublimated very largely in intellectual combat," according to Glover. In 1938 Kubie had helped establish the new professional standards for the American Psychoanalytic Association. What he regarded as his own contumacious-

ness was matched by a "compulsive benevolence." He was also remarkably productive, and was particularly concerned with evidence and scientific method.[4]

(Like Glover Kubie was the youngest of three siblings.)

Although, again like Glover, Kubie served in multiple official capacities, including the presidency of the New York Psychoanalytic Society, Kubie was thoroughly independent-minded; having helped many of the continental analysts to emigrate to New York, once they were established in power it was possible for them to brush him aside. The Europeans overwhelmingly cited mainly each other's work. Although at an earlier period he could be considered a "heresy hunter," in connection with Karen Horney and Sandor Rado for example, by the end of his life he was one of psychoanalysis's freest thinkers. "Later he rejected many of the new developments in Anna Freud's and Heinz Hartmann's ego psychologies because they seemed too abstract yet also too anthropomorphic and less explanatory than a theory of conflicting drives. And it is ironic that as a result, Kubie came to feel alienated from the New York education committee where ego psychology by then held sway."[5] Kubie was also notable for having proposed the creation of a wholly new profession of medical psychology, embracing the humanities as well as the sciences, so that the development of psychoanalysis would not be cut off from its roots.[6]

At the time Kubie first contacted Glover in 1928, Kubie was 32 years old, married, the father of his first child and expecting a second one in the fall. Kubie had graduated from Harvard College in 1916, and then Johns Hopkins Medical School in 1921. Kubie had spent three years in the Henry Phipps Psychiatric Clinic at Johns Hopkins under the then famous Adolf Meyer.[7] Kubie's laboratory interests drew him also in the direction of neurophysiology and neuropathology, and he had been finishing two years at the Rockefeller Institute in New York. He felt divided between his organic and psychiatric interests, and had a Medical Research Council Fellowship to study in London where Kubie also proposed to be analyzed by Glover. (Kubie had discussed his choice of Glover with his analyst friends.) As was the custom then, Kubie wrote in June to see if Glover might have an analytic space open for the fall; Glover indicated his availability, and Kubie spent two years in analysis in London.

In those days there were no psychoanalytic institutes set up in America; abroad the most popular alternatives were either the Berlin or the Vienna Psychoanalytic Institutes. While in London Kubie does not seem to have had any formal relations with the newly founded British Institute. As Glover commented in response to Kubie's 1930 news of his application, once Kubie had returned to America, for membership in the New York Society:

> With regard to your relations to the Training Committee in New York, it seems to me that as the present situation stands in America, you are perfectly justified in adopting the course you have taken. The situation is very similar to that which existed in England as recently as 1925. Officially speaking, it is no doubt heretical of me to say so, but I do not think you will find any great drawback in not having had any experience of a literature course in England. This is to a certain extent also true of the Control Courses, because I believe if you have any flair for analysis at all (and it is my opinion that you have), you can make up for any disadvantages of this sort by individual application and careful discussion of your cases with some experienced analyst in America.[8]

It will be remembered that Glover was also writing as a leader of the IPA, and therefore in a position to give good professional advice. By the fourth quarter of 1930 Kubie was accepted as an associate member in New York, where he could finish up his training through appropriate clinical supervisions; within months he was moved up to full active membership there. Glover was confident that Kubie's self-understanding would increase thanks to his clinical work:

> with regard to your own analysis, I think it is extremely probable that you will find yourself attempting to expand this through analysis of your patients, and of course in controls, but however that may turn out, I think it is likely that at the end of a year you ought to have a shrewd idea of the nature of any stumbling blocks, and be able to come to some final conclusion as to the professional policy to pursue.

However detached Glover might have sounded about Kubie's possible need for further analysis, Glover was wryly able to encourage Kubie in continuing to move away from his physiological interests: "I will say that I think it is very difficult to run organic interests with psychological ones, and in saying so, I admit I am not very much concerned with the possibility that your organic technique may be blunted."[9] Glover was clearly on the side of the furtherance of Kubie's psychoanalytic inclinations.

Glover and Kubie kept regularly in touch for the rest of their lives. Even in the early 1930s they seem to have been like-minded on a variety of issues. For example, as Kubie put it in 1932:

> [I]n gloomy moods . . . I begin to wonder which has the greater curative value, analysing others or being analysed one's self. Then I look at the analysts around me and wonder how many of them could function in any other milieu. . . . [T]here are among us those whose neuroses seem to me completely unresolved and for whom life would be impossible except as analysts. For the others, life would have been possible, even had they never been analysed and had they been working in some other sphere. And the most disturbing thing in the picture, perhaps, is that it is out of the first group that some of the most gifted analysts seem to come.

Kubie also wrote about his concern that his seeing patients non-analytically, perhaps sitting up, would jeopardize later working with them in a more strictly analytic manner. Kubie felt "sure . . . that if these patients had been faced with the alternative of analysis or nothing at the start, they would have sought some other kind of help." Although Kubie thought there was a contrast between analysis as practiced in Berlin as opposed to London, he still thought that as far as technical recommendations went "the two most helpful things that I have read and reread on technique have been your lectures and Miss Sharpe's."[10]

Glover thought that:

> The whole point is whether you have enough cases with whom to pursue pure analytic methods. If you have, the argument that other cases cannot get any treatment unless of the shortened kind, is not

any longer valid. It is useful, however, to acquire experience of this kind; I have done so myself and occasionally do so still in response to urgent pressure from professional friends who may have some protegé in a position similar to that you describe.

Kubie had written that remaining in New York seemed an "absurd" setting, but that offers from Yale, Chicago, or Harvard had not yet materialized. Glover wisely responded that "in a deep sense, all settings are equally absurd, and I shall not feel that you are likely to make a major blunder even if you do remain in New York." And "if there is any legitimate comparison between Yale or Harvard and Oxford or Cambridge, I can only say that life for a psycho-analyst under these conditions is largely a thankless pioneering task made palatable by a gilded ginger-bread atmosphere."[11]

Kubie seemed to have a genuine human relationship with Glover; even during his analysis, at the 1929 Oxford Congress, Kubie was distressed to learn about difficulties the Glovers had had the preceding winter with their daughter's health. Kubie would in the 1930s continue to hear of future health problems of Ann's, and express his solicitude. Kubie's marriage was in trouble, and his first wife (Susan) had in London gone for awhile to Miss Sharpe; this analysis had an "unsatisfactory outcome," since Kubie and Susan were each determined to prove that the other was ill. She went to Vienna for a further analysis with Helene Deutsch. Kubie wrote a letter himself to Dr. Deutsch, sending a copy to Glover, who was

> very much impressed by the clearness of the situation as you present it, even more so I think than when the same story filtered through the process of analysis. At any rate it is clear to me that at your age and with your definite urges to married life as well as that can be done, it was impossible to allow the situation simply to remain in suspense. It is to my mind a definite turning point.[12]

Glover's words brought Kubie "a good measure of reassurance,"[13] and there can be no doubt of the special sort of friendly relationship that Glover and Kubie had established. (In a 1933 letter of Kubie's to Helene Deustch he referred to his own "unconscious purpose [vis-à-vis Susan] which made much trouble for me in my work with Glover."[14] Deutsch seems to have felt that the problem was that Susan was afraid of Kubie. By the mid-1930s the Kubie marriage had ended in divorce; on and off he continued to write Glover about how the two Kubie children were doing.)

In late 1932 (December 29) Kubie had written about a specific professional issue, connected with the "fracas between Jones and the Quarterly." Jones had taken great objection to the creation of the *Psychoanalytic Quarterly* in America, which seemed to him a reproach and a threat to Jones's own *International Journal of Psycho-Analysis*. Brill had asked Kubie "to serve" editorially on the *International Journal*, and Kubie was confident that Glover would be "judicial"; knowing how closely Glover was allied to Jones, however, Kubie wrote: "If, however, you don't feel free to discuss the matter, I will readily understand the local considerations which might make it inadvisable." Glover replied on January 1, 1933:

> The best plan is for me to tell you what I know personally about this "Quarterly-Journal" affair. In so far as this involves quoting other people's opinions, it is of necessity confidential.
>
> I first heard of the Quarterly when E.J. expressed strong feeling not only against its originators but against continental colleagues for hurrying to join its board. A purely American quarterly would have been all right in his eyes provided it had been arranged for officially, was sanctioned by the Association and did not overlap in regard to material with the Journal, i.e. publish articles on which the journal has—by official agreement—first rights. I believe the Journal actually has translation liens on all *Zeitschrift* and *Imago* stuff. He objected to its being brought out without previous discussions or official sanction, its attempt to make an international appeal rather than a national, its co-option of foreign collaborators (who are already bound by agreement to the Journal), its overlapping, i.e. translating foreign articles on which the Journal has first legal claim. In short if American, why not American; if international, what is wrong with the "International" Journal.
>
> He has never abated these objections. Recently I was invited by Dr. Feigenbaum to join the Board of the Quarterly, submitted this naturally to E.J. and found that he was strenuously opposed

to my doing so on the grounds I have summarised. I therefore refused the invitation as tactfully as I could.

My difficulty in advising you is increased by the fact that I don't quite know what is the official attitude of the American Association to the Quarterly. I gather from the fact that Brill invited you to review for the I.J. that the Quarterly is not regarded in administrative quarters as official. But I don't really know. In general I should have said that if the Quarterly is officially supported by the American Association, no one on the I. Journal could take exception to your joining the Quarterly staff. If it is not recognized, then the only person in England who would feel strongly on the subject would be E.J.

Other points that occur to me are a) whether the Quarterly is going to maintain a high standard b) whether it is likely to be a success or to fizzle out.

A practical point would be the following: assuming that the Quarterly continued to be offensive in the eyes of the English editor and that you joined its staff, would articles written by you and sent to the English Journal be liable to be crowded out. Personally I don't think so.

(Much to Jones's horror Freud had lent support to the new quarterly, by sending some of his own articles to be translated, for example, and Kubie did publish reviews there. Flügel somehow risked Jones's wrath by becoming an editor of the new quarterly.)

One further professional issue arose just before the outbreak of World War II. On June 15, 1939, Glover wrote Kubie about an impending voyage to America.

About the trip to America, this is the actual state of affairs as far as I personally am concerned (again unofficial). When Jones first made the tentative suggestion to [Franz] Alexander, he had not in fact asked if I would go—but rather took it for granted. Now actually I'd quite like to go over a) if I had a decent spell off to visit all the people I'd like to meet again b) if I could take the family over with me. You see I always look on the summer holiday as a time to make up to Gladys and Ann for leading a heavy professional life during the rest of the year.

And it isn't practicable this year to do this. Jones's scheme of dashing over from 10th Sept., staying New York 5 days & dashing back (without the family) doesn't at all appeal to me. And quite frankly I wouldn't be sorry if I had a reasonable cause to back out. It's a question of professional duty vs. personal disinclination.

I mention all this so that you will understand the personal aspect of the situation if it should happen that I finally decide not to come.

I was myself in favor of preliminary exchange of plans by letter and then a brief visit to the USA next year about whatever to complete them. And I still would prefer this. The difficulty is increased because, following on Jones's suggestion, your people naturally started making all their plans accordingly and it would look like discourtesy if now he were to back out. And he seems keen that I should come with him.

It's a nuisance and I feel torn about the whole thing. Anyhow that's enough grumbling for the day.

By the end of August political and military events had overwhelmed all psychoanalytic planning:

August 31, 1939

My dear Kubie,

It was not until 11 p.m. last night (*30th Aug*) that Dr. Jones and I met under circumstances of urgency and were reluctantly compelled to call off our visit to New York—a decision, notice of which was called to Alexander within the next hour, of the circumstances leading up to that decision (viz, the imminence of war) I shall not speak now, since my immediate purpose is to add this letter to the copy of Dr. Jones's speech (prepared in advance for our projected conference) and to get both posted in time to catch the "*Ile de France*" service. As suggested in the cable sent to Alexander we hope very much that despite our unforeseen absence your committee will nevertheless meet and confer; and it is in this expectation that the enclosed set of proposals is sent to you. Before leaving the personal side of the matter however, I feel I must add a few comments of my own. In the first place we trust you will all realize how bitterly disappointed we are that extrinsic circumstances should have, at the very last moment, made it impossible for us to travel.

I ought to say also that this is particularly true of our president. As you know I had some obstacles to overcome before arranging to travel, but, from the very first, Dr. Jones has had his heart set on the purposes of the journey, namely, the building up of a new and better understanding between the American Association and the European groups, and the strengthening of the bonds between analysts in all countries at a time when most international relations were losing some of their juice and good will. In short Dr. Jones was ready to make any personal sacrifice to bring about a closer unity in the psycho-analytic movement and I can testify to the depth of his disappointment that the meeting he has looked forward to so eagerly should have had to be cancelled.

In the second place I should ask you to excuse the somewhat scrappy and ill prepared state of this letter. It is written in a hurry and cannot do justice to the importance of the occasion. I would nevertheless be glad if you would have it copied *in extenso* and distributed, with the other enclosure, to the members of your Committee.

Glover could count on Kubie's transcribing all Glover's corrections to his text. Differences over the matter of lay analysis were the main issues between the Americans and Europeans.

I feel that the most useful contribution I can make to his discussion is to present a few personal impressions of the situation, leaving Dr. Jones's communication to serve as a more formal basis of negotiation. Ever since I became Secretary of the International Association (and indeed for some years previously) I have, from time to time, asked Dr. Jones to outline to me the growth of the International Movement and in particular the relations existing between European and American colleagues. In process of doing so Dr. Jones has often told me of the nature of various difficulties that have cropped up. But I must confess (in spite of its being no tribute to my capacities as a Secretary) that I have had always the very greatest difficulty in remembering all the ins and outs of these difficulties. As against this amnesia I have the very liveliest memories of all my contacts with American colleagues since I first met them at the Berlin Congress of 1923 [sic]. I recall with pleasure their friendliness of disposition; their active scientific interest in all that concerned psycho-analysis; their readiness to cooperate willingly in any piece of work that might be suggested, and their capacity to maintain contact (including scientific relations) for years after the first meeting. These contacts were, it is true, personal contacts and the members concerned were scattered over different branches in the U.S.A. but they represent to me the most valuable of my American associations. In fact some of my closest and most cherished friendships are bound up with America. And it does seem to me not only that this state of affairs is worth maintaining on a larger if more formal scale but that there should not be any great difficulty in preserving simultaneously a) the interests of psycho-analysis b) scientific contact in an international organization and c) the possibility of intimate exchanges between colleagues however far separated by domicile. It is to secure these three aims that I feel every effort should be made. In my view no sacrifice except of course that of psycho-analytic principles is too great to be made to secure them.

Now to the proposals made in Dr. Jones's speech. It seems to me that they have one outstanding merit, viz., that not only would they automatically eliminate all frictions of an administrative type, but would permit each of the continental organizations to go about their own legitimate scientific business without feeling that there was the remotest possibility of an "interference" which would run contrary to the spirit and letter of scientific method. I must confess however that for my own part I would prefer a still closer form of international organisation. For one thing I don't like very much a redundancy of officials. Good officials in touch with current events are not as plentiful as blackberries and the work of congresses would be facilitated if the arrangements were in the hands of the more active officebearers of clinical organisations. In the next place I do not think that the science of psycho-analysis is as yet so firmly grounded that it can afford to imitate too closely the international organisations of other branches of science. P.A. is still a young vulnerable science, vulnerable in the sense that it would not be difficult for many of its most precious traditions to become weakened without a constant and close intercommunication on e.g. the various methods of research and training. But although this is my personal opinion, I realise that situations might arise due to legitimate differences in local conditions when a too close organisation might have its disadvantages *to both sides*. And it is for this reason that I have waived my own views in favor of those presented by Dr. Jones on behalf of the Committee.

May I add of course that whatever organisation is built up should have the courage of its main convictions. If there is to be any international organisation it must be in a position to do all it can to further the interests of psycho-analysis and of psycho-analysts in all countries. And it seems to me that for this reason alone, it is very desirable that whatever can be, should be done, to solve the perplexing problem of "migration" of analysts originally recognized as competent by their own competent branches. This may not be a problem for all time but it is certainly a problem of the present day a solution to which would in my opinion make the task of international organisation extremely simple.

May I mention also a pet concern of my own. I have always dreamed of a really first-class scientific bulletin, concerned less with domestic affairs of branches than with the spread of scientific information in a convenient reference form (containing for example, a three line digest to the content of papers given in Societies but not published in the Journals). This Bulletin service could be worked in conjunction with a Bibliographical Service as suggested in Dr. Jones's letter. To be successful it would require very close and constant cooperation between responsible officials.

I mention this as one only of the numerous arrangements that could be arrived at. There are many others. And this brings me to my last point. As you can well imagine, the speech prepared by Dr. Jones was drawn up on the natural assumption that the hundred and one details arising from its considerations could be dealt with point by point in personal conferences. As this is no longer possible it seems to me all the more urgent that two special steps should be taken by your committee in addition to considering our main suggestion and formulating if necessary alternative schemes. Those additional steps are (a) a tabulated list should be made of all possible sources of friction past, present or future. These should not, I imagine, take the form of generalisations but be, rather, as concrete as possible (b) in the case of any scheme that may be forwarded by your Committee, whether that suggested by us or any other preferred scheme, a rough outline should be made of the statutes intended to regulate it.

I must close this letter rather abruptly to catch the mail.

This particular letter of Glover's is of course a long one, written to Kubie as both a friend and a fellow leader in psychoanalysis; perhaps nothing else by Glover so graphically shows his studied efforts to remain loyal to Jones's various positions without violating his own personal views. Above all it shows how personally accommodating Glover could be, which was no doubt one of the sources of his being such a good administrator. In nothing that Glover wrote Kubie was there any unusual partisan intent or bitterness.

Kubie's reply (September 13) was addressed to both Glover and his wife; Kubie was hoping that the Americans might be in the war soon, but disappointed not to be seeing the Glovers in peacetime. The next surviving letter (October 7, 1939) we have is another of Glover's— at the top is the sentence "Please excuse the drunken handwriting, it is written in a train." Glover was writing in answer to the personal note, in addition to having acknowledged an official letter from Kubie. "We all (Gladys & Ann & self) were most disappointed not to be able to come to see you. (Did I ever thank you for all the trouble you took over the landing difficulties.)" Despite all his own reservations Glover had been planning to come over with Jones on a quick trip to the States, accompanied by his family. After the outbreak of the war Glover had sent his wife and daughter for safekeeping some 56 miles southwest of London, and he travelled up and down to work so that they might not feel too lonely. Most analysts had lost their practices, but Glover was doing better in that he still had a third of his "load left."

Kubie replied, as usual on a typewriter, by November 2, 1939; he regularly addressed himself: "My dear Glover." Kubie was frustrated by the forced inaction imposed on the American analysts. Kubie actually had to inquire whether he could legally send a small contribution for the Clinic Glover was planning to start in order to help deal with the neurotic problems of the London wartime population. Kubie was also chafing over the inability of America to take the political leap that would not be accomplished for almost two years, by the Japanese bombing of Pearl Harbor and Hitler's declaration of war against the U.S. In the meantime Kubie wrote: "Around every dinner table the fight rages; with the majority somewhat uncomfortably silent—and the main battle coming between some articulate proponent of our neutrality, and some equally articulate proponent of intervention. Personally I can't believe this head-in-the-sand position can go on indefinitely."

Kubie had remarried, and minded that Glover and his wife had been unable, due to the cancellation of the trip, to meet his bride and the children involved. "On the side" Kubie reported having been "as usual . . . engaged in a little warfare—that is, with regard to the New York Society."

> Unheeded, two factions were gathering a good deal of strength within the Society—one around Rado, and the other around Horney. I'm no heresy hunter; but it wasn't very healthy to see young people going through the Institute and having in their training literally no influence but the one-sided influence of some particular faction. I allowed myself to be drafted into the battle last spring, and although it's been rather trying and bitter, we do seem to have made some headway in establishing a much sounder curriculum and in forcing all students to have a fairly conservative basic training in their first years, with ample opportunity to be exposed to every shade of divergent opinion when their training is a little more mature. . . . Out of it all, however, comes one very firm conviction—namely, that something must be done to draw into psychiatry and into analysis a less frantically neurotic and anxiety-ridden type of human being.

Kubie sent along to Glover later that month (November 22) the outline of the curriculum that the New York Institute was "trying out" that year.

> I think I hinted to you that this curriculum was the fruit of a pretty violent struggle, in the course of which I was quite unwillingly erupted into the presidency of the Society and into the midst of a rather unpleasant scrap. The situation which lay behind it was

briefly that we were developing four cliques not only among the Society members, but among the students: a group of students who were under exclusive Horney influence, another group under exclusive Rado influence, another group under Kardiner's influence, and a group that had a more general classical training. Each group was more or less hermetically sealed from the other, and you can imagine how much confusion, lopsided and inadequate training, and mutual distrust and hostility all of this generated.

This curriculum was designed in order to insure some kind of reasonable orderliness in the sequence of the students' studies, and to make it certain that every student would have to be exposed to all possible influences.

Kubie felt passionately about the beleagured British situation:

I am constantly outraged at the inertia, the cowardice, and the myopic vision of the American people; and even more ashamed of the way in which the average comfort-loving, profit-hungry American citizen has rationalised his ease by stressing every past British and French blunder.... On innumerable occasions Roosevelt has said everything that he dared.... [E]xcept at the moments of crisis, and up until the collapse of France, our country like yours maintained the *belle indifference* of a typical hysteric.

Kubie's politics sound admirable; he was also to be militantly against racial segregation in the American armed forces during World War II.

A year later Glover was appealing (November 29, 1940) to Kubie to secure funds for alleviating the "straightened circumstances" of London colleagues. In early January of 1941 Kubie sent Glover a long article from the influential Popular Front newspaper *PM* based on an interview the editor (Ralph Ingersoll) had conducted with Anna Freud, and also Glover, about how Londoners were coping with the air raids.[15] Anna Freud explained to Ingersoll the specific survival measures she and others at the house Freud had died in had to take during the Blitz. She had not yet set up her Clinic for young children separated from their mothers. Glover reported the surprising news that the Clinic they had scheduled to open for three days a week for those who were emotionally broken down by the terror of the bombing had had to close "because we had no patients." Glover tried to explain the paradox that Londoners were not being made depressed or ill by being bombed. "As long as there is always a daylight when things are not so bad it makes a great difference."

> Dr. Glover is an enormous man and very Scotch. He speaks with a broad burr. He said that when it began they wanted him to go in the Ministry of Information and he turned the job down. He said, "I work with them but if I took an official position I couldn't call my soul my own. I can now. For instance, when it started people lost their heads a little and began locking everybody up. They took two or three of my assistants who were foreigners. I could go and raise hell with them and I did. My people are where they belong—back with me now."

Glover subsequently edited a shortwave broadcast series to North America on "Inside the Nazi Mind." Glover gave the opening and closing talks; Flügel, Anna Freud, Ella Sharpe, and the great sociologist Karl Mannheim were also in the series. Kubie read the news of the London colleagues to a meeting of the New York Society. Glover and also Kubie shared respective family developments.

When Glover resigned from the British Society in early 1944, he sent copies of his resignation material to Leonard Blumgart as President of the New York Society, and they were circulated among members of the governing Educational Committee. (He included mimeographs of his January 24 and February 1 letters to Sylvia Payne, as well as copies of the memorandum he submitted to the British Training Committee in late January 1944.) On June 30, 1944, Glover wrote at length to Kubie; before then evidently Glover had been silent about the Controversial Discussions.

> The inner history of the recent Society upheaval would, like all inner histories, take a long time telling—but it wouldn't really alter the main outline.
>
> The cardinal blunder we made (though for the past 10 years I have tried to redeem it) was allowing the Klein group to gradually build up prestige & authority. And now that I am no longer Jones [sic] 1st Lieutenant (as I was for about 16 years during which

I never criticised him) I can say quite openly that I think Jones by his timid flattery of Klein and Riviere was responsible mostly for letting the situation get out of hand.

Anyhow our middle group was always spineless. When the Vienna contingent arrived I thought the position had been saved & indeed it was until about 10 of them left for the USA. Thus we lost ground again. In addition the younger men (mostly with psychiatric leanings) were ready to get rid of the old gang (Jones and myself) and they combined with the Klein group to gain authority. We started an investigative series on the Klein ideas but this cut no ice. It was purely partisan. So after about 2 years continual squabbling I foresaw that on votes the Klein party would retain authority. Training in the meantime became a farce. (2 to 3 separate groups all training in their own systems. Klein, Freud & Middle Groupers.) And suddenly last summer I decided to get out. For many years I fought for balanced training & I was at first loath to let the Clinic Institute and Journal go to the other side but once I decided to do it it was effortless & I have been enjoying a complete emancipation from squabbles, meetings and party politics. As for the future I don't intend doing anything until I see how things shake down. It may end in my forming a Freudian group, but it will be a long fight to get it well founded. And I won't start unless it is going to be a good group.

All the same I want to retain my connection with the International and if some American branch made me an honorary member I would not only be personally grateful but saved the necessity of insisting on "direct membership" of the International.

By August 8, while mainly commenting on helping get a birthday gift to Kubie's son in the army, Glover also observed that he thought "our position is still obscure & the real trends in the Society will not show up for awhile."

Kubie had been in close enough touch with the Jones–Glover team to be in a position to appreciate how Glover could have borne the burden of Jones's prior autocracy. The myth that later arose within the British Society about the crisis that took place in 1944 was that Glover had been unusually arrogant (in contrast, one wonders, to people like Masud Khan, Jones, Melanie Klein, and Anna Freud?)

and Glover was guilty of blocking the rise of a more democratic Society.

> Glover, one of the main protagonists in the quarrel, was disliked for his high-handed, anti-democratic running of the Society.... Jones ... was President continuously for twenty-seven years.... What is more, both Jones and Glover were thought to be aloof and high-handed in their handling of relations with the public and other professions.... Perhaps because of his rather ignominious role in the Controversial Discussions and his subsequent departure from the British Society, Edward Glover is not much quoted by later Independent writers, but his scholarly influence was great throughout the 1920s and 1930s.[16]

It was alleged that Jones and Glover had kept the British Society "in rather lofty isolation from those other institutions, like the Tavistock Clinic," and that the 1942–1943 "revolt against the policies of Jones and Glover, particularly their isolationist attitude toward the community at large" had finally triumphed with Glover's exit from the Society in 1944.[17]

But Glover was after all only Jones's second-in-command, which had not prevented Glover from playing such a leading role in the creation of the ISTD and Portman Clinic. Psychoanalysts have not been known for their peaceableness; to complicate matters, an educated Scot (like Glover) could admire America while looking down on the English, who in turn could patronize a Welshman like Jones. No group likes someone who has resigned from it, especially when the resignation is made a matter of formal principle; such withdrawals are more apt to be politically familiar in Britain than America. But the British do also tend to favor institutionalizing a row, and then doing nothing about it; they can appoint a Royal Commission, and then proceed to do little about implementing the recommendations. (For years the Balfour Declaration about a Zionist state was just a pious intention.)

However the British chose to deal with Glover, and I would argue that he got singularly stigmatized as a malevolent influence, the international psychoanalytic community was necessarily also implicated. Jones wrote to Brill in New York on July 22, 1944:

> The best thing to do with the Glover affair is to leave it to time to become forgotten. Counter-argument is only advertisement and keeps such things alive. You may take it from me that it is essentially a personal affair, and rather sordid at that. I can tell you all about it when we meet next.

Jones's use of the word "sordid" was designed to help in what became, I think, the demonization of Glover.

Jones also wrote to Franz Alexander on July 2 (1945?) in response to Alexander's letter to LeRoy Maeder:

> I have the copy of your letter to Dr. Maeder concerning what you call the Glover–Jones affair. It is news to me that there is supposed to be one and I will tell you all I know about the matter. After I had resigned office and ceased to attend the Society meetings I heard to my surprise that Glover had resigned from the Society. I know of course something of the background and thought it was a very unnecessary action, that it was his affair and he did not speak of it to me.

Jones was lying on several counts; he did not relinquish his office as President until mid-1944, and Jones had in fact participated at some of the proceedings of the Controversial Discussions. Although Glover had not "spoken" to Jones about the resignation, he had written to him about it.

Jones went on to Alexander:

> Some time afterwards application was made to me for permission for him to join the Swiss Society under the misapprehension that I had the power to grant this. I replied to Dr. Sarasin that on the contrary the last congress had expressly forbidden the President to exercise this power which he had previously had (there being one exception which is irrelevent here). So there was nothing I could do about it. The next congress can of course alter this rule again if it wishes to, although personally I do not think it a good

thing that an analyst whenever he quarrels with his local Society should be free to join a foreign one. It is surely better that he makes an effort to compose his difference. However, the whole matter has really nothing to do with me personally. I do not know what version you got from Princess Marie, but perhaps you would think it well to show this letter to Dr. Maeder.

Jones was of course disguising the support Glover had had from Anna Freud as well as the Swiss. (And we know that only after Jones stepped down as IPA President did Glover's Swiss membership sail through. It does rather take one's breath away how Jones could write, "The whole matter has really nothing to do with me personally.")

As of March, 1945, Glover had still been hoping to avoid the necessity of trying to stay in the IPA as a "direct member," a practice which when he was Secretary he had frowned on. Glover wrote Kubie on the 14th:

> I am hoping that soon we shall be able to constitute a Freudian Society: it is on its way (this still unofficial). I expect you will be soon or have already seen my digest of the Klein Controversy. [It appeared in Vol. I of *The Psychoanalytic Study of the Child*.] In a previous letter of yours you spoke of the possibility of my being made an Hon member of the Amer. Association or even of the New York Branch. Either eventuality would gratify me very much—& of course both together would delight me. But I leave all that to you & if there is any difficulty I shall quite understand.

Kubie was in a position to be able to help Glover, but appropriately cautious; he was about to undertake a mission on the continent and also London for the U. S. Surgeon General, and would be coming over with three other prominent American analysts (John Romano, Leo Bartemeier, and Karl Menninger): as Kubie wrote Glover on April 7,

> I am most interested to learn of your plans to organize a Freudian Society in London. I hope our coming will help, in some indirect fashion. Your name has been submitted to the American Psychoanalytic for honorary membership; but because of the war there will be no meeting of that Association this spring. Consequently

no action can be taken on this until the next meeting of the Association occurs. I hope there will be no such delay in similar action on the part of the New York Society; but some few feel that in spite of full sympathy and agreement with you it is not a good precedent for one society to set itself up as judge in the problems of another group, or to take sides by a personal gesture of this kind. This is the only possible obstacle that may occur.

Kubie was abroad with his colleagues for three months, and of course had his own professional (and personal) problems. Kubie wrote Glover on September 10, 1945: "My own hopes at the moment are to disengage myself from my various 'extra-curricular activities' as quickly as possible, so as to concentrate again on problems of technique. For instance, I want to see how it would influence analytic therapy if I could intersperse analytic sessions of controlled dissociative regression and customary analytic sessions." As dogmatic as Glover is sometimes alleged to have been, Kubie seems to have known Glover better, and there was no objection from Glover to any such technical innovation. Kubie also wrote that "before leaving for my vacation, I was able to secure an invitation for Dr. Schmideberg from Youth House, an excellent institution for delinquent boys here in New York City. I hope that by now she will have heard from them directly and that this will make it possible for her to take the trip which she contemplated."

At this time Anna Freud's own arrangements with the British Society were still uncertain; it was only in the early summer of 1946 that the negotiations between Anna Freud and Sylvia Payne's little committee were finalized. Even before things were settled on that front Melitta Schmideberg was heading abroad. (The Executive Council of the American Association met in May and unanimously endorsed Glover's nomination as an Honorary member, but this could not yet be acted on by the Association since it had not yet assembled.) In the spring of 1946 Kubie could review Glover's essay on David Eder for the *Saturday Review of Literature*. (Glover was even tempted to write a small study on the science and art of biography, but this project never came to anything. Jones, in the meantime, was starting to undertake what became his three-volume biography of Freud.)

Glover (April 15, 1946) was intrigued by Kubie's proposed use of chemical substances for therapy. But Glover argued that "group therapy is to be taken with several grains of salt as far as dynamics is concerned. To me it seems a combination of a short-cut and an escape from the undoubtedly difficult job of analyzing resistances. That the method gets good therapeutic results doesn't count. I doubt it resolves many social resistances sooner than p.a.: in that sense it's a kind of 'Ferenczi' technique." Glover complained that the Tavistock Clinic, and perhaps Bowlby, were engaging in a "watering down" spell in Britain.

> As for p.a. training I still hold that a fundamental analytical training is the first essential but that candidates are on the whole much too *ignorant* of cognate sciences: e.g. they ought to know more about the pharmacology of mental interference. These *special bits* of study should however be "picked out" and given some prominence so that the candidate is not overwhelmed with e.g. irrelevant . . . detail. Candidates are even more ignorant however of life and literature, and something should be done about that. They are ignorant of "selected" anthropology and something should be done about that. And sometimes they are bloody fools into the bargain and nothing can be done about that. So there we are.

(This letter does communicate a tone expressive of haughtiness.) Anna Freud was still convalescing from pneumonia, and about to deal with Payne's proposals. Glover worried that Anna's illness "may reduce her fighting morale because to my view . . . psychoanalysis needs all the strength it can gather to meet the next twenty-five years."

Kubie's next letter (April 26, 1946) reported his harsh appraisal of Schmideberg, tactfully expressed within parentheses, which Glover chose not to comment on:

> (Let me say in passing . . . that I gave her the devil for other matters. I may do her an injustice, but nothing makes me madder than being taken in. I almost never recognize it when anybody is lying to me, but always assume that folk are being frank and truthful, and then I am surprised and mad as hell when I have to face the fact that someone has been pulling the wool over my eyes. When I talked to Schmideberg in London I asked her whether she really was

interested in coming here in order to carry on studies in the field of criminology as she said, or whether she really wanted to come over here to live. I would have been ready to help her in either case; but the method of helping would have differed, and if the latter had been her acknowledged purpose I would not have spent a lot of time and energy writing and phoning and interviewing people about possible jobs and research opportunities. However, she was wide-eyed and disingenuous in her protests that she was not even thinking of staying here for more than two or three months, and that she was coming solely for the reason she had stated. So I believed her and spent quite a lot of time lining up jobs, all of which she turned down; and within ten days or two weeks of her arrival she was taking patients and telling people that she was preparing to stay. She has made a rather unfortunate impression on her colleagues here, from whom rather uncomplimentary reports filter back to me from time to time. When she came to see me recently, I told her quite frankly that I considered that she had behaved badly, that there had been no reason why she should not have been frank with me, and that I personally would have no further dealings with her. I am telling you all of this, just because I do not want a distorted version of it to go to you without correction. Other than that it makes no difference to me, and I am sure it will make none to her. The need for competent technicians is so great that she will get along perfectly well in spite of her quirks.)

However disheartened Glover may have felt by Kubie's report, Kubie went on about other better news: "You may not know it, but some years ago, when we were getting rid of Rado, I raised the question of whether we might be able to induce you to come to New York." (Rado had left Berlin in 1931 in order to found the New York Psychoanalytic Society's first Institute; even though Brill had raised $50,000 to fund the Institute, his New York colleagues were agreed he was not the person qualified to run it. Although in London some analysts also crowed about having got rid of Glover, neither Kubie or Glover perceived any possible analogies to Rado's case.) Kubie said there were other possibilities for Glover at Chicago, Cleveland, Rochester, California, Topeka, and also Canada.

I have been making discreet inquiries in all of these places dropping a hint that they might be able to get you or someone like you to come here at least on a visiting lectureship for a few months, out of which might grow plans for the development of a full-time training and research institute. I did this without consulting you because I wanted to be able to tell all of them that I had not the faintest idea whether you would be interested, and that this was something entirely out of my own head. Nothing may come of any of these leads; and you may in fact be interested in none of them: but I can assure you of one thing, namely that the American scene would welcome you with open arms and with an open heart.

Kubie was puzzled by the news about the Tavistock Institute:

You put your finger on their weakness, but I am not as pessimistic about the outcome as you are. The old group there has always ducked the full challenge of the unconscious; but the younger group is better and more nearly analytically trained. I think that the strange misalliance between the official Kleinian analytical crowd in London and the Tavistock group may conceivably go in either of two ways; it may reinforce the quirks of both, or iron them out. What puzzles the life out of me is why the Tavistock group, with its really healthy and good-hearted and responsible social orientation, has fallen for the fantastic Kleinian theoretical structure, with its ultra-extreme isolation of the individual from social influence. It is very perplexing to me.

There was just so much influence Kubie or anybody else could exert in behalf of Glover, but Kubie was not just strategically placed to be looking around in Glover's behalf, but as well put together personally (and socially) as one could imagine anyone to be. (Kubie was secure and had no special reason to be worried that Glover's problems in Britain might somehow damage his own psychoanalytic lineage.) The best prospect for Glover turned out to be in Toronto—with liaisons planned at a variety of Canadian universities. (Unknown to Glover was the fact that there would be difficulty in bringing over his "feeble-minded" daughter because of "strict" Canadian immigration rules.)

Glover acknowledged his reluctance to leave England, although he conceded that he would be tempted to get out of London for a clinical and university teaching appointment at Oxford, Cambridge, or Glasgow because of the prospect of "influencing oncoming generations." Against accepting an appointment abroad was of course all the personal attention that his daughter Ann required; in addition,

> (1) I am at the top of my professional career here with a busy and for the time being lucrative practice
> (2) I have acquired some respect in scientific circles, for independence and soundness of judgment
> (3) I have a lot of books to write and I want to write them
> (4) I don't want to uproot either Gladys or Ann who are both London-lovers—Ann's development in particular depends on her personal contacts; I think it would be a traumatic effect to break them for more than a spell.

On the other hand, Glover looked forward to taking part in

> the development of mental science—in particular planting and building up p.a. organizations. [I have no regrets at my separation from the British Official Group: it is deadwood for the next 10–20 years anyhow. I can do more outside as in any case I didn't do any training for some years before the war (barring lectures of course).] I would enjoy contacts with sincere people. (It has been a constant process of dissimulation, pretending for the sake of official appearances that I liked this thoroughly second-rate and arriviste gang in p.a. here.)

Glover thought he could "organize and inspire still; but I can't do hard donkey work (which would be necessary)"; yet "I have an unsatisfied itch to absorb new lands." If he were younger Canada would be attractive; "U.S. is a different proposition; it has a civilisation. Canada is I take it just about to build one." (Jones had been in Toronto before World War I.) Glover then told Kubie that he had refused an offer of a Professorship in Australia and another in New Zealand "for the same reason." A "longish" visit seemed more feasible than any "life job" even in the U.S.[18]

In Kubie's circularized letters to various friends in positions of psychiatric power he indicated that Glover had been

> caught in a squeeze play between two intransigent groups in London: the Viennese group on the one hand the Melanie Klein group on the other. After years spent in an effort to reconcile them on scientific grounds, he found the situation deteriorating so badly that he turned his back on the whole business. Consequently at the moment he is isolated, and pretty unhappy at seeing the London Society and Institute to which he has really devoted his life in such hands. He is a man of exceptional intellectual distinction and has been the scientific spark-plug of everything sound in British analytic circles for many years, always trying to hold in check the excesses of the Klein school. He failed to do this because of the conscienceless exploitation of the preparatory analyses of which Klein was guilty, since she used it to make personal proselytes and personal devotees out of her students.

Kubie thought that anyone interested in Glover should read his 1940 investigation of psychoanalytic technique, and "his own judicious comments on the replies which came to him from his colleagues in response to the questionnaires on which the book is based. It is in his evaluation of these replies that you get the best insight into the quality of the man's mind." Kubie also alerted people to "the feeble-minded" child, "to whom he and his wife devote much of their time (because of the fact that in England there have been no adequate private facilities for taking care of a child of that kind)."

Kubie did have success in the Honorary Membership in the American Association coming through, clearly gratifying to Glover. But Glover reported (June 28, 1946) that

> After prolonged secret negotiations between the Middle Group led by Payne and on the other hand the Anna-Viennese group, the Society have appointed a Committee to fix the details of a *double-training* system—i.e. 2 separate training groups within the Society.

> Payne is keen on this because she's keen on an 'official' unity—Anna because she's now frightened of the position of the Viennese if she works apart. Her own followers are split. They don't like a false rapprochement but don't want to refuse her. So there it is: it will keep a façade going for a year or two. What Anna doesn't realise is that this would not have come about but for my bringing it to a head by resigning. It is my intention still to keep aloof until I see whether this double training system works. I don't think it will, so long as the Klein group have power in the Training Committee and can influence allocation of candidates.

(Anna Freud may have feared that if she had rejected Jones's invitation to be IPA Secretary she might have invited the sort of vengeance Jones was attempting to wreak on Glover.) In Glover's next letter (July 15, 1946), after discussing some publishing queries, he came back to the Society's new regime:

> Latest news from PA battle front. The Society have passed a resolution authorizing the organisation of 2 sets of training under the same umbrella—or did I tell you this in my last letter, i.e. for the first time in its history the Society has officially recognized that differences exist strong enough to justify separate training. Well, that is something. What has really been wrong with this group for years has been a combination of timidity and a sort of face-saving that is very near to hypocrisy.

In September, 1947, Kubie came up with the suggestion of Glover becoming Clinical Director of the New York Psychoanalytic Institute. Hartmann was mentioned as part of the "universal enthusiasm." (It remains to be seen what Anna Freud might have been writing around this time to her old Viennese allies in the New World.)

> We can probably offer a flat salary of $20,000 to $25,000 a year for a three year period, plus the right to have two or three analytic patients which should add another $9,000 to $12,000 to your income. If there is any chance that you would be interested, we would start the ball rolling at once. I understand the many difficul-

ties for you in contemplating such a change; but I keep hoping that we may succeed in tempting you to take up the challenge anyhow.

In the end Kubie wrote that the funding for that position did not materialize, but student and mentor were certainly thinking along similar lines. As Kubie wrote (October 2, 1947),

> Over the years I had seen enough of the work of my colleagues (even the best of them) to make me feel deeply concerned over the defects of our analytic technique. It was no longer possible to believe that a bad therapeutic result could be explained away as due either to inadequate training or to inferior analytic ability. I had been forced to accept the fact that it was often the result of certain basic inadequacies in the therapeutic leverage of even the best and most skillful analysis. Nowhere is this more evident than in the therapeutic results of our training analyses, where for many obvious reasons our therapeutic leverage is even less than with our patients. All of this bothered me deeply, both about the progress of analysis as an art and science, and even more because of the tendency of mature colleagues to develop overt neurotic character disorders with the passing years. I sensed something of the same feeling in you when we talked in England two summer ago. Perhaps the time has come for a frank facing of this problem within our own analytic circles. That is another reason why I hope that you will bring out and amplify the full implications of your investigations on technique.

Kubie's second marriage was in serious trouble (they finally divorced), and Kubie had gone back into analysis with Herman Nunberg, "for whom I have always had high regard . . . and with whom I have purposely avoided any extensive social relationships." (Glover was thoroughly supportive of what he thought of as Kubie's continuing maturation and independence, an expression of a combination in Kubie of vitality and frustration.)

Before finally hearing that the New York proposal had fallen through (without it being offered to anyone else), Glover replied (January 6, 1948) that he had taken counsel from 3 people: Ernest Jones (who hates my guts ever since I resigned from the Society but whom I treat exactly in the same way as before), Anna Freud and JR Rees [at the Tavistock Clinic]. They were all against my going!!! E.J. because he is anti-American (why so I've never understood; personally I've always had the most cordial feeling for the U.S., for U.S. folk and for U.S. works: perhaps he was annoyed at the offer). Anna just didn't want me to go. Rees thought it was a young man's job. Personally I was going to try and buy you off with an offer of a 3 months visit including a tutorial course to candidates either on technique or theory. But on second thoughts I can see that I'd have to do some economic thinking before committing myself even to this.

Glover was proving a stubborn fighter within the IPA; and he forwarded to Kubie a supportive letter from Sarasin in Basle about Glover's becoming a full member of the Swiss Society. (The American delegates to the 1949 IPA Congress in Zurich were supporting Glover's position, which went through at the same time that Jones had been succeeded as IPA President by Bartemeier.)

The politics of international psychoanalysis were such that Franz Alexander, whom one would not have thought as ideologically well-disposed to Melanie Klein, was critical of Glover's having resigned from the British Society. Glover addressed Alexander's objections in a lengthy July 3, 1949, letter to LeRoy Maeder of the American Psycho-analytic Association; the only reason this letter is accessible is that Maeder sent a copy to Kubie.

> Naturally I appreciate very much Dr. Alexander's friendly references to my psycho-analytic standing and his desire that no avoidable technicality should stand in the way of my being recognized by the President as a member of the Swiss Society. . . . Dr. Alexander, however, goes on to say that the staff of the Chicago Institute are not in sympathy with the motivation of my resignation from the British Society. I quote some of his comments: ". . . we feel that differences of opinion in a scientific society are not only unavoidable but highly desirable" . . . "complete agreement . . . in the field of science . . . would be contrary to scientific development." Dr. Alexander main-

tains further that I expect a scientific society to have "a homogeneous attitude about scientific matters which are still in flux" and he is in favour of "a freer, self-critical and non-dogmatic attitude among psycho-analysts."

I need hardly say that I agree unreservedly with everything Dr. Alexander says regarding the necessity for a scientific attitude to questions of controversy and I believe I may claim that throughout my twenty-years membership of the British Society, during the greater part of which I acted as Scientific Secretary and Director of Research, most of my energies were devoted to securing scientific standards of research and training. I realize that it is not easy for colleagues living at a distance to understand the actual state of affairs existing at the time of my resignation and as it still exists in the British Society. At the time I resigned I sent a full account of my reasons to the Society and a number of copies to the Secretaries of other branches of the International. But I can well understand that with the passage of time it is difficult to keep the details of a distant controversy in mind. Hence I wish to state as briefly as possible the decisive reason for my resignation. *It was that the training of psycho-analysis in Britain was being organized on a tendentious, non-scientific basis which whether those responsible realised it or not (only a few did not realise it) meant that psychoanalytic training in Britain and consequently the future of psychoanalysis in Britain would be determined by factors of political (i.e. numerical) power rather than by an appreciation of the basic principles of psycho-analysis.* I omit for the moment the influence of transference factors.

This, I may say, was not a hastily formed impression on my part. I had been a member of the Training Committee from its inception, was for many years its Secretary and latterly its Chairman; and had watched the developments that took place from about 1935 onward with a good deal of anxiety and, I confess freely, a good deal of distaste. As you may have gathered the difficulty became acute when following the adumbration of Melanie Klein's *later* theories, the question arose whether those theories should be officially taught as part of psycho-analysis and inculcated during training analyses by members of the Klein group. It was my view that they should not; and that every step should be taken to secure a basic Freudian training for all candidates. When that possibility faded I resigned. Needless to say I took every step possible to avoid this course. I proposed that all principals holding opposed views* should abstain from conducting training analyses, leaving them to be conducted by "middle-groupers" or "non-partisans."

I proposed (and still propose) that travelling scholarships should be founded to enable students to be analysed in the U.S. and other countries, thereby eliminating to some extent the existence of bias. But to no effect. And it is significant that my resignation from the Society was followed by Anna Freud's resignation from the Training Committee, and that, until a "political compromise" was reached, largely through the assiduous efforts of Middle-Groupers, a state of actual cleavage existed in the work of the Society.

I shall not burden this letter with a recapitulation of the Klein controversy. The simple fact remains that to this day if you ask any member of Anna Freud's group what he thinks of the Klein theories, you will find that they regard them as not only unsound but in contradiction to *basic* Freudian principles. For myself, I think they (her later theories) are not only wooly, garbled and unscientific but resemble the systems of Jung and of Rank in many important respects. (Compare Jung's archetypical phantasies with Klein's "3 month old" depressive phantasies of sin and Rank's "birth trauma" with Klein's traumatic (depressive) theory of mental disorder.)

Now it was was never considered unscientific or dogmatic on Freud's part to repudiate either Jungian or Rankian theories. On the contrary, most analytic groups have been at pains to insist on certain *basic* Freudian principles and theories as essential to psycho-analysis, and to reject any attempt to over-throw these principles. Whether the attempt originated within or without analytic circles. I maintain that the present issue is of this order. If Klein is right, many of Freud's basic theories are wrong. Personally I do not think they are wrong and I regard modern Kleinian theory as non-analytic in content, tendency and therapeutic application.

*The issue had previously been debated for about 18 months in the Society and there had been a total and irreconcilable cleavage between, on the one hand, former members of the Vienna Society together with a number of British members, and, on the other hand, members of the Klein group.

Glover could not break free of the Freudian legends about deviants:

> Now to the transference element. It would not have mattered seriously except to the reputation of the British Society to give house room to the most absurd theories. But it does matter when, through the process of training analyses and official instruction such theories are canonized and inculcated. Candidates have no serious defence against "transference-suggestion," as every psychotherapist knows. And in fact to the extent that Kleinian theories were accepted, the lever was in most cases that of training analysis and control analysis.
>
> Finally it is to be noted that the "solution" of the impasse at present accepted by the British Society is in fact no solution. To form two training groups, whether called "A" and "B" or, for that matter "X" and "Y," deceives nobody, not even the outside world. Irreconcilable differences still exist and the outcome depends on the rapidity with which the respective groups train candidates and so spread their influence and ultimately achieve administrative power. This is a perfectly hopeless scientific situation and no one knows this better than Dr. Jones. It is a situation that has proven more and more acute since 1935; and when at the end of 1943 I decided to protest against it, I found that the only effective course I could take was to resign from the Society. I could not and would not be a party to any attempt to conceal the deplorable condition into which psycho-analytic training in Britain had fallen. And I believe that my resignation has at least called attention to the urgent necessity of subjecting training methods to scientific control.

If one might be inclined to think that I have gone into Glover's reply to Alexander at too great length, it seems notable that Alexander felt obliged to respond. It seems a bit odd that Alexander was pursuing the point just when Glover was about to triumph in getting his Swiss membership finally accepted at the 1949 IPA meetings at Zurich. (It was a poignant moment when Glover wrote Kubie what it was like to witness the Berlin analysts, after the Nazi period, reappplying for admission to the IPA.) Alexander had "never any doubt that Anna Freud's contentions were sound, while Melanie Klein's were untenable." (Alexander, like Glover, had known Klein in Berlin.) But still

Alexander did not want to go into the business of trying "to establish whether one author is more Freudian than another." Alexander accepted the idea that in scientific life deviations from Freud would occur. "I am convinced that psychoanalysis today no longer needs to settle theoretical controversies by way of secession." This "is customary only with religious sects, where the disciples have to subscribe to certain fundamental beliefs."

> My attitude is one of the utmost humility toward the unknown and I feel that in our field we have only begun to scratch the surface and that many of our theoretical views are still extremely crude and of quite transitory nature. No matter how much I agree with your criticism of Melanie Klein's ideas, I do not feel the necessity of trying to exclude her from our field, to which she has made some contributions.
>
> Ever since I have been a psychoanalyst, I have always deplored the secessionist movements in our field. They may have been unavoidable in the very early years of psychoanalysis when a certain amount of uniformity was necessary—an agreement on basic issues—to allow free collaboration and exchange of ideas among the workers. By now our field has advanced sufficiently to tolerate crucial divergences in opinion concerning theory. As long as a person uses our established modes of observation and the generally accepted principles of reasoning, there is no need to exclude him from our community even if his theoretical views appear untenable. It is true that Melanie Klein's reasoning is not convincing and she has little sense for what is scientific evidence. She has, however, a sense for the unconscious and has described the content of some infantile phantasies which were corroborated by others.
>
> It is more difficult to take a proper stand regarding the teaching activites of analysts whose theoretical views are so highly questionable. On the whole, I am inclined to trust the critical faculty of the psychoanalytic student of today and leave it up to him to discover the weakness of a teacher's point of view rather than to interfere with the principle of academic freedom.

However powerful Alexander's arguments may seem, his reputation is today as marginalized in America as Glover was then in England.

After the end of World War II Alexander would be denounced by Kurt R. Eissler for heresy, which may have made Alexander even more wary of psychoanalytic dogmatism.[19] (The problems Alexander suffered had their effect in the degree to which a subsequent analyst in Chicago, Heinz Kohut, scarcely breathed a word about Alexander's own innovations, theoretical as well as technical.) But although it was Glover who finally resigned from the British Society, as we have seen someone like Adrian Stephen was proud of having helped drive Glover out.

In late 1949 Kubie had an acquaintance who was interested in conjecturing about whether Klein was diabetic or not; it is unknown what the basis was for this query, but Glover reported (January 25, 1950) about such information that "it isn't easy for me to obtain it directly from her as when we pass at close quarters she maintains a complete state of oblivescence." Glover's implication was that he would not react that way himself. He had hopes of finding the answer out from Klein's "niece." Apparently Kubie's acquaintance, with a special interest in psychosomatic medicine, had correctly deduced from Klein's theoretical system that she herself must have been diabetic.

One curiosity that arises in the exchanges between Glover and Kubie touches on the character and thinking of Lionel Trilling, whom Jones wrote to Anna Freud so disparagingly about. Kubie (December 3, 1953) did not share Jones's contempt for Trilling:

> I know Lionel Trilling quite well. He is one of the most brilliant of our literary critics; and in addition to that is extraordinarily incisive in his understanding of psychoanalysis and of the interplay between psychoanalysis and literature. His critical reviews of Horney have been precise, mature, informed and devastating. [Neither Kubie nor Glover thought well of Horney.] His recent review of Jones' [sic] biography of Freud was equally fine. He is an extremely good lecturer to boot.

Kubie had for some time been a Clinical Professor of Psychiatry at Yale School of Medicine; one of his former patients was persuaded to set up the Foundations Fund for Research in Psychoanalysis.[20] But by the early 1960s Kubie was prepared to chuck private clinical practice, and concentrate on a hospital training position. Kubie became Clinical Professor of Psychiatry at the University of Maryland Medical School, where he also assumed the post of editor-in-chief of the *Journal of Nervous and Mental Disease*. Kubie was aware that he was working at odds with the psychoanalytic "mainstream." As he wrote Glover on January 22, 1960:

> My emphasis on pre-conscious processing in recent papers has led some to say that I am denying the Unconscious; but that is the usual nonsense of fuzzy-minds who are literally terrified if you deviate by a hair from those mental ruts which they mistake for thinking. However, this only makes me sad for analysis and sad for them, because it includes some folk of whom I am fond.

Kubie was finding out for himself what it was like being in the minority like Glover.

Kubie continued to remain attached to Glover's way of thinking, and they both shared a radical skepticism about what others in the field were doing, even as they continued to think of themselves as fundamentalists. As Kubie wrote Glover (September 27, 1961):

> What I would like would be a little working conference of our own, to sit down with a psychoanalytic dictionary and an ink eraser to see how many terms we could get rid of, thus producing a kind of international psychoanalytic Esperanto of basic terms alone. In some measure you have done this; but it needs even more pruning. . . . A copy of this note is going to Bert Lewin. If you and he think well of it, send me the name of a couple of people who would have the kind of tough-mindedness that I have in mind and that I personally ascribe to you and Bert as well, but frankly not to many others among us.

Lewin was one of the real "brains" in American psychoanalysis.

Kubie had become aware of his own "heretical biases," as he admired those exceptions in analysis who had had "the courage to break with the past, as Freud did, and you did."[21] At one point, in reading a 1968 book of Glover's, Kubie wondered whether a footnote meant that Glover was criticizing ("excommunicating") Kubie. Glover had written:

> I am not concerned here with those accredited psycho-analysts who indulge themselves in negative transference orgies by denying the concept of the libido or of Freud's conception of the instincts or who, bypassing the dynamic unconscious, live in a cloud of preconscious formulations such as any Jungian might enjoy or any of our modern novelists exploit. I have never been able to conceive how anyone with pretensions to scientific integrity can cut Freudian theory to ribbons and yet, undisturbed by pangs of scientific conscience blandly continue to pay his annual subscription to membership of any psycho-analytic society.[22]

(Kurt Eissler would carry on in similar embattled terms.) Glover explained to Kubie, however, that "my Papal Bull in the footnote was directed against Hartmann. . . ." Glover thought that "the truly egregious Hartmann [had] substituted for a brave try by Freud . . . a lot of cotton-wool verbiage. . . ."[23] Glover and Kubie exchanged numerous letters in connection with their biographical essays about each other. Glover proposed tongue-in-cheek that "we ought to constitute ourselves a Society of two—with a few selected psycho-analytic associates who however have no voting rights."[24]

The last letter from Glover to Kubie is dated July 12, 1970. After knowing Kubie for over forty years, Glover finally had been addressing him as "My dear Lawrence." (Kubie's American friends used to refer to him as "Larry.") By 1970, when Glover was 82, he was entering an exquisitely lonely period of his life in London. Gladys had already died, and he was left taking care of their daughter Ann. Of course Glover had his contacts with ISTD people and the Portman Clinic; the *British Journal of Criminology* also provided him with stimulating human contacts. But the life of a clinical psychoanalyst, with all the burdens of the troubles of others, is an isolated one; it is so easy to think one has no real friends, only former patients, who after all do not see one as one is. Glover had heaps of people he could count on to assist taking care of Ann, but they were those who he had helped in some way or another; instead of his wide acquaintances being a source of comfort, it could also underline just how alone he really was.

And so Glover's letter writing grew more literary than ever; he allowed himself to be freer in his letters than beforehand. In this last letter to Kubie, Glover asked him about a certain Reuben Fine, who had "pontificated at the Rome Congress." Glover wanted to know who Fine was. (Fine was an American clinical psychologist who became the first president of Division 39 of the American Psychological Association, and later wrote a dreary history of psychoanalysis.[25]) And who was Charlotte Fine? "His wife, his mother, his mistress, his daughter or his 'niece' . . . I wish to God analysts did not insist on marrying their Grandmothers in analysis, despite all the warnings of the Church of England. How wise indeed is the Church of England—for what comes of this incestuous orgy—nothing but misery, backbiting and spurious analytic theory." Analysis was, Glover supposed, inherently incestuous; it seemed to be an intrinsic aspect of the profession. The final words of Glover's last letter to Kubie are typical. "*Very, very secret, please*," as Glover went on to inquire whether a colleague they both thought extremely well of was perhaps "depressive?" "A really fine head and a first class clinician (send him cases if you can) but too God damned perfectionist. Poor dear. I'm glad I never married him." Underneath all the polemics, and right on the surface I think if one met Glover even casually, he was an unusually nice and caring person. Whatever the other failures Glover may have felt about his life, Kubie was as a student one of Glover's outstanding successes.

Epilogue

The fact that there is still so little literature about someone as interesting as Glover, who played such a pivotal role in a crucial stage of British psychoanalysis, is in itself telling about how rich a subject for intellectual historians psychoanalysis can be. One unusually conscientious German author of a history of depth psychology, writing in the 1950s, thought that Glover's "investigations" entitled him to be regarded as "the most important and certainly the most critical representative of Freudian psychoanalysis within the British group."[1] When the time comes, although somehow the history of psychoanalysis in Britain has not attracted even one book yet, Glover will deserve a significant role.

The circumstances surrounding his resignation from the British Society, combined with his continuing ability to function within world psychoanalysis, amounts to a unique story in the tale of the spread of Freud's school. Glover does not easily fit into any of the stereotypes that have grown up to characterize leading psychoanalytic figures. As a critical voice his views still deserve to be heard. Although it has not been in anybody's particular organizational interest to keep his work and thoughts alive, aside from London's ISTD or the Portman Clinic, I believe he still has something important to teach. I have not proposed discussing him in an uncritical way. An in-depth look at his thinking should, I hope, make highly questionable the way recent myths about the Freud–Klein controversy have treated his role.

Glover was a man who "combined great energy and determination with high intelligence and gentleness"[2]; his withdrawal from the British Society cut him off from becoming one of the immediate founders of today's psychoanalysis in Britain. Even his work on forensic psychiatry would have benefited from "the post-Kleinian evolution of ideas."[3] But his detachment from organizational life gave him a special sort of vantage point, enabling him to stand back from all aspects of the psychoanalytic conventional wisdom of his day.

One possible interpretive line would be that Glover had started out working as his brother James's assistant; then, following James's premature death, Glover successfully became next-in-command to Jones. But after Freud's move to England, and Glover hearing from the creator of psychoanalysis that he was right in thinking that Klein's work was indeed a "deviation," Glover mounted a sustained effort as Freud's assistant, even though this meant a clash with Jones as well as others in the British Society. In hindsight Glover might seem to have made a muck of being a British psychoanalytic leader, and perhaps he had been unduly inflated (to use a Jungian term) by Freud's encouragement and the arrival in Britain of the Viennese contingent. But he succeeeded against odds in remaining within the IPA, and functioned harmoniously at the ISTD and the Portman Clinic.

From the point of view of those who can easily thrive within organizations, Glover can look like an odd man out. And he continued to attract the resentments of those he had left behind at the British Society. Yet for other creative analysts he served as a model of independence and integrity. To take one notable example, the late Charles Rycroft, who at one time served as Secretary of the British Society, was over a generation younger than Glover, but he felt that his own career as an analyst had been ruined by the respective dogmatisms of Anna Freud and Melanie Klein. Rycroft, one of the most brilliant and subtle minds in the British Society, eventually quietly resigned from the British Society. Like Glover he had been, besides making his own original contributions, one of the most successful publicists on psychoanalytic subjects.

The unfortunate destruction of Glover's own psychoanalytic files and so many other of his personal papers means that it is unlikely that any much more comprehensively satisfactory biographical presentation of Glover as a pioneering figure can ever be possible. But the liveliness of what I hope I have been able to present from my interviews with him will, I hope, when combined with the documentation I came up with, help ensure that he survives in the general tale of the development of the depth psychology associated with Freud's name. Until now Glover has been the object of far too much scapegoating connected to his role in the struggle over Klein within British psychoanalysis. Glover has been "the subject of obloquy, and finally a man left professionally isolated and out in the cold."[4] He did get an L.L.D. from the University of Glasgow in 1956, and was an honorary fellow of the British Psychological Association. But his "great professional isolation" did exist, and was "handled with the same quiet dignity and lack of complaint which he showed in every aspect of his personal life."[5]

In addition to all the other unfortunately one-dimensional accounts of Glover, it has recently been proposed that "regrettably, Edward Glover, a great figure on other counts, played a destructive role in ... [the] crisis" occasioned by the Freud–Klein controversy during World War II. Even if it is true that Klein had helped establish "relatedness as central to life," by "promoting a view of human beings that was radically different from that of Freud," one would expect substantial controversy. It should indeed be so that "psychoanalysis thrives on arguments of whatever quality."[6] But it is not enough to ignore the merits of what Glover was trying to say and how far-seeing, about the problem of training analyses for example, he could be. If there was a "trial atmosphere" in London, it would hardly be the first time in the history of psychoanalysis. The crisis precipitated by Freud over Adler's ideas before World War I was even more of a trial.[7] And it does not seem to me fair to summarize the tone of the interventions of Anna Freud and others as having been "nothing if not inquisitional." Nor would it be adequate to conflate "the diatribes of Glover and Melitta Schmideberg."[8]

Seeing Glover as a fallible human being, caught in the midst of forces which were beyond his capacity to control, should make the dilemma of his situation more humanly compelling. By his resignation (although he chose to stay within the IPA) he was willing to pay a price for his convictions. There was a limit to his fanaticism—he contested his beliefs through his writing rather than by training disciples. His personal success in surviving professionally is a tribute to his personal courage, and the successful reputation he continued to earn as a writer and clinician. The only remaining question is whether the long-standing polemics association with the Freud–Klein struggle can be surmounted enough so that Glover's historical individuality is allowed to emerge.

It sometimes seems as if the history of psychoanalysis consists only of a series of recurrent blow-ups, each of which plays a part in the general mythology about the story of the growth of psychoanalysis. I think that these well publicized, if still little understood, difficulties repeatedly have arisen because of an inadequate degree of normal give-and-take within psychoanalytic communities. For if differences of opinion were more of a commonplace matter, and people were encouraged to disagree without its involving stakes of personal friendship, loyalty, and, above all, transferences, then volcanic kinds of eruptions would be less likely to break out. But I realize that Glover might not have approved of my way of presenting him here. Perhaps he might have agreed that the peculiar insecurities implicit in the practice of psychoanalysis led to multiple false certitudes.

In order to have succeeded in intellectual history up until now, perhaps Glover had not been messianic enough; instead of just seeing him as malevolent over Klein, I am reminded how some of the most gentle figures in psychoanalysis have tended to be those who have been forgotten. It is schools of thought that get most easily remembered, and even minor individuals have been unduly elevated thanks to their association with successful streams of thought or triumphant bureaucratic organizations. Glover's own fascination with deviance meant that some of Glover's writing was "marred by an acerbic and vehement quality which often brimmed over into contempt." We "can learn . . . some things to try to avoid: to wit, his fundamentalism in certain areas of his work, and his authoritarianism, which ended up stifling the movement and flow of ideas, and against which people rebelled."⁹ In his uncompromisingness Glover got hoisted in his own petard. But Glover's having become a victim of his own belief in the merits of intolerance does not mean that we should perpetuate that sort of belligerence. In a sense, with the isolation of his last years, he had reaped what he had sown.

There are abundant ironies, as well as exaggerations, associated with the original struggle over Kleinianism in Britain. I am not sure that the distinctions between the theoretical positions of Glover and Anna Freud, as contrasted with that of the Kleinians, were always sound and down-to-earth enough. As a matter of fact, like James Strachey I think that both sides in this dispute were almost equally theological. If I had to pick one over the other, and I would only do so with the greatest reluctance, I would probably steer clear of the Kleinian position, for her concepts were too often in principle unverifiable, and she was throughout this contest engaged in a substantial power move. (An observer noted of Klein: "Like her opponent Edward Glover, in everyday life she was mild mannered but again like Glover when roused she became a different person."¹⁰ In print intellectuals are capable of seeming vicious.)

Both Klein and Glover had the flaws of their certainties; Glover had unusual powers of exposition, while she was able to get others to do it for her. In hindsight both of them appear too sure of themselves. But I believe I know something of how admired Klein was as a therapist and how fruitful her concepts have proven to be in enlivening psychoanalytic thinking, and in adding a needed correction to psychoanalysis as Freud originally conceived it. She was, for example, able to make religious feelings more understandable than earlier psychoanalytic thinking would have permitted. A passage about Klein from Virginia Woolf's diary is worth quoting: "A woman of character, & force & some submerged—how shall I say—not craft, but subtlety: something working underground. A pull, a twist, like an undertow: menacing. A bluff, grey-haired lady, with large, bright, imaginative eyes."¹¹

My personal reaction is mainly colored by what I take to have been the editorial stacking of the deck for Klein throughout, for example, *The Freud–Klein Controversies*. To take a small example, when Anna Freud presented a paper on May 5, 1943, before the British Society, we are not even told the title of her presentation. Critiques of Kleinianism too often go unmentioned in the text. To repeat what I mentioned at the outset: Glover's own 1945 "Examination of the Klein System of Child Psychology" gets ignored in the bibliography (even though Kleinian formal papers presented during the Controversial Discussions, amended or not later, get cited in the form of their subsequent publication). And only pro-Klein literature after the 1940s gets listed. One has to assume that psychoanalytic religiosity lies behind such partisan editorializing; the ambitiousness of Klein's objectives, in relative contrast to those of Freud, is in itself memorable. To the extent that psychoanalysis and its history is centrally concerned with rival conceptions of what people ideally might be like, and the objectives they should pursue, then there is reason to think that the confrontation that took place in the Controversial Discussions will endure as an interesting aspect of intellectual history. But I am hoping that Edward Glover's name will in the future be less likely to be the subject of partisan abuse, and the singularity of his career and ideas be more broadly appreciated.

I have to wonder whether it could be that the mixture of motives I have seen in Glover—private generosity combined with public tenacity, and political weakness expressing itself as tactical blunders—can be also seen in other participants in different psychoanalytic struggles, even ones more famous than that of the Controversial Discussions. It would not be the first time in the history of ideological squabbling that tender human qualities get somehow associated with doctrinaire commitments. One social anthropologist at the London School of Economics thought Glover, whom he knew in the 1950s and 1960s, was in a perpetually combative mode, and compared him to a Presbyterian minister preaching hellfire and damnation.

In an interview Ronald D. Laing commented:

> You should read a paper by Edward Glover which is a virulent denunciation, a sustained denunciation of Melanie Klein's theory, claiming that it was a secular re-done-up version of the old Calvinist and Augustinian Christian doctrine of original sin. He said we had

gone back to the constitution of genetic original sin with her idea of constitutional envy. It was against the evidence, there was no warrant for it in psychoanalytic experience, and it was a complete projection of her mind. However, even if it was projected onto hapless infants, she did project a remarkable personal world view, which had some profundity about it. It might be profoundly psychotic or profoundly odd but it was of a serious engaging interest to anyone who was interested in that sort of thing.[12]

The lessons from studying the history of psychoanalysis may lead to a form of skepticism that questions all zealotry in the humanistic sciences. An appreciation of these sorts of complexities should promote less partisanship and polemicizing, about others as well as Glover. I am afraid that my argument implies that some compassion is in order even for ideologues and heresy hunters.

At home Glover loved savoring the pleasures of good wine, and once he and his wife Gladys had been "addicted" theatergoers. He took fine writing and great literature for granted. In 1934 he once suggested handing medical students over to "those masters of intuitive psychology whose discoveries have been set out in an imperishable form in the literature of this and other lands."

> Ella Sharpe once suggested that all psychoanalytic students should be fully conversant with, amongst many other masterpieces, the tale of the *Three Blind Mice*. . . . A good grounding in the stories of the Tin Soldier or Rumpelstiltzkin or the Sleeping Beauty will do more to initiate the student into the mental functioning and phobias of early latency than a formal study of the "acquired habits" of writing and knitting.
>
> With this grounding he may advantageously go on to read Thomas Mann or D. H. Lawrence in order to gain some insight into the fixation processes of girls and boys respectively, fixation processes which will be his active concern from the first day he enters a psychological out-patient department. For more precise clinical studies let him turn to, shall we say, Forster, for hysteria; Hamsun, sometimes Proust, for obsessional states; Thomas Mann, for unconscious male homosexuality; Hamsun, or better still

Meredith, for some of the finest studies in character pathology. When he comes to orient himself in borderline states or actual psychoses the range is even wider: Cronin on paranoia; or Richardson; or Dovstoievsky on epileptic insanity. Should taste and tradition limit him to earlier masterpieces, let him study the borderline psychoses described by Shakespeare through the mouthpiece of Hamlet or Richard II or Macbeth or Lear.[13]

Glover confessed privately that his pleasure in Shakespeare had been marred by too early school drilling. Toward the end of Glover's life a younger friend of his (Dr. Paul Byers) would take light literature out of the libraries, several books a week, so that Glover would have something to relax with at night. We have seen enough examples of Glover's own capacities as a writer to appreciate his sensibilities and talents. (By accident we know from a letter to Glover's executors that a former patient had been the American writer William March, and that his novel *The Tallons* had been dedicated to Glover.) Writing is an exquisitely autocratic pursuit, beyond the capacities of some of the most sensitive and empathic psychologists.

But Glover was also a rare form of psychoanalyst who had trouble getting his patients, even rich ones, to pay their bills. His rather beat-up cars were given to him by the husband of an ex-patient for services rendered. (He left a modest estate of £23,000, which was to take care of Ann, who first went to a niece of Glover's and later died in a facility. The malice of ideological politics about Glover would be hard to top; Klein's biographer flat-footedly told the public: "Many analysts have commented on his seeming refusal ever to accept that there was anything wrong with the child, and she accompanied him even to international congresses."[14]) He remained modest about his attainments, and could claim toward the end of his life that he was "decidedly *not* 'world famous,' or if I am, that is due to the world's lack of judgment.... I am just a competent Scottish peasant ... masquerading as a professional scientist and therefore always busily engaged in concealing my ignorance."[15]

Above all I am trying to contend in attempting to describe Glover that humaneness deserves its central place in intellectual history. I have not tried to rescue Glover from a kind of oblivion in order to blacken others with blame. Jones, for instance, may have been justly criticized lately: "the only way he could stand his ground against Freud was on behalf of someone else's supposed originality—that of Melanie Klein."[16] But Jones is the one person who can be credited with having created British psychoanalysis; it might be sentimentalist to think that he could have accomplished that objective without iron determination and single-mindedness of purpose. And Jones—knowledge of whose pack of troubles with women before his final successful marriage first made him humanly sympathetic to me—had been courageous in rescuing Freud and his entourage from Vienna, and in coping with his own final illness. Jones's biography of Freud, no matter how tendentious it has proven to be, did more to enhance the study of the history of psychoanalysis than any other work aside from Strachey's *Standard Edition* of Freud's psychological works.

Reinstating Glover may inevitably serve to tilt the scales of historical justice against others. But in keeping with the objective of trying to look sympathetically at events from the points of view of all the participants that were involved: Melitta Schmideberg could feel rightly put upon by her unusual upbringing; Melanie Klein understandably felt threatened and unappreciated; Freud's daughter Anna was legitimately offended by how those who claimed to be her father's intellectual heirs were capable of offhandedly treating her; Adrian Stephen, put upon by his sisters and his wife, had momentarily been able to assert himself in the fight within the British Society. And so on. The conflict that took place during the Controversial Discussions does now seem an unavoidable one. Every biographer, other than traitorous ones, becomes a kind of advocate, and my central purpose is to try to extend charity toward Glover's final predicament entailed by the world around him as well as his inescapable contradictions.

Paul Byers, a medical colleague who was close to Glover, happened to stop by his flat during the final days of Gladys's illness; she was terribly sick, also incontinent, and Glover so dutifully caring for her that Byers could not stand it and marched to the telephone and ordered an ambulance to take her immediately to hospital. The obituary of Glover in the *British Journal of Criminology* accurately highlighted how he had a "manifestly loving and caring quality as a husband and father."[17] (Glover wrote a pack of almost grandfatherly letters to Byers and his wife.) According to the *Times* obituary, Glover had in his student days helped put forward the name of the socialist Keir Hardie as Lord Rector of Glasgow, and later Glover kept a "fatherly eye" on undergraduate socialists.[18] People are capable of encapsulating inside themselves wide inconsistencies, and in Glover this meant what looks like almost a double personality encompassing his many kindnesses with his occasional fervors. The historical evidence will not sustain the glib generalizations about Glover's character that have appeared so often in the literature. I am proposing this thesis even though it conflicts with the received Family Romance among British analysts, which concentrates on linking Klein's ideas to Abraham.

History is too often written solely from the perspective of the immediate victors. Kubie credited Glover with being an advocate of "vigorous heterodoxy,"[19] and such informed dissent added a special dimension to the history of psychoanalytic ideas. Those whom Glover wounded intellectually—Jungians as well as Kleinians—still wince at what he did. But these systems, if they deserve to survive, should be able to withstand the most rigorous scrutiny.

Scholars should not take ideological sides in history, except in maintaining the purpose of broadening and enhancing our awareness. I doubt that Freud, or Glover, with their respective fighting spirits would agree with the standpoint that I consider appropriate at the beginning of the twenty-first century. But the future of toleration in psychoanalysis cannot be enhanced by upholding the kind of mythology that has been polemically associated with Glover's name. The creators of any original system of thought, and their immediate disciples, may be entitled to the one-sidedness necessary to implement their ideas. The clashes that have taken place in the history of psychoanalysis can be seen as part of the genuine vitality of this system of thought. But it is important that as students of the life of the mind we do nothing to fan the flames of intolerance, but instead try to come as close as possible to the standard of impartiality that we know ahead of time we will be incapable of accomplishing.

Toleration should not be considered a reflection of any lack of intellectual ability, or incapacity to choose between alternatives, but rather can become an energizing ideal in its own right. Freud's legacy can be interpreted to mean that the deepest truths about human beings come from the closest possible examination of life as it has been experienced, and it is in that spirit that I am offering what I have been able to understand about Edward Glover. The judgment of Frances Partridge, the last survivor of the old Bloomsbury group who put in her diary that she had found Glover "charming,"[20] deserves being remembered. Freud taught us how little we understand about ourselves, which should also imply that others can be even more mysterious.

Notes

INTRODUCTION

1. For instance, see Frederick C. Crews, *The Memory Wars: Freud's Legacy in Dispute* (New York: A New York Review Book, 1995) and Frederick C. Crews, ed., *Unauthorized Freud: Doubters Confront A Legend* (New York: Viking, 1998).

2. Edward Glover, *The Technique of Psychoanalysis* (New York: International Universities Press, 1955); Edward Glover, *Freud or Jung?* (New York: Meridian Books, 1956; reprinted, with a Foreword by James William Anderson, Evanston, Illinois: Northwestern University Press, 1991). Other books by Glover include: *War, Sadism & Pacifism: Three Essays* (London: George Allen & Unwin, 1933); *Psycho-analysis: A Handbook for Medical Practitioners and Students of Comparative Psychology* (London: Staples Press, 1949); *On the Early Development of Mind: Selected Papers on Psychoanalysis*, Vol. 1 (New York: International Universities Press, 1956); *The Roots of Crime: Selected Papers on Psychoanalysis* (New York: International Universities Press, 1960); *The Birth of the Ego* (New York: International Universities Press, 1968); *The Psychology of Fear and Courage* (London: Allen Lane, 1940).

3. Phyllis Grosskurth, *Melanie Klein: Her World and Her Work* (New York: Knopf, 1986).

4. *The Freud-Klein Controversies 1941–45*, ed. Pearl King and Riccardo Steiner (London and New York: Tavistock/Routledge, 1991), pp. 680, 914.

5. Peter Rudnytsky, "Tough Morsels," *London Review of Books*, Nov. 7, 1991, p. 13.

6. John Forrester, "Freudian Power Struggles," *Times Literary Supplement*, July 12, 1991, p. 10.

7. Paul Roazen, "Book Review of *The Freud–Klein Controversies 1941–45*," *Psychoanalytic Books*, Fall 1992, pp. 391–398.

8. J. Zelmanowits, "Obituary: Edward Glover," *British Journal of Medical Psychology*, Vol. 46 (1973), p. 191; "In Memoriam," *British Journal of Criminology*, Vol. 13, No. 2 (April 1973), p. 86; *The Times*, Aug. 18 and 24, 1972. See also Paul D. Byers, "Edward Glover," *British Medical Journal*, Vol. 3 (1972), p. 534.

9. Interview with Sylvia Payne, Nov. 10, 1966.

10. See for example Hannah Segal, *Introduction to the Work of Melanie Klein* (London: Hogarth Press, 1973), and Hannah Segal, *Klein* (London: Fontana, 1979).

11. Lawrence Kubie, "Edward Glover," *Psychoanalytic Quarterly*, Vol. 38 (1969), p. 528.

12. Nicholas Wright, *Mrs. Klein* (London: Nick Hern Books, 1988), pp. 6, 47.

13. For a bibliography of Glover's writings, see *Psychoanalytic Quarterly*, Vol. 38 (1969), pp. 532–548.

14. Rudnytsky, *op. cit.*, p. 14.

1. AN OUTSIDER ON WIMPOLE STREET

1. C. G. Jung, *Letters*, Vol. II, ed. Gerhard Adler, translated R. F. C. Hull (Princeton: Princeton University Press, 1975), p. 31. I am grateful to James Anderson's edition of Glover's *Freud or Jung?* for bringing to my attention this letter of Jung's.

2. James William Anderson, "Foreword," *Freud or Jung?*, *op. cit.*, p. 6.

3. Frank McLynn, *Carl Gustav Jung* (New York: St. Martin's Press, 1996), p. 265.

4. Richard Noll, *The Jung Cult: Origins of a Charismatic Movement* (Princeton: Princeton University Press, 1994); Richard Noll, *The Aryan Christ: The Secret Life of Carl Jung* (New York: Random House, 1997); see in contrast Sonu Shamdasani, *Cult Fictions: C. G. Jung and the Founding of Analytic Psychology* (New York: Routledge, 1998).

5. See Edward Glover, "Psychoanalysis in England," in Franz Alexander, Samuel Eisenstein, and Martin Grotjahn, eds., *Psychoanalytic Pioneers* (New York: Basic Books, 1966), pp. 534–545; Edward Glover, "The Position of Psychoanalysis in Great Britain," in *On the Early Development of Mind*, *op. cit.*, pp. 352–363; Charles William Wahl, "Edward Glover: Theory of Technique," in *Psychoanalytic Pioneers*, *op. cit.*, pp. 501–507.

6. Paul Roazen, *Meeting Freud's Family* (Amherst, MA: University of Massachusetts Press, 1993).

7. Paul Roazen, *Freud: Political and Social Thought* (New York: Knopf, 1968; third edition, with new Introduction, New Brunswick, NJ: Transaction, 1999).

8. Paul Roazen, *Helene Deutsch: A Psychoanalyst's Life* (New York: Doubleday, 1985; with a New Introduction, New Brunswick, NJ: Transaction, 1992), pp. 254–255.

9. *The Diary of Sigmund Freud 1929–39*, ed. Michael Molnar (New York: Scribner's, 1992), p. 276.

10. Glover to Mrs. Thelma Lebeaux, Oct. 18, 1965.

11. Glover to Mrs. Thelma Lebeaux, Feb. 20, 1967.

12. Glover to Laurence S. Kubie, April 21, 1968.

13. Glover to Mrs. Thelma Lebeaux, Feb. 20, 1967.

14. Glover to Mrs. Thelma Lebeaux, Jan. 19, 1966.

15. Lawrence S. Kubie, "Edward Glover: A Biographical Sketch," *International Journal of Psycho-Analysis*, Vol. 54 (1973), p. 85.

16. Paul Roazen, *How Freud Worked: First-Hand Accounts of Patients* (Northvale, NJ: Jason Aronson, 1995), Ch. 9.

17. Edward Glover to Lawrence S. Kubie, March 6, 1968.

18. Edward Glover to Lawrence S. Kubie, April 16, 1968.

19. Kubie, "Edward Glover: A Biographical Sketch," p. 91.

20. Edward Glover, *The Technique of Psychoanalysis* (New York: International Universities Press, 1955), p. 24.

21. Glover to Mrs. Thelma Lebeaux, Oct. 18, 1965.

22. Edward Glover, "Introduction," *A Psychoanalytic Dialogue: The Letters of Sigmund Freud and Karl Abraham*, ed. Hilda C. Abraham and Ernst L. Freud, translated by Bernard Marsh (pseudonym) and Hilda C. Abraham (New York: Basic Books, 1965), pp. ix–xvi.

23. See Susan Quinn, *A Mind of Her Own: The Life of Karen Horney* (New York: Summit Books, 1987); Bernard J. Paris, *Karen Horney: A Psychoanalyst's Search for Self-Understanding* (New Haven: Yale University Press, 1994).

24. Paul Roazen, *Freud and His Followers* (New York: Knopf, 1975; New York: Da Capo, 1992), Parts V–VI.

25. C. P. Oberndorf, *A History of Psychoanalysis in America* (New York: Grune & Stratton, 1953).

26. Interview with Dr. Abram Kardiner, Oct. 12, 1965.

27. K. R. Eissler's Interviews with Franz Alexander (Library of Congress).

28. Paul Roazen, "Review of Cooper's *Speak of Me As I Am: The Life and Work of Masud Khan*," *Psychoanalytic Books*, Spring 1995.

29. Roazen, *Freud and His Followers*, pp. 378–381; see also Lavinia Edmunds, "His Master's Choice," *Johns Hopkins Magazine* (April 1988), pp. 40–49.

30. Paul Roazen, "Tragedy in America," *Clinical Studies*, 1999.

31. Alexander Etkind, *Eros of the Impossible: The History of Psychoanalysis in Russia*, translated by Noah and Maria Rubins (Boulder, CO: Westview Press, 1997), p. 382.

32. Edward Glover, "Psycho-analysis and Psychotherapy," *British Journal of Medical Psychology*, Vol. 33 (1960), pp. 73–82.

33. *The Technique of Child Analysis: Discussions with Anna Freud*, Joseph Sandler, Hansi Kennedy, and Robert Tyson (Cambridge, MA: Harvard University Press, 1980), pp. 70, 96, 111.

34. Edward Glover, "Psycho-analysis and Psychotherapy," p. 80.

35. See Glover, *The Technique of Psychoanalysis*, pp. 353–366. Also, Malcolm Pines, *Circular Reflections: Selected Papers on Group Psychoanalysis* (London: Jessica Kingsley, 1998), p. 143.

36. *The Correspondence of Sigmund Freud and Sandor Ferenczi*, Vol. I, *1908–14*, ed. Eva Brabant, Ernst Falzeder, and Patrizia Giampieri-Deutsch, translated by Peter T. Hoffer (Cambridge, MA: Harvard University Press, 1993), p. 489. See Paul Roazen, "Review of Vol. I of *The Correspondence of Freud and Ferenczi*," *The American Scholar*, Spring 1994; Paul Roazen, "Review of Vol. II of *The Correspondence of Freud and Ferenczi*," *The Psychohistory Review*, Winter 1998; Paul Roazen, "The Freud–Jones Letters," in *Behind the Scenes: Freud in Correspondence,* ed. Patrick Mahony, Carlo Bonomi, and Jan Stensson (Oslo: Scandinavian University Press, 1997), pp. 273–287. See Paul Roazen, *The Historiography of Psychoanalysis* (New Brunswick, NJ: Transaction, 2000), Part III.

37. Glover to Lawrence S. Kubie, November 17, 1969.

2. ERNEST JONES AS A LEADER

1. Interviews with Anne Geismar. See also A. A. Brill to Ernest Jones, May 24, 1930, July 9, 1930, Oct. 17, 1930, Sept. 24, 1931, Nov. 9, 1944, May 8, 1946.

2. Ernest Jones, "The Theory of Symbolism," in *Papers on Psychoanalysis*, Fifth Edition (Boston: Beacon Press, 1961), pp. 87–144.

3. *The Freud–Jung Letters*, ed. William McGuire, translated by Ralph Manheim and R. F. C. Hull (Princeton, NJ: Princeton University Press, 1974), pp. 145, 164; Elisabeth Young-Bruehl, *Anna Freud: A Biography* (New York: Summit Books, 1988), p. 171.

4. *The Complete Correspondence of Sigmund Freud and Ernest Jones*, ed. R. Andrew Paskauskas (Cambridge, MA: Harvard University Press, 1993), p. 61.

5. Lisa Appignanesi and John Forrester, *Freud's Women* (New York: Basic Books, 1992), p. 238; *The Complete Correspondence of Freud and Jones*, p. 491.

6. Carlo Bonomi, "Flight into Sanity: Jones's Allegation of Ferenczi's Mental Deterioration Reconsidered," *International Journal of Psycho-Analysis*, Vol. 80, Part 3 (June 1999), pp. 507–542.

7. Roazen, *How Freud Worked*; Roazen, *Freud and His Followers*, Part IV.

8. Roazen, *Freud and His Followers*, Part VI, Chs. 6–7.

9. *The Complete Correspondence of Freud and Jones*, p. 721.

10. *The Clinical Diary of Sandor Ferenczi*, ed. Judith Dupont, translated by Michael Balint and Nicola Zarday Jackson (Cambridge, MA: Harvard University Press, 1988); see Paul Roazen, "Review of *The Clinical Diary* of Sandor Ferenczi," *American Journal of Psychoanalysis*, Dec. 1990.

11. Interview with Dr. Smiley Blanton, Jan. 25, 1966.

12. *The Correspondence of Freud and Ferenczi*, Vol. I, p. 493.

13. Ernest Jones to Anna Freud, April 20, 1956 (Library of Congress).

14. Interview with Dr. J. R. Rees, Nov. 21, 1966.

15. Ernest Jones, "Hanns Sachs: Obituary," *International Journal of Psycho-Analysis*, Vol. 27 (1946).

16. Katherine Jones, "A Sketch of Ernest Jones's Personality," *International Journal of Psycho-Analysis,* Vol. 60 (1979), p. 271.

17. Interview with Rees.

18. Edward Glover, "Eder as Psychoanalyst," in *David Eder*, ed. J. B. Hobman (London: Gollancz, 1945), pp. 89–116.

19. *Letters of Sigmund Freud*, ed. Ernst L. Freud, translated by Tania and James Stern (New York: Basic Books, 1960), p. 427.

20. Ernest Jones, *Free Associations: Memoirs of a Psychoanalyst* (New York: Basic Books, 1959; New Brunswick, NJ:1 Transaction, 1990), p. 137.

21. Sigmund Freud, "Foreword," *David Eder*.

22. *The Complete Correspondence of Freud and Jones*, pp. 328, 331, 332, 335.

23. Erich Fromm, *Sigmund Freud's Mission* (New York: Harper, 1959), p. 65.

24. *The Complete Correspondence of Freud and Jones*, p. 416.

25. John C. Burnham, *Jelliffe: American Psychoanalyst and Physician* (Chicago: University of Chicago Press, 1983). See Paul Roazen, *Encountering Freud* (New Brunswick, NJ: Transaction, 1990), pp. 195–197.

26. Edward Glover, "In Praise of Ourselves," *International Journal of Psycho-Analysis*, Vo. 50, No. 4 (1969), p. 499.

27. R. D. Hinshelwood, "Psycho-analysis in Britain: Points of Cultural Access, 1893–1918," *International Journal of Psycho-Analysis*, Vol. 76 (1995), p. 140.

28. Ernest Jones, "James Glover," *International Journal of Psycho-Analysis*, Vol. 8 (Jan., 1927), p. 2.

29. Etkind, *Eros of the Impossible*, p. 205.

30. Jones, "James Glover," p. 3.

31. Ella Freeman Sharpe, *Dream Analysis: A Practical Handbook for Psychoanalysis* (London: Hogarth Press, 1937); Ella Freeman Sharpe, *Collected Papers on Psychoanalysis*, ed. Marjorie Brierley (London: Hogarth Press, 1950).

32. Athol Hughes, ed., *The Inner World of Joan Riviere: Collected Papers, 1920–58* (London: Karnac Books, 1991), pp. 5, 10.

33. Bruno Bettelheim, *Freud and Man's Soul* (New York: Knopf, 1982); see also Paul Roazen, "The Rise and Fall of Bruno Bettelheim," *Psychohistory Review*, Spring 1992.

34. James Strachey, "Joan Riviere: An Obituary," *International Journal of Psycho-Analysis*, Vol. 44 (1963), p. 230.

35. *The Complete Correspondence of Sigmund Freud and Ernest Jones*, p. 635.

36. Jean MacGibbon, *There's the Lighthouse: A Biography of Adrian Stephen* (London: James & James, 1997).

37. Karin Stephen, *The Wish to Fall Ill* (Cambridge: Cambridge University Press, 1933).

38. Phyllis Grosskurth, *Melanie Klein*, p. 289.

39. Robert Skidelsky, *John Maynard Keynes*, Vol. I, *Hopes Betrayed, 1883–1920* (New York: Penguin, 1994), p. 428.

40. Ernest Jones to A. A. Brill, March 7, 1927.

41. Maurice Walsh to Lawrence S. Kubie, July 17, 1972; Ernest Jones to A. A. Brill, Dec. 26, 1912.

42. See Ray Monk, *Ludwig Wittgenstein: The Duty of Genius* (London: Jonathan Cape, 1990).

43. *The Complete Correspondence of Sigmund Freud and Ernest Jones*, p. 491.

44. See Paul Roazen, "Review of Ornston's *Translating Freud*," *American Journal of Psychoanalysis*, June 1998, pp. 241–242. See also Roazen, *The Historiography of Psychoanalysis*, Part VIII.

45. Paul Roazen, *Helene Deutsch: A Psychoanalyst's Life, op. cit.*, pp. 212–213.

46. Paul Roazen and Bluma Swerdloff, *Heresy: Sandor Rado and the Psychoanalytic Movement* (Northvale, NJ: Jason Aronson, 1995), pp. 72, 75, 78, 94, 111, 151, 157, 164, 166, 167, 173.

47. Jones, *Free Associations*, p. 239.

48. Maurice W. Walsh, "The Scientific Works of Edward Glover," *International Journal of Psycho-Analysis*, Vol. 54 (1973), p. 98. See also, Ernest Jones, *The Life and Work of Sigmund Freud*, Vol. 3 (New York: Basic Books, 1957).

49. Bernard Hart, *The Psychology of Insanity*, 5th edition (Cambridge: Cambridge University Press, 1962).

3. THE CONTROVERSIAL DISCUSSIONS–I
"A NEW *WELTANSCHAUUNG*"?

1. Edward Glover, "An Examination of the Klein System of Child Psychology," reprinted from *The Psychoanalytic Study of the Child*, Vol. I (New York: International Universities Press, 1945). This reprint, brought out by The Southern Post, Ltd., replaced some omitted paragraphs and restored footnotes to the original placing. See also Edward Bibring, "The So-Called English School of Psychoanalysis," *Psychoanalytic Quarterly*, Vol. 16 (1947), pp. 69–93; Marjorie Brierley, "Problems Connected with the Work of Klein," in *Trends in Psychoanalysis* (London: Hogarth Press, 1951), pp. 57–89; Otto Kernberg, "A Contribution to the Ego-Psychological Critique of the Kleinian School," *International Journal of Psycho-Analysis*, Vol. 50 (1969), pp. 317–333; Ralph Greenson, "Transference: Freud or Klein," *International Journal of Psycho-Analysis*, Vol. 55 (1974); Clifford Yorke, "Some Suggestions for a Critique of Kleinian Psychology," *The Psychoanalytic Study of the Child*, Vol. 26 (New York: International Universities Press, 1971), pp. 129–155.

2. "On the History of the Psychoanalytic Movement," *Standard Edition*, Vol. 14, p. 66.

3. Roazen, *Freud and His Followers*, Part VIII; Paul Roazen, "Tola Rank," *Journal of the American Academy of Psychoanalysis*, Summer, 1990; See also Roazen, *The Historiography of Psychoanalysis*, Part V.

4. Glover, "An Examination of the Klein System of Child Psychology," pp. 31, 42, 43.

5. See, for example, J. C. Flugel, *The Psycho-analytic Study of the Family* (London: Hogarth Press, 1960); J. C. Flugel, *The Psychology of Clothes* (London: Hogarth Press, 1930); J. C. Flugel, *Man, Morals, and Society* (New York: Viking, 1961).

6. *Bloomsbury/Freud: The Letters of James and Alix Strachey, 1924–25*, ed. Perry Meisel and Walter Kendrick (New York: Basic Books, 1985), p. 294.

7. Riccardo Steiner, "Some Thoughts About Tradition and Change Arising from An Examination of the British Psychoanalytic Society's Controversial Discussions (1943–44)," *International Review of Psycho-Analysis*, Vol. 12 (1985), p. 46.

8. Grosskurth, *Melanie Klein*, p. 355.

9. Sylvia Payne to Melanie Klein, March 16, 1942 (Wellcome Institute).

10. Quoted in Grosskurth, *Melanie Klein*, p. 297.

11. Glover, "An Examination of the Klein System of Child Psychology," pp. 38, 43.

12. Quoted in Grosskurth, *Melanie Klein*, p. 354.

13. Grosskurth, *Melanie Klein*, p. 214.

14. Sylvia Payne to Anna Freud, May 26, 1966 (Library of Congress).

15. Grosskurth, *Melanie Klein*, p. 423.
16. *The Freud–Klein Controversies 1941–45*, pp. 93–94. See also Paul Roazen, "Review of *The Freud–Klein Controversies*."
17. Melitta Schmideberg, "A Contribution to the History of the Psychoanalytic Movement in Britain," *British Journal of Psychiatry*, Vol. 118 (Jan. 1971), p. 63. See also Francis Baudry, "Kohut and Glover: The Role of Subjectivity in Psychoanalytic Theory and Controversy," *The Psychoanalytic Study of the Child*, Vol. 53 (New Haven: Yale University Press, 1998), p. 16.
18. *The Freud–Klein Controversies*, p. xix.
19. Pearl King, "Melitta Schmideberg," *International Dictionary of Psychoanalysis*, ed. Alain Mijolla, in press.
20. Quoted in Grosskurth, *Melanie Klein*, p. 343.
21. Letter from Sylvia Payne to Melanie Klein, March 30, 1942 (Wellcome Institute).
22. Letter from Sylvia Payne to Anna Freud.
23. Quoted in Young-Bruehl, *Anna Freud*, p. 260.
24. See Paul Roazen, "Review of Sandler, Kennedy, and Tyson, *The Technique of Child Analysis: Discussions with Anna Freud*," *Journal of the History of the Behavioral Sciences*, July 1991.
25. *The Freud–Klein Controversies*, p. 85.
26. Ibid., pp. 32–33.
27. Glover, "An Examination of the Klein System of Child Psychology," pp. 18, 42.
28. See R. D. Hinshelwood, "The Elusive Concept of 'Internal Objects' (1934–1943): Its Role in the Formation of the Klein Group," *International Journal of Psycho-Analysis*, Vol. 78 (1997), pp. 877–897.
29. Schmideberg, "A Contribution to the History of the Psycho-analytic Movement in Britain," p. 66. See Roazen, *Freud and His Followers*, pp. 478–488.
30. *The Freud–Klein Controversies*, p. xiii.
31. Young-Bruehl, *Anna Freud*, p. 269.
32. Clifford Yorke, "Freud Or Klein: Conflict Or Compromise," *International Journal of Psycho-Analysis*, Vol. 75 (1994), p. 383.
33. Jean MacGibbon, *There's the Lighthouse*, pp. 158–159, 161–162.

4. THE CONTROVERSIAL DISCUSSIONS–II
"DOUBLE-BARRELLED TRAINING"

1. See Roazen, *Freud and His Followers*, Part IX, Chs. 1–2; Paul Roazen, "Review of Rank, *A Psychology of Difference*, ed. Robert Kramer, *Journal of the History of the Behavioral Sciences*, Winter 1998.
2. *The Complete Correspondence of Sigmund Freud and Ernest Jones*, p. 579.
3. Ibid.

4. *Ibid.*, pp. 619–620.
5. *Ibid.*, pp. 624, 633, 641, 743. See "Civilization and Its Discontents," *Standard Edition*, Vol. 21, pp. 130, 138.
6. *The Freud–Klein Controversies*, p. 690.
7. Riccardo Steiner, "Some Thoughts About Tradition and Change Arising from an Examination of the British Psychoanalytic Society's Controversial Discussions," pp. 40, 46.
8. Joan Riviere, ed., *Developments in Psycho-analysis* (London: Hogarth Press, 1952).
9. Grosskurth, *Melanie Klein*, p. 433.
10. *The Freud–Klein Controversies*, p. 100.
11. Richard Wright, in Richard Crossman, *The God That Failed* (New York: Bantam Books, 1950), p. 150.
12. Paul Roazen and Bluma Swerdloff, *Heresy: Sandor Rado and the Psychoanalytic Movement*, p. 156.
13. MacGibbon, *There's the Lighthouse*, p. 151.
14. Quoted in Grosskurth, *Melanie Klein*, p. 256; Rudnytsky, "Tough Morsels," p. 13.
15. Pearl H. King, "The Life and Work of Melanie Klein in the British Psychoanalytic Society," *International Journal of Psycho-Analysis*, Vol. 64 (1983), p. 257.
16. William Gillespie, "Ernest Jones: The Bonnie Fighter," *International Journal of Psycho-Analysis*, Vol. 60 (1979), p. 278.
17. Vincent Brome, *Ernest Jones: Freud's Alter Ego* (London: Caliban Books, 1982), p. 208.
18. *Ibid.*, p. 202.
19. Ernest Jones to A. A. Brill, Oct. 17, 1930.
20. Eve Saville, with David Rumney, *"Let Justice Be Done!": A History of the I.S.T.D.* (London: Institute for the Study and Treatment of Delinquency, 1992), p. 4.
21. *Ibid.*, p. 36.
22. *Ibid.*, p. 49.
23. Christopher Cordess, "Pioneers in Forensic Psychiatry. Edward Glover (1888–1972): Psychoanalysis and Crime—A Fragile Legacy," *Journal of Forensic Psychiatry*, Vol. 3, No. 3 (1992), p. 519.
24. *Ibid.*, pp. 509–530.
25. "In Memoriam: Edward Glover," *British Journal of Criminology*, p. 88.
26. Edward Glover, *Basic Mental Concepts* (London: Imago Publishing Co., 1947).
27. Francis Braudy, "Revisiting the Freud–Klein Controversies Fifty Years Later," *International Journal of Psycho-Analysis*, Vol. 75 (1994), p. 372.

28. Helen Walker Puner, *Freud: His Life and Mind* (New Brunswick, NJ: Transaction, 1992).

5. FREUD IN EXILE AND TECHNIQUE

1. Geoffrey Cocks, *Teaching Mind and Body: Essays in the History of Science, Professions, and Society Under Extreme Conditions* (New Brunswick, NJ: Transaction, 1998), p. 98.
2. Melitta Schmideberg, "A Contribution to the History of the Psychoanalytic Movement in Britain," p. 64.
3. Paul Roazen, *Meeting Freud's Family*, p. 62.
4. Helene Deutsch, "Control Analysis," in Helene Deutsch, *The Therapeutic Process, The Self, and Female Psychology*, ed. Paul Roazen, translated by Eric Mosbacher and others (New Brunswick, NJ: Transaction, 1992), pp. 239, 246; see "Introduction," pp. liii–lvii.
5. Roazen, *Freud and His Followers*, pp. 272–276.
6. "In Memoriam: Edward Glover," p. 88.
7. Kubie, "Edward Glover: A Biographical Sketch," p. 86.
8. Paul Roazen, *Erik H. Erikson: The Power and Limits of a Vision* (New York: Free Press, 1976; Northvale, NJ: Jason Aronson, 1997), pp. 70–72, 182, 191.
9. Esther Menaker, *Appointment in Vienna: An American Psychoanalyst Recalls Her Student Days in Pre-War Austria* (NewYork: St. Martin's Press, 1989), p. 18.
10. Quoted in Roazen, *Freud and His Followers*, p. 273.
11. *The Freud/Jung Letters*, ed. William McGuire, translated by Ralph Manheim and R.F.C. Hull (Princeton: Princeton University Press, 1974), pp. 534–535.
12. Celia Bertin, *Marie Bonaparte: A Life* (New York: Harcourt Brace, 1982), p. 176.
13. "The Interpretation of Dreams," *Standard Edition*, Vol. 4, p. 142.
14. Henri Ellenberger, "The Story of 'Anna O.': A Critical Review With New Data," in *Beyond the Unconscious: Essays of Henri Ellenberger in the History of Psychiatry*, ed. Mark S. Micale (Princeton: Princeton University Press, 1993), Ch. 9.
15. Roazen and Swerdloff, *Heresy: Sandor Rado and the Psychoanalytic Movement*.
16. Pines, *Circular Reflections*, p. 188.
17. Edward Glover, "Some Recent Trends in Psychoanalytic Theory," *Psychoanalytic Quarterly*, Vol. 30, No. 1 (1961), pp. 86–107.
18. Edward Glover, "Freudian or Neo-Freudian," *Psychoanalytic Quarterly*, Vol. 33 (1964), pp. 97–109.

6. STAR PUPIL: DR. LAWRENCE S. KUBIE

1. Lawrence S. Kubie, *Neurotic Distortion of the Creative Process* (New York: Noonday Press, 1961); Lawrence S. Kubie, *Practical and Theoretical Aspects of Psychoanalysis* (New York: International Universities Press, 1950); Lawrence S. Kubie, *Symbol and Neurosis: Selected Papers* (New York: International Universities Press, 1978).

2. Lawrence S. Kubie, "Edward Glover: A Biographical Sketch," *International Journal of Psycho-Analysis, op. cit.*

3. Edward Glover, "In Honor of Lawrence Kubie," *Journal of Nervous and Mental Disease*, Vol. 149, No. 1 (1969), pp. 5–18.

4. Nathan J. Hale, Jr., *The Rise and Crisis of Psychoanalysis in the U.S.: Freud and the Americans, 1917–85* (New York: Oxford University Press, 1995), p. 137.

5. *Ibid.*, p. 138.

6. Lawrence S. Kubie, "The Independent Institute," *Bulletin of the American Psychoanalytic Institute*, Vol. 8, No. 2 (May, 1952), pp. 205–208; Lawrence S. Kubie, "The Pros and Cons of a New Profession: A Doctorate in Medical Psychology," *Texas Reports on Biology and Medicine*, Vol. 12 (1954), pp. 692–737.

7. Paul Roazen, *Canada's King: An Essay in Political Psychology* (Oakville, Ontario: Mosaic Press, 1998), Ch. 2.

8. Edward Glover to Lawrence S. Kubie, Nov. 11, 1930.

9. *Ibid.*

10. Lawrence S. Kubie to Edward Glover, Feb. 17, 1932.

11. Edward Glover to Lawrence S. Kubie, April 5, 1932.

12. Edward Glover to Lawrence S. Kubie, June 6, 1933.

13. Lawrence S. Kubie to Edward Glover, July 18, 1933.

14. Lawrence S. Kubie to Helene Deutsch, June 15, 1933.

15. *PM*, Sunday, Dec. 1, 1940.

16. Eric Rayner, *The Independent Mind in British Psychoanalysis* (London: Free Association Books, 1990), pp. 19, 30.

17. *Ibid.*, p. 259.

18. Edward Glover to Lawrence S. Kubie, May 16, 1946.

19. Kurt R. Eissler, "The Chicago Institute of Psychoanalysis and the 6th Period of the Development of Psychoanalytic Technique," *Journal of General Psychology*, Vol. 42, First Half (Jan. 1950), pp. 103–157. See also Paul Roazen, "The Tausk Problem," in *Encountering Freud: The Politics and Histories of Psychoanalysis* (New Brunswick, NJ: Transaction, 1990), pp. 95–119.

20. Hale, *op. cit.*, p. 252.

21. Lawrence S. Kubie to Edward Glover, May 1, 1968.

22. Edward Glover, *The Birth of the Ego: A Nuclear Hypothesis* (New York: International Universities Press, 1968), p. 14.

23. Edward Glover to Lawrence S. Kubie, Oct. 3, 1968.
24. Edward Glover to Lawrence S. Kubie, June 29, 1969.
25. Reuben Fine, *The History of Psychoanalysis*, new expanded edition (NewYork: Continuum, 1990).

EPILOGUE

1. Dieter Wyss, *Depth Psychology: A Critical History* (London: George Allen & Unwin, 1966), p. 191.
2. "In Memoriam: Edward George Glover," *British Journal of Criminology*, Vol. 13, No. 2 (April 1973), p. 90.
3. Cordess, *op. cit.*, p. 516.
4. *Ibid.*, p. 515.
5. Lawrence S. Kubie, "Edward Glover: Biographical Sketch," p. 92.
6. Roy Schafer, "One Perspective on the Freud–Klein Controversies 1941–45," *International Journal of Psycho-Analysis*, Vol. 75 (1994), pp. 359–365.
7. Paul Roazen, *Freud and His Followers*, Part V.
8. Roy Shafer, "One Perspective on the Freud–Klein Controversies 1941–45."
9. Cordess, *op. cit.*, pp. 523, 527.
10. Vincent Brome, *Ernest Jones*, p. 208.
11. Quoted in Jean MacGibbon, *There's the Lighthouse*, p. 150.
12. Bob Mullan, *Mad To Be Normal: Conversations with R. D. Laing* (London: Free Association Books, 1995), p. 161.
13. Edward Glover, "Medical Psychology Or Academic (Normal) Psychology: A Problem in Orientation," *British Journal of Medical Psychology*, Vol. 14 (1934), p. 45.
14. Grosskurth, p. 197.
15. Glover to Mrs. Thelma Lebeaux, Feb. 20, 1967.
16. Adam Phillips, "The Unimportance of Being Ernest," *London Review of Books*, August 5, 1993, p. 10.
17. "In Memoriam," *British Journal of Criminology*, p. 86.
18. "Obituary of Edward Glover," *The Times*.
19. Kubie, "Edward Glover: Biographical Sketch," p. 93.
20. Frances Partridge, *Everything to Lose* (London, Gollancz, 1985), p. 55.

Acknowledgments

I am grateful to the following people for their kindnesses in critically reading an earlier draft of the manuscript of this book: Dr. James W. Anderson, Dr. Robert G. Andry, Rosemary Dinnage, Dr. André Green, Dr. André E. Haynal, Dr. Robert D. Hinshelwood, Dr. Linda B. Hopkins, Dr. A. E. Hughes, Dr. Peter Lomas, Dr. Malcolm Pines, Dr. Eric Rayner, and Professor Michael P. Rogin. Mrs. Thelma Lebeaux was kind enough to send me copies of Glover's many letters to her. I am also indebted for the chance to talk recently with the following people: Adrian Arnold, Dr. Paul Byers, Professor David Downes, Dr. William Gillespie, Dr. Mervin Glasser, Dr. Robert Hale, Mrs. Robert Hinshelwood, Pearl King, Sarah Miller, Professor Terence Morris, Sonu Shamdasani, Professor J. E. Hall Williams, and Dr. Clifford Yorke. Professor Lawrence J. Friedman was kind enough to send me copies of two letters I needed from the Wellcome Trust in London. Jill Duncan and Riccardo Steiner cooperatively facilitated my use of material from the archives of the British Psychoanalytic Society; Michael Molnar helpfully came up with documents from the Freud Museum; Henry Cohen was a critical help to me in connection with the Glover–Kubie and Glover–Jelliffe correspondences at the Library of Congress; Dr. Daisy de Saugy, Archivist of the Swiss Psychoanalytic Society, did her best to try to help me track down the files of Dr. Philipp Sarasin; Dr. Nellie Thompson at the Brill Library of the New York Psychoanalytic Institute answered the questions I had; and Marvin Kranz and Fred Bauman facilitated my work in the Manuscript Room of the Library of Congress. At the Centre for Crime and Justice Studies at King's College, London, I had critical help about the history of the ISTD from Una Padel, Shirley Anderson, and Julie Grogan. Now that I have moved back to Cambridge, Massachusetts, it is a pleasure once again to be regularly relying on the facilities at Harvard's Widener Library, and those of the Boston Psychoanalytic Society. For me it has proved true that living away from Boston has been one way of getting to appreciate the comforts of home.

Index

Abraham, H., 17
Abraham, K., 20, 28, 112, 116
    and Freud, 16–17, 26
    and Glover, 10, 15
    influence of, 15–16
    and Klein, 54
Active therapy, 120
Adler, A., 18, 46, 101
Alexander, F., 20–21, 137–138
    Glover's criticism of, 109–111, 129
    and Glover's resignation from British Psychoanalytic Society, 158–163
American Psychoanalytic Association, 105, 131
    Glover's membership in, 149–150, 155
American Psychoanalytic Society, Glover as honorary member of, 12
Army psychiatrists, Glover's criticism of, 77–78

Balint, M., 27
"Basic Mental Concepts" (Glover), 104
Berlin Psychoanalytic Institute, 15, 21
Bernfeld, S., 40
Bibring, E., 105
Birth Theory, 75, 80
Blanton, S., 123
Bloomsbury group, 35–36, 38–40
Blumgart, L., 145
Boehm, F., 127
Bonaparte, M. (Princess of Greece), 92, 95, 125–126
Bowlby, J., 49, 151
Breuer, J., 126
Brierley, M., 83–84, 127
Brill, A. A., 21, 24, 93, 152
Britain, 103
    distinctiveness of psychoanalysis in, 9, 108
    emphasis on neurology in, 18, 20
    Glover consider emigrating from, 152–155
    psychoanalysis in, 36, 47, 130
    psychoanalytic training in, 116–117
    Viennese psychoanalysts in, 62–63, 86, 114–115

British Journal of Criminology, 42, 101–102
   Glover's obituary in, 175–176
British Journal of Delinquency, 101–102
British Psychoanalytic Institute, 38–39
British Psychoanalytic Society, 31, 95, 112
   and Anna Freud, 95–100, 114–115, 150–151
   criticism of Glover's resignation from, 109–110, 158–163
   divisiveness in, 18, 28–30, 42, 84
   effects of Glover's resignation from, 147, 168
   factions within, 62, 82–83
   gender in divisiveness of, 56, 82
   on Glover addressing Conference of European Psychoanalysts, 88–90
   Glover as deputy President of, 55–56, 146–147
   Glover not trying to split, 74–75, 84
   Glover's resignation from, 12, 64–65, 71–72, 74, 78, 107–108, 121–122, 145
   Glover's role in referrals within, 50–51
   Jones as President of, 82, 90–91, 93
   Jones's role in, 23–43, 47, 148
   Kleinians *vs.* Freudians in, 51–53, 62–65, 81–83, 86, 168
   members of, 10–12
   officers of, 85, 88, 107, 146–147
   and publication of Controversial Discussions, 106–108
   response to split over Klein's doctrines, 72–73, 76–77
   role of training in schisms within, 67–71
British Society of Criminology, 103

Brunswick, R. M., 79
Bullitt, W. C., 55
Burlingham, D., 87
Byers, P., 175–176

Canada, job opportunities for Glover in, 152–154
Centre for Crime and Justice Studies (King's College), 104
Chadwick, M., 33–34
Chemical substances, for therapy, 151
Child psychoanalysis, 34, 58–59
Children, psychosis in, 48
Civilization and Its Discontents (Freud), 81
Cole, E., 127
Committee, of British Psychoanalytic Society, 25–26
Committee of Research (IPA), 105
Conference of European Psychoanalysts, 88–89, 104
Connolly, C., 2–3
Controversial Discussions, 63
   bias toward Klein during, 83, 172
   examining Klein's doctrines during, 72–73
   Glover writing to Kubie about, 145–146
   Jones as President during, 55–58, 148
   publication of, 106–108
Countertransference, 24, 123
   in training analysis, 62, 66
Couples, analysis of, 37
Crime, Glover's work on, 100–104
Culture, and development of psychoanalysis, 12–13, 18–19

De Saussure, R., 43
Death instinct, 46, 60
Delinquency, Glover's work on, 100–104

Deutsch, H., 112, 135–136
Developmental stages, Kleinian vs. Freudian, 104–105

Eder, D., 29–31, 150
Ego psychology, 127, 129, 132
Eissler, K. E., 110, 163, 165
Eitingon, M., 19–20, 26, 55, 116–117
Elasticity, of principles vs. application, 121
Ellis, H., 101
England. *See* Britain
English school. *See* Kleinianism
Erikson, E., 124, 127
European analysts, 47, 76
  support for Glover, 89–90
  vs. American, 31–32, 139
  worship of Freud by, 109, 112
"Examination of the Klein System of Child Psychology" (Glover), 172
Eysenck, H. J., 128–129

Federn, P., 111–112
Fenichel, O., 111
Ferenczi, S.
  analysands of, 21, 38
  and Freud, 115, 120
  and Jones, 21, 26–27
Fine, R., 166
Fleiss, W., 16, 114
Flügel, J. C., 116, 119, 137, 145
Fordham, M., 2
Forsyth, D., 41–42
France, 13, 47
Free association, play therapy compared to, 58
French Society, 89
Freud, A., 13, 115, 175
  in controversy with Klein, 49, 61, 80, 83, 87, 171–172
  Glover's relation with, 4, 104–106, 115–116
  in IPA, 105, 156
  and Jones, 80, 86
  on Melitta Schmideberg, 58
  on mother's role in development, 79
  Payne mediating between British Society and, 95–99, 150–151
  projects of, 87, 144–145
  and publication of Controversial Discussions, 106–108
  resignation from Training Committee, 63, 71–72, 77–78
  status in England, 86, 114–115
  support for Glover, 89–95, 104–105
  on techniques with children, 58–59
Freud, E., 116
Freud, M., 106, 116
Freud, O., 89
Freud, S., 20, 40, 82, 101
  and Abraham, 15–17
  analysands of, 29, 34–35, 38, 41, 116
  and Anna, 80, 116
  biographies of, 105–106
  cancer of, 32, 62, 109–110
  choosing successors, 19, 128
  cult around, 110–114, 127
  defense of lay analysis, 22
  and divisiveness within psychoanalysis, 18, 49
  in England, 86, 110
  Glover's relationship with, 109, 113–114, 129
  and idealism of early analysts, 45–47
  Jones's biography of, 4–5, 24–25, 150, 175
  and Klein's theories, 49–50, 60, 80–81, 83–84

Freud, S. (*continued*)
  personality of, 126–127
  and psychoanalysis in U.S., 18–19
  and psychoanalytic organizations, 26, 30, 32, 85
  and psychoanalytic press, 41, 137
  and psychoanalytic techniques, 26, 120, 123, 125–126
  pupils of, 123–124
  referrals by, 40
  relations with family, 113, 115–116
  translation of writings, 34–35, 40
  as unanalyzed, 62
Freudians, 3, 83
  Glover wishing for society of, 63, 115
  and Jungians, 128
  lack of referrals to Independents, 84–85
  similarities to Kleinians, 79
  training through British Psychoanalytic Society, 97–99, 119
  vs. Kleinians in British Psychoanalytic Society, 62, 72–73, 130, 159–160
Freud-Klein Controversies, The, 55, 71, 171–172
Frink, H. W., 19
Fromm, E., 14, 30

Geismar, M. and A., 24
Gitelson, M., 105
Glover, A. (daughter), 11–12, 154–155, 165–166, 174
Glover, C. (wife), 11
Glover, E.
  analysands of, 55–56, 132–133
  analysts of, 15
  background of, 7–9
  bust of, 104
  clinical competence of, 122
  demonization of, 146–148, 169
  family of, 11–12, 154–155, 165–166, 174–176
  influence of, 1–2, 167–177
  interviews with, 3–4, 6, 14–15, 130
  introduction to Freud-Abraham correspondence by, 16–17
  isolation of, 12, 165–166, 171
  obituaries for, 11, 175–176
  office of, 6–7
  personal life of, 173–174
  personality of, 1, 7, 51–52, 54, 84, 128–130, 142, 166, 168, 170–171
  training of, 15
Glover, G. (wife), 11–12, 165, 175–176
Glover, J. (brother), 8, 11, 32–33, 37–38
  and deviations from psychoanalysis, 75, 80, 129
Gorer, J., 5–6
Grotjahn, M., 124
Group therapy, 151

Hadfield, J. A., 27–28
Hampstead Child Therapy Clinic, 87, 114–115
Harnick, J., 127
Hart, B., 42
Hartmann, H., 156
  and conflict-free sphere, 104–105
  Glover's criticism of, 111, 129, 165
Heimann, P., 82–83, 84, 90
Hiller, E., 41
Holland, psychoanalytic group in, 14
Horney, K., 47, 55, 163
  Glover's criticism of, 17–18, 111
  in New York Society, 143–144

Hug-Hellmuth, H. von, 127
Hysteria, 121, 123

Idealism
  of early analysts, 45–47
  Glover's, 130
Independents. *See* Middle Group, in British Psychoanalytic Society
Inexact interpretations, 21, 120
"Inside the Nazi Mind" (radio series), 145
Institute for the Study and Treatment of Delinquency (ISTD), 100–104, 147, 167–168
International Journal of Psycho-Analysis, 11, 32, 41, 110, 136–137
International Psycho-Analytic Association (IPA), 105
  Anna Freud as Secretary of, 87–88, 156
  Glover as Secretary of, 1–2, 87, 91–95
  Glover's membership in, 104, 146, 149, 158
  and Glover's membership in Swiss Society, 90, 105, 148–149
  Glover's roles in, 1–2, 12, 105
  Jones's role in, 31–32, 87, 90–95, 105
International Psychoanalytic Congress (1922), 109
International Training Commission, 116–117
Interpretations, inexact, 21, 120
Isaacs, S., 82

Jacobson, E., 129
Japan, psychoanalytic group in, 13
Jelliffe, S. E., 31
Jews, as psychoanalysts, 13–14, 128
Jones, E., 63, 86, 101, 111, 116, 175
  analysands of, 36, 42, 119
  analysis with Ferenczi, 21
  and Anna Freud, 80, 156
  biography of Freud by, 4–5, 24–25, 105–106, 150
  in British Psychoanalytic Society, 23–43
  as British Psychoanalytic Society President, 55–58, 77, 82, 90–95, 146–147
  on divisiveness within British Psychoanalytic Society, 18, 146, 148
  and Glover, 83, 90, 137–141, 158, 168
  and Glover's membership in Swiss Society, 105, 148–149
  in IPA, 31–32, 87, 90–95, 105
  and Klein, 49–50, 61, 80
  and Melitta Schmideberg, 55, 59
  personality of, 23, 25, 27–30, 30, 156
  and *Psychoanalytic Quarterly,* 136–137
Jung, C. G., 18, 62, 79, 101, 118, 122, 160
  and Freud, 25, 46, 112, 128–129
  Glover's criticism of, 2–3, 111
  on techniques, 124–125
Jungians, 3, 29, 128

Khan, Masud, 5, 19
Klein, M., 86, 120, 155, 163, 171, 175. *See also* Controversial Discussions; Kleinianism; Kleinians
  analysands of, 39, 83
  and Anna Freud, 61, 81, 87
  competence as therapist, 60–61

Klein, M. (continued)
  and divisiveness in British Psychoanalytic Society, 18, 28, 35, 68
  Glover's disagreements with, 45–78, 169
  Glover's initial support for, 47, 107
  influence of, 34, 47, 50, 61, 64–65, 79
  Jones's support for, 49–50
  personality of, 34, 48–49, 56
  power politics by, 83, 171–172
  relation with daughter, 53–56, 58–60
  work with children, 34, 48, 58–59
Kleinianism
  as deviation from Freud, 23, 45–46
  Glover's criticism of, 2, 159
  over-theoreticalness of, 81–82
  on personality development, 80
  rejection of theories, 76, 171
  similarity to Jung, 128
Kleinians, 16
  lack of referrals to Independents, 84–85
  leadership of, 82–83
  similarities to Freudians, 79
  training through British Psychoanalytic Society, 85, 97–99, 119
  vs. Freudians in British Psychoanalytic Society, 62, 72–73, 130
Kohut, H., 163
Kris, E., 43, 104
Kubie, L. S.
  analysis with Glover, 135–136
  in factionalism within New York Society, 143–144
  personality of, 131–132, 164–165
  positions of, 163–164
  and *Psychoanalytic Quarterly*, 136–137
  on psychoanalytic techniques, 150–151
  relationship with Glover, 4, 134–135, 142–143, 145, 164–166
  on Schmideberg, 151–152
  support for Glover, 149–150, 152–153, 156–157
  training of, 132–133
Kubie, S., 135–136

Lacan, J., 47, 62
Laforgue, R., 89
Laing, R. D., 172–173
Lamda, P., 104
Lampl-de Groot, J., 105
Lay analysis, 22, 32, 139
Lewin, B., 164
London, 130, 153
  during WWII, 63, 144–145
London Psychoanalytic Society, 30
Low, B., 35–36, 83

Maeder, L., 148
Mannheim, H., 101
Mannheim, K., 145
Medical model for psychoanalysis, 32
Medical psychology, 132
Medical studies, required to become analysts, 37, 39–40
Medico-Psychological Clinic, 32–33
Metapsychology, Kleinian vs. Freudian, 73, 104
Meyer, Adolf, Kubie training under, 132
Middle Group, in British Psychoanalytic Society, 62, 83–84, 119
  inability to heal split, 70, 73
  and split, 146, 159–160
Miller, E., 42–43, 101

Mitchell, T. W., 43
Mosbacher, E., 17
Mothers, 46, 53, 79–80
Mrs. Klein (play), 54

Negative therapeutic reactions, 122
Neo-Freudian, general dislike of term, 129
Neurology, relation to psychoanalysis, 18, 20
Neurotic Distortion of the Creative Process (Kubie), 131
New York, Glover's visit to called off, 137–139
New York Psychoanalytic Institute, 156–158
New York Psychoanalytic Society, 132
  factionalism in, 143–144, 152
  and Glover, 145, 150
New York Training Institute, Glover invited to be Director of, 105
Nunberg, H., 157

Oberndorf, C., 18–19
Oedipus complex, in Klein's theories, 46, 80
One Hundred Years of Psychology (Flügel), 119

Pailthorpe, G., 100–101
Partridge, F., 177
Payne, S., 33, 36, 49, 84
  on dual training system, 155–156
  on Glover, 55–56, 64, 122
  on Jones, 30, 43, 55–56
  and Klein, 61, 81
  mediating between Anna Freud and British Psychoanalytic Society, 95–100
  mediating between Glover and Klein, 51–53
  and publication of Controversial Discussions, 106–108
  roles in British Psychoanalytic Society, 83, 86–87
Penrose, L., 40
Personality development, 80
Play therapy, and free association, 58
Portman Clinic. *See* Institute for the Study and Treatment of Delinquency
Practical and Theoretical Aspects of Psychoanalysis (Kubie), 131
Pre-conscious, Kubie's work on, 164
Pregenitality, 79, 108
Pre-oedipal phases, 79
Psychiatry, 20, 128
Psychoanalysis. *See also* Britain, distinctiveness of psychoanalysis in; Science, psychoanalysis as; U.S., psychoanalysis in
  contributions to, 129, 140
  controversies in history of, 169–170
  and cult around Freud, 110–112
  culture and development of, 18–19
  culture's effect on development of, 12–14
  deviations from, 111, 129, 162–165
  divisiveness in, 17–18, 49, 128–129
  element of artistry in, 118
  failures of, 122
  fear of dilution of, 3, 95, 151
  and Glover, 128, 159
  Glover's desire to maintain purity of, 75–76, 91, 111, 129, 160–161

Psychoanalysis (*continued*)
  international *vs.* national organizations of, 140–141
  Klein's theories as deviation from, 75–76, 91
  length of, 20–21, 82
  principles *vs.* application in, 81–82, 121
  relation to other fields, 20, 128
  response to deviations in, 50
  responses to deviations in, 45–46, 176–177
  results of, 21, 45–46, 54, 111, 122–123
Psychoanalysts, 115, 126, 127, 133
  finances of, 9, 24, 117, 174
  financial cost of political stands, 84–85, 121–122
  Glover's and Jones's proposed visit to U.S., 137–139
  humanity of, 174–175
  idealism of early, 45–47
  intensity of conflicts among, 65
Psychoanalytic Quarterly, 32, 136–137
Psychoanalytic Study of the Child, The, 45
Psychology of Insanity, The (Hart), 42
Psychopaths, Glover's work on, 103
Psychopharmacology, 118
Psychosis, in children, 48
Publishing, psychoanalytic, 10, 41, 171–172
Puner, H. W., 105–106, 111

Rado, S., 127, 143–144, 152
Rank, O., 62, 101, 160
  criticism of, 46, 75–76
  and Freud, 26, 120
  on pre-oedipal phases, 79–80

Referrals
  by Glover, 50–51, 64
  Independents losing out on, 84–85
  matching patients to analysts in, 117, 127
Reich, W., 49
Reik, T., 22
Resistance, overcoming, 16
Rickman, J., 38–39, 83, 90, 111
Rivers, W. H. R., 128
Riviere, J., 34–35, 39, 146
  and Klein, 49, 61, 81–82
Rosenberg-Zetzel, E.. *See* Zetzel, E. Rosenberg-
Rosenfeld, E., 83
Rycroft, C., 168

Sachs, H., 20–22, 26, 28, 34, 36
Sarasin, P., 95, 105, 158
Saville, E., 102
Schmideberg, M., 52–60, 113, 175
  and Glover, 10, 64, 107
  Kubie's appraisal of, 151–152
Schmideberg, W., 60
Schmidt, V., 33
Science
  British Psychoanalytic Society moving away from, 76–77, 85
  Klein's theories as deviation from, 46, 72–73, 91
  psychoanalysis as, 31, 78, 111, 118, 140, 159
  incompatibility of compromise in, 75, 84
Scott, C., 57, 83, 90
Searl, N., 33, 84
Self-analysis, 112, 114
Sharpe, E., 32–34, 134, 145
  analysands of, 37, 55, 107
  in British Psychoanalytical Society split, 64–65, 83–84, 100

Simmel, E., 32–33
Social science, in Britain, 103
Socialism, 111, 176
Standard Edition, Strachey's translation of Freud in, 17, 40
Stephen, A., 36–38, 175
  in British Psychoanalytic Society split, 83, 97–98
  opposition to Glover, 77–78, 85, 88, 163
Stephen, K., 36–38, 85
Storfer, A. J., 41
Strachey, A., 39, 123
  and Klein, 48, 60
  and translation of Freud's writings, 34–35
Strachey, J., 39, 78, 83
  on Freud-Abraham correspondence, 16–17
  on Klein, 60, 61
  on psychoanalytic training, 63, 65–66, 70
  and translation of Freud's writings, 34–35
Superego, child *vs.* adult, 80
Swiss Psychoanalytic Society
  Glover's and Anna Freud's membership in, 86, 95–96
  Glover's membership in, 12, 88, 105, 148–149, 158
  opposition to Glover joining, 90, 93–95, 109–110

Tausk, V., 22, 62
Tavistock Clinic, 39, 95, 151, 153
Technique, psychoanalytic, 16, 34, 118
  with children, 58–59
  dissent over, 26, 65–70
  Glover on, 121–123, 155
  influences on, 15–16

Jones's, 23–24
Kubie on, 134, 150–151, 157
rigidity of, 121, 124–125
Sachs on, 21–22
use of couch, 124, 126
"Therapeutic Effect of Inexact Interpretation, The" (Glover), 21
Thompson, C., 37
Totem and Taboo (Freud), 129
Traditionalists, in psychoanalysis, 3, 80, 129. *See also* Freudians
Training, psychoanalytic, 20–21, 114, 120. *See also* Training analysis; Training Committee, of British Psychoanalytic Society
  curriculum of New York Institute, 143–144
  dual systems of, 62, 155–156, 161
  European *vs.* American thought on, 31–32
  Freudians *vs.* Kleinians on, 62, 72–73, 86
  and Glover, 85, 96, 106, 116–118, 151
  Glover *vs.* Strachey on, 65–71
  Glover's resignation over, 72, 74
  influence through, 64–65, 85
  Kubie's, 132–133
  medical studies required in, 37, 39–40
  need for well-rounded reading in, 173–174
  split in British Psychoanalytic Society over, 31–32, 85, 96–97, 119, 146
Training analysis, 24, 56
  analyst's influence limited by forbidding, 47, 63
  in Freudians *vs.* Kleinians, 72–73, 76–77

Training analysis (*continued*)
  influence through, 49, 61–62, 64–65, 76–77, 117–118
  results of, 85, 120
  transference during, 50–51, 62, 66–68, 76, 161
Training Committee, of British Psychoanalytic Society
  and Anna Freud, 71–72, 86, 98–100
  Glover's criticism of, 67, 69
  Glover's resignation from, 71–72
  report on controversies on training, 63, 65–66, 73–74, 77
  response to divisiveness, 63, 76–77
Transference
  in psychoanalysis with children, 58–59
  during psychoanalytic training, 65, 117–118
  therapists' handling of, 122–123
  during training analysis, 50–51, 62, 66–68, 76, 161
Trilling, L., 27, 163

Unconscious, of analysts, 51, 54
U.S.
  and Glover, 105, 139–140, 142, 152–154
  Glover's and Jones's visit to psychoanalysts in, 137–139
  psychoanalysis in, 17–19, 36, 140
  psychoanalysts in, 112, 118, 142–143
  psychoanalytic training in, 31–32, 117
  psychoanalytical dogmatism and tolerance in, 17–18, 162–163

Viennese psychoanalysts
  in Britain, 62–63, 86, 114
  Freud's denigration of, 112

Wells, H. G., 101
Winnicott, D. W., 39, 89–90, 90
World War I, treating shell-shock from, 13
World War II
  effects on British, 142, 144–145
  effects on British analysts, 63, 138–139, 142, 144

Yaekichi Yabe, 13
Young Girl's Diary, A. (Hug-Hellmuth), 127

Zetzel, E. Rosenberg-, 24, 84
Zilboorg, G., 105